W9-ASJ-646

Children's

Faces

oking Up

Children's Faces Looking Up

Program Building for the Storyteller

DOROTHY DE WIT

In creating this lively and informative book Dorothy de Wit draws upon almost 20 years of dedicated library work with young children, a good many of them spent in designing and carrying out storytelling programs.

While there are many books describing various techniques of storytelling, this is probably the first work that delves into the rich background of folklore—often overlooked as a source of story material—describing techniques for adapting this material to creative storytelling programs. Ms. de Wit shows how themes latent in one story can be pursued by telling related stories. The themes chosen, for example, may recall holidays, seasons, or the various special interests of childhood. Story programs are built around themes, and the planning of these programs requires a sensitivity and skill that this book will help to develop in its readers.

The author's principle aim throughout the book is to inform the young or new storyteller of the characteristics of a sound program. She includes six sample programs and shows how the stories in each program, taken together, employ balance, rhythm, pacing, and variety. Readers can use these programs while learning from them how to prepare their own. An extensive list of sources of program materials is provided to guide the novice storyteller.

Children's Faces Looking Up will provide a wealth of information for enriching storytelling programs in libraries, community groups, and schools.

Children's Faces Looking Up

Program Building for the Storyteller

Dorothy de Wit

AMERICAN LIBRARY ASSOCIATION

Chicago 1979

Library of Congress Cataloging in Publication Data

De Wit, Dorothy.
    Children's faces looking up.

    Bibliography: p.
    1. Story-telling. I. Title.
LB1042.D4   372.6′4   78-10702
ISBN 0-8389-0272-3

Printed in the United States of America

For the beloved compatriots of the
storyroad, Adriaan, Erica, Rick,
Brian, and Carolyn, my family.

Contents

Acknowledgments

Special recognition should be given to John Rowell of Case Western Reserve University, for his initial encouragement; to Margaret Skiff, Charlotte Gallant, and Annette Shockey of the Cuyahoga County Public Library system for their help; to Arlene Mosel, author, for her interest; and to Ruth Bay for her skill in setting up the manuscript. Perhaps the warmest thanks should go to the many children in Maple Heights, Ohio, who have shared innumerable story hours with me. Theirs are the faces in the background of CHILDREN'S FACES LOOKING UP.

Introduction

What can I do in my story programs? For weeks, this question buzzes around in my mind as I look toward another year of storytelling in a regional public library. My feeling is not one of dread, nor reluctance to plunge into the enormous amount of searching for just the right tale; nor is it lack of energy to go through uncounted anthologies, indexes, and collections, nor uncertainty in choosing an intriguing theme. Perhaps it is primarily a fervent wish to make this year's storytelling program so vital, so absorbing for both children and teller that it will leave an ineradicable trace of delight on those who tell and those who listen.

But realizing that objective involves hours of hard searching, combing narrative materials, and then building the materials into story programs that will be tantalizing, cohesive, appropriate, varied in appeal, contrasting in approach, and eminently "tellable." For this reason, I have pulled out of the bag of my experience with children in many after school programs (grades 1 through 6), with school visitation programs in the community, as well as in special and summer library programs, those ideas and suggestions that should prove to be a springboard for richer and more imaginative storytelling programs for all storytellers, especially those just beginning.

Storytelling is a deeply satisfying well, and those standing on the brink, inexperienced and perhaps hesitant, need both encouragement and practical help. It is primarily to these compatriots on the storyroad that this sheaf of ideas is addressed, with the earnest hope that they may bring in a rich harvest of ideas and satisfying programs.

Although most storytellers rely on the traditional narrative material found in folklore, because of its timelessness, antiquity, and capacity to elicit laughter, tears, or bravos, modern fantasy or creative literary tales are also often valuable sources for programming, especially for children in the elementary grades. Because the average child at the end of a school day finds it difficult to sustain attention for very long, the traditional story hour is usually only a half or three-quarters of an hour in duration. With this time span in mind, and the principles of balance, rhythm, and mood to consider, the storyteller may decide to abridge, adapt, or amplify particular choices. He or she may also choose to retell a tale. But for best results, the storyteller should write out such material ahead of time, and not trust the sheer inspiration of the moment.

At its simplest, program building is relating appropriate story materials, within a given period of time, to reach a predetermined goal. The purpose of this book is to suggest guidelines and source materials to gain that end, and to strengthen and develop skills in programming, so that telling stories to boys and girls may be more meaningful, more enjoyable. Adequate space, good facilities, an experienced teller, and children of the same age, background, and experience enhance storytelling. Yet the inherent worth of the story hour lies in no one of these factors, nor is it destroyed by the lack of them. It is my conviction that it is the choice and arrangement of material, presented zestfully and with a sense of sharing, that overrides the competence of the storyteller, important as it is to have a sound technique in that art.

It is not my purpose to go into the techniques of storytelling at length, although some pointers will be included in chapter 7. Rather, I shall ex-plore programming for storytellers, including a brief background on storytelling and how it evolved, the definition of the tellable tale, recognition of good story material and how to find it, and especially, the process of relating stories in creative and imaginative designs. Finally, a few tips for beginners in programming story hours will be included.

Experience has delivered bumps and hard knocks, but it has also developed a compulsion to encourage others to enter the world of oral narrative—of storytelling. Given time, patience, an abundant source of supply, and imagination, there are few limits to what one can do with stories. After a story hour or a planning session, you may realize how very much storytelling can do for *you*, the teller. The luck o' the road to ye!

Part 1

BUILDING THE
STORY HOUR

About the Author

Dorothy de Wit is Head of Children's Services, Maple Heights Regional Library, Cuyahoga County Public Library, Ohio. She has been actively involved in children's library work since 1960. Ms. de Wit's educational background includes an M.S. in library science from Case Western Reserve University and a B.S. from Schauffler College of Religion and Social Work. She is a book reviewer for *School Library Journal* and *Top of the News,* and author of the children's book *The Talking Stone* (Greenwillow, 1978).

1

Of Storytellers and Storytelling

Storytelling is an ancient art, an oral art born of the experiences of men and women as they first became aware of themselves, their outer world, and the strange inner world each person saw with the eyes of the mind and could not help sharing with others. At first, perhaps, this sharing was an account of one's own prowess, the bare retelling of an event, or an incident in which that person had an important part. To the brief fact, was then added some individual ideas, emotional reaction, and some background color; and with repetition to others beyond the immediate circle, the storyteller supplied imaginary details. When the story was retold, the details might change.

Among primitive tribes today, the tales of physical achievements follow much this same pattern, and so it is not difficult to imagine that as one nomadic group moved to another place, it left behind some of its tales, and as one well-known figure in the group died, another took the place as raconteur. In retelling the stories, the new storyteller added personal touches to the narrative. Historical events were thus gradually changed in color, background significance, and the protagonists involved. The details that linked individuals to specific areas or times became blurred and generalized, yet the verity of the tale lived on. If it contained the qualities which provoked laughter, tears, or another emotion close to the human heart, it was warmly received, retold, and thus perpetuated down the generations. In time the initial vitae became so indefinite that accurate identification was no longer possible, the tale became anonymous, and might begin: "In far off days, there once lived a man who was brave in deed and mighty in heart. . . ."

But if the details were blurred, the quintessence of the tale was far from dead. It affected listeners and called forth spontaneous words of approval or derision. Perhaps it elicited a refrain, a repetition, or a proverb from everyday life, and at the beginning or at the close, listeners might respond orally, sometimes in unison: "A story, a story! . . . let it come, let it go. . . ." or "Crik crak . . . break my back!" Such phrases were incorporated into the woof of the story fabric as formulae or rituals. Even today, in Africa and Asia, listeners participate in the storytelling in this manner. *Gassire's Lute* (Jablow), an epic known in West Africa for centuries, illustrates the rhythmic antiphonal refrain chanted by listeners. Often a response is accompanied by a tambour, lute, drum, flute, or other primitive instrument, such as the thumb-piano of Africa. Sometimes the teller, or perhaps a wise listener, tacked on a proverb, moral precept, or group ethic, thus weighting the story for the young. Some folklorists feel that this oral interpersonal exchange was the genesis of ritual, liturgy, and later sophisticated bardic and heroic sagas. Even today clapping, stamping, and swaying accompany ballads and folk songs and attest to the pull of rhythm in the oral narrative, an eloquent expression of universal longing for social interaction and identification with others who share common fears, griefs, joys, and aspirations.

Thus stirring, significant stories evolved, and gradually the retelling of them fell to the lot of one who could declaim them most vividly, the individual who showed a desire to pass them on. That person then assumed the role of the group teller-of-tales and through practice built up a repertoire as well as a distinctive approach stamped with the individual's personality. With the recognition as official storyteller came honors; with the rise of royalty, the storyteller became a member of the ruling household. From time to time the storyteller listened to tellers from other places, marked their patterns of speech, their formulae. Over the years guilds of storytellers were built up through association, groups that held storytelling festivals attracting people from near and far. Different storytellers specialized in specific types of tales; for instance, tradition allocated certain tales to designated Celtic shenachies, and they alone might tell them. In Germany, during the time of the guilds, a high standard of storytelling was reached, periodic contests were held, and mastersingers vied with each other in the oral art. Wagner's music drama, *Die Meistersinger*, is based on this theme.

And so they marched down the ages—the skalds of Iceland and Scandinavia, the bards and pinkerdds of Wales, the trouvères and troubadours of France, the gleeman, scops, and minstrels of England, the ollamhs and shenachies of Ireland, and the minnesingers and meistersingers in Germany—bearing their treasury of ballads, heroic stories, epics, and sagas of kings and warriors. Wandering harpers in ancient Egypt and Greece chanted their odes; friars and monks joined pilgrims on their journeys over Christendom; caravans, merchants, traders, sailors, crusaders, the conquered and the conquerors—all carried with them their literary merchandise and exchanged it freely along the roadways of the world, in the decades between the eleventh and sixteenth centuries in Europe and Asia. The dawn of the age of exploration sent ships and crews all over the globe, and stories from the Old World reached the New. Voyageurs plying Canadian rivers met Indian shaman and medicine men; fur traders discovered soothsayers and wisemen telling tales around Arctic fires. The oral tradition counted among its bearers gypsies, immigrants, peddlers, tinkers, cobblers, grannies, frontiersmen, and indentured servants in America. Over and over the power of the storyteller bridged the gap of time, perpetuated tradition, and underscored the ethics of group action to formulate ideals and introduce new ideas. The deeds of past heroes and the folktales of countless little people linked the known to the unknown. In strange new lands it was the source of security and continuity. To people far from home stories brought reassurance; to newcomers, diversion; to the old, reaffirmation. In *Bag o' Tales*, Effie Power speaks of the heritage of the storyteller as a living voice moving across the centuries to amuse, warm, and cheer people through the oral art, transmitting thought, language, and literature.

The skalds of Iceland, the troubadours of France, the minstrels of England have long since gone, but their tales live on. In the busy life of the twentieth century, television, radio, and the theater have taken their places. Thousands of books are published each year, and the traditional storyteller has been pushed to the fringes of those societies where there is little organized education, or where printed matter is difficult to procure for a large majority. The picture storyteller can still be found in remote parts of Japan, calling the children with wooden clappers to gather and listen. Busy market places in Morocco and the Near East count storytellers between the booths, holding eager listeners spellbound among the bazaars. The shadow puppeteer of Indonesia performs Wa-jang stories, the village teller of tales recites stories in Nigeria. In remote areas of South Africa, Ethiopia, the islands of the Pacific, fishing areas of the North Sea, the highlands of North and South America, Arctic villages in sparsely settled parts of Russia, the sun-warmed atolls and islands of the Caribbean—in these places stories still come alive to link past and present with magic.

And, in the public libraries in our country, the oral tradition is alive and flourishing as well. Teachers may read aloud, the media may dramatize, but the library teems with eager children sharing preschool story hours. Boys and girls arrive to delight in after-school programs where adventure, humor, and fantasy interweave with folk and fairy lore. Girl Scouts working on badges for storytelling, folklore, or puppets gather with the children's librarian to explore old tales. Brownies, Cubs, Bluebirds, and Pixies choose library storytellers to enrich their programs. Indian Guide fathers and sons reach back into the rich treasury of the history, myth, and legends of Native Americans through the recreation of an enthusiastic storyteller.

But the children's librarian is not content in the library sphere only. In countless public and parochial schools he or she carries on a regular storytelling program for all ages, making use of longer stories and more sophisticated material with homogeneous groups; supplementing curriculum units, and enriching special study groups. Children's Book Week, National Library Week, assemblies—these call for special storytelling, as do sleep-ins, festivals, workshops, or campfires. Storytelling is a tool used with skill in special schools, in hospitals, and among handicapped children. Vacation church schools draw on the rich store of religious legends and traditions; playgrounds often include "chucklebait" adventure from Grimm, Jacobs, and Andersen passed on by a storyteller savoring these treasures.

In everyday contacts, the children's librarian constantly creates minitales as he or she relates books to readers or gives short book talks. But formally accumulating and disseminating the oral heritage—in short, storytelling—offers more than mere pleasure to endorse it. Through storytelling programs, children attune their ears to the flow of language, the imagery of words, the rhythm of speech, and patterns of reading long before they are capable of meeting these through reading print for themselves. Both before and after reading, a child's imagination is enriched and stimulated as people and places of long ago and from distant shores are found in stories. The child experiences emotions and feelings common to all humans; the ability to laugh at one's self, and at the funny situations in which people embroil themselves, is charged. On the child's own terms culture is confronted by hearing stories of other peoples; the ethics and ideals of his or her own, as well as another's, society emerge through legends and myths. Children stretch their horizons through well-designed storytelling hours, and they are more at ease in a world growing increasingly smaller. Carefully chosen stories develop their sympathies and sense of identification with others, and the child begins to appreciate the humor, bravery, and beauty of people he or she does not yet know, but finds reflected in their stories. Many tales that accomplish these ends exceptionally well are now out of print, and it is only as a skillful storyteller finds them and brings them alive that they will be remembered by boys and girls.

Finally, from a practical point of view, the librarian can find no better way to help children belong to the library community and feel at home within library walls than through storytelling. The children's librarian knows that the warm sense of friendliness and rapport established with these patrons is one of the most important aspects in making children and books mutual friends.

Is storytelling a lost art? Not yet! A well-told story is ageless, penetrates many age levels, and gives immeasurable delight. In Cloyd Bowman's book *Winnebojo*, the old grandmother reproves her young grandson, Thunder Stone, for his reluctance to tell her a familiar small child's tale: "No very old story is childish! They very often carry deep truths. . . ." If they did not, we would not still be telling them after these thousands of years! And they are likely to be with us as long as there are lips to tell and ears to listen.

2

The Tellable
Tale

What is a tellable tale? Some people have an almost instinctive sense for recognizing a story that will be enhanced by oral presentation, but most of us need to cultivate this selective faculty. However, we have criteria which can act as guidelines to develop a "sense of story," in J. R. Townsend's phrase; for in the vast inheritance of literary material not everything can be used in oral presentation. Storytelling is not indicated for material with the following characteristics: stories with complicated plots and subplots; long passages of philosophizing, or stream-of-consciousness soliloquy; stories with brittle, rapid-fire repartee; stories with discourse, or dialogue that is complex, lengthy, or does not really further plot development; tales with long passages of description; tales with characters that are analyzed, characters that are extremely complex, or characters that need extended narrative to become real, because they need to reveal growth and development; fragments, brief anecdotes, or selections from long narratives that depend on previous or later information to have meaning; stories that stop, without any kind of conclusive ending or resolution; or, finally, stories whose effectiveness depends on the precise style and vocabulary of the author. Indeed, the value of such literary material may be decreased by oral presentation.

The analogy of the picture frame and the canvas may be useful here. If telling is merited by the quality of the story, and if the telling enhances the inherent beauty and flavor of the story as a frame sets off a canvas, then the time and effort needed to prepare the story for telling is justified. One of the pertinent aspects of storytelling is the participation of the child in this literary treasure long before the printed symbols can be interpreted through his or her own language skills. Moreover, story structure, vocabulary, imaginative ideas, creative thought, and the flow of language are meaningful to the child well before reading begins, and these sink deeply into his or her unconscious. Unknowingly, the child is caught up in the spirit of the story, enters into the mood of fantasy or adventure, and responds to the verbal character that is focused on his or her mind. Since verbalization is such an important part of the growing child's life, children constantly imitate speech patterns, heard through storytelling as well as in their daily living. "Say that again" is a familiar phrase the world over. It may be the "feel" of the story, but it may also be the specific phraseology that worms its way, with penetrating power, into the subconscious of the child.

Since folktales embody part of the accumulated wisdom of the culture from which they spring, a tellable tale is also identifiable in part by the strength of its theme, by its universal significance. Construction is simple; events clearly lead to an encounter with some problem involving a situation or a person, one that must be satisfactorily resolved. The beginning must evoke anticipation, the characters must be vivid, the language artistic or earthy depending on whether one is using Grimm, Andersen, Pyle, or Gág. The spice of humor, whimsey, sly wit, or idiomatic language should be present; stories that have lasted for centuries are imprinted indelibly with oral speech patterns that are like wooden kitchen utensils used for many years, smoothed, shaped, and practical. Many times folk wisdom, proverbs, and colloquialisms dot the dialogue. For example, see "What the Good Man Does Is Always Right" (Anderson—tr. Paull). Riddles or folk sayings may be sprinkled through the story.

The pattern of repetition predominates in tellable tales—repetition of names, rhymes, or descriptive phrases; repetition within the plot in cycles of three or four, often separated by "runs" or "points of rest," as Padraic Colum terms it. In old days, the storyteller speeded up the action here, telescoping action to heighten suspense for what should come afterwards. Seumas MacManus uses this device, and Howard Pyle adopted it in his tales: "Oh, there was no trouble about that—it happened thus and so, and then the old soldier told them all about it. And after that the others went home. . . ." Skim through Pyle's *Pepper and Salt* and *Wonder Clock*, and see.

Another characteristic of the tellable tale is its frequent use of a symbolic object that becomes identified with an individual character, such as, for example, the gusly of the Russian minstrel, Sadko; or the sword of Arthur; or the doll of Vasilissa; or the cap of Pekka; or the boots of Puss-in-Boots. This helps the listener to recognize and imprint more firmly on his or her mind that special character. Feathers, gloves, rings, colored threads—many such may be recalled.

Folk and fairy tale characters are two-dimensional, posterlike, and they represent abstract qualities by using extremes. For example, good lads are all good, witches are all bad, or the fool of the family is witless in the extreme until fate conspires to bring his innate cunning to the fore. Heroines are too beautiful to describe, and wealthy kings have more money than you could shake a stick at. It is the "extreme" quality which differentiates folk

characters from literary or theatrical characters. The latter are usually complex and develop throughout the work; they may be read, reread, pondered, or returned to over and over by reading or viewing. But, posterlike though a folk character may be, each must strike a note of authenticity; it must, within the framework of the story situation, be really believable. The listener must be able to nod, and say, "Yes, yes! That is the way it is!" Even when the most unbelievable actions are portrayed, they must retain an inevitable logic within the demands of the story, and must be motivated by more than mere caprice. In folklore, characters become the vehicles for such abstractions as beauty, truth, sorrow, evil, hatred, or love.

Obviously storytelling is, in some respects, a dramatic art, because it is a recreation of events in which another shares vicariously; but storytelling is also a self-contained art, with its own nutrients for listener and teller. It does not depend on lights, costumes, staging, or sound effects. An example of the timeless vitality of the oral tradition is the thousands-of-years-old treasury of epigrams, anecdotes, fables, and animal stories, the Indic *Panchatantra*, that has been recreated orally to the delight of innumerable children in its native culture and has served as a fount for Western fabulists as well. With or without the didactic commentary of the original, the stories are vital and dramatic. And no well-told story has to have its moral exhumed for the listener. No less a figure than Sigmund Freud pointed out that the mythmaker and the fabulist had anticipated the insights of psychologists long before psychology laid claim to them.

Constant reading and experimenting with stories gradually builds up a recognition of what is good and what is tellable, and though guidelines can help, only working with story materials, and with the "stuff" of oral tradition, can provide skill in story use or story making. Finland's great epic *The Kalevala* (Deutsch) evolved when Elias Lönnrot and Zacherias Topelius gathered up fragments discovered in every part of the country and wove them into a continuing narrative of power and beauty. Andersen, Perrault, and Pyle, in particular, molded the stuff of oral tradition, and with it created distinctive and new tales.

But very few of us can create stories like those of Andersen, Pyle, or Perrault, and we must learn to discover what is tellable, and use it as best we can. Some further delineation of a tellable tale may then be suggested. In most folk and fairy lore, the basic theme does not pop up in the opening paragraphs, but is led in with a formula or ritual often unspecific and general in time and place: "Once upon a time," or "Long ago and far away, over seven seas and seven mountains and across seven plains, there reigned a tsar. . . ." Time, telescoped, moves quickly, and thus pushes the plot steadily forward with credibility, even when supernatural forces or objects are utilized. Incidents are sparse, rather than compacted, and contained in one main plot; graphic, vivid phrases sketch the characters in quintessential, rather than detailed, portraits.

Repetition—the reiteration of certain words, phrases, and incidents—builds suspense and enhances the flow and the rhythm of the story. A rhyme appears and reappears, a couplet appears over and over, a given task or trial is repeated and a spell or chant utilized several times. Native American stories have these in series of four, emphasizing the four directions, the four elements, the four winds, and the four seasons; Western European stories prefer threefold definition, perhaps the influence of Christianity and the Trinity.

Note that in most folktales or fairy tales the center of attention is often divided between two characters, two influences, or two objects interacting to underscore the element of contrast; face to face; good versus evil; the hero opposed to the heroine; the villain against the agent of good; happiness versus misery; fortune against misfortune. As the plot unfolds, the least likely character gradually takes the center of action, such as the most stupid, the youngest, the most ill-treated, the poorest; and that character, then, evinces the most worth as the vessel of fortune, or the winner of the trial, or the one who wins the princess, or claims the reward, or earns the kingdom.

The closing is also flavorful, with pithy, appropriate, colorful description used either as a ritual or as a formula: "Three apples fell from heaven—one for you, one for me, and one for him who comes after!" Or: "This is my story which I have told to you; if it be good take some, and let some come back to me." Or: "Snip, snap, snover, this story's over!"

The young storyteller stands on the shore of a sea of stories. How shall they ever be sorted out? Perhaps some rough classifications can be suggested.

Stith Thompson developed the term "basic motif" to indicate that one single, recognizable element in a story, the motivating factor. For example, story separations could be made with the idea of magic as a basic element:[1]

1. The magic of smallness—"Tom Thumb" (Steel), "Issun Boshi, the Inchling" (Haviland—*Japan*), *Thumbelina* (Andersen), "Peter Pea" (Grishna), "Pyelkin" (Gottschalk).

2. The magic of sleep, either as a condition, as in "Briar Rose" (Hutchinson—*Chimney Tales*), "Brunhilde and the Magic Fire" (Henderson), *Snow White and the Seven Dwarfs* (Grimm), or "Sadko" (Downing); or as a telescoping of the years, as in *Rip Van Winkle* (Irving), "Keel-Wee" (Jewett), "Urashima" (Lang—*Pink*), "The Seven Sleepers of Ephesus" (Westwood).

3. There may be a magic disguise, as in "The White Cat" (Arbuthnot—*Fairy Tales*), "The Frog Prince" (Grimm—*Household*), "The Gull" (Deutsch—*Tales*), or "Beauty and the Beast" (Dalgleish—*Enchanted*).

4. The protagonist may have a magic token such as *The Dancing Kettle* (Uchida), "Clever Peter and the Two Bottles" (Pyle—*Pepper*), *The Magic Listening Cap* (Uchida), or "The Magic Drum" (Burton).

5. The magic of shape-changing may be present, as in "The Clever Student and the Master of the Black Arts" (Pyle—*Wonder*), "Niilo and the Wizard" (Bowman and Bianco).

6. It may be a magic ability, such as unusual sight, strength, or wisdom, as, for example, "Long, Broad, and Sharpsight" (Manning-Sanders—*Wizards*), "The Black Bull of Norroway" (Jacobs—*More English*), *The Fool of the World* (Ransome).

Other motifs suggest themselves: a task to do, as "The Princess Nobody Could Silence" (Hutchinson—*Candlelight*), "The Golden Bird" (Kavcic), "The Princess on the Glass Hill" (Asbjornsen—*East*); a wily cunning, as *The Valiant Tailor* (Werth), "Bajan Budiman" (Courlander—*Kantchil*), "The Legend of Knockmany" (Jacobs—*Celtic*), "Bouki Buys a Burro" (Courlander—*Piece*),

1. In the lists that follow, the anthology in which each story is found is indicated by the name of the compiler, editor, or translator under whose name it is listed in the bibliography. When more than one work is listed, an identifying word or phrase has been added to the parenthetical reference.

"Jack and the Beanstalk" (Jacobs—*English*), "Molly Whuppie" (Jacobs—*English*); the motif of numskull logic that wins out in the end, as in "Buttercup" (Undset), "Silly Jean" (Duvoisin), "Just Say Hic!" (Walker), "Clever Grethel" (Grimm—*Household*), "Prudent Hans" (Grimm—*Household*). See how, by picking out the central motivating idea of the plot, stories may be grouped more accessibly; also, study *The Folktale*, by Stith Thompson, for sheer delight as well as profit.

Long before Stith Thompson coined his motif theory, however, storytellers grouped stories for convenience in selection. Think of all the stories which center around wishing: *The Three Wishes* (Jacobs), "The Fisherman and His Wife" (Lang—*Green*), "Hidden Laiva" (Arbuthnot—*Fairy Tales*), "The Quern at the Bottom of the Sea" (Asbjornsen—*Norwegian*), or "How the Good Gifts Were Used by Two" (Pyle—*Wonder*). Often the wishes were misused. Or consider the store of tales where an action is turned topsy-turvy in interpretation, as in "Nazar the Brave" (Khatchatrianz), "Greedy Anansi" (Fisher), "The Bear and the Leak" (Sugimoto—*Japanese*), *The Coconut Thieves* (Fournier), "The Race between the Hare and the Tortoise" (Aesop), in its endless variants, or "Hereafterthis" (Jacobs—*More English*).

Again, one may group stories about supercreatures—"Drakestail" (Hutchinson—*Fireside*), "Red Chicken" (Duvoisin), "Mighty Mikko" (Fillmore), "Puss in Boots" (Perrault—*French*), "The Little Rooster and the Turkish Sultan" (Ross—*Lost*), or *The Cock and the Ghost Cat* (Lifton). Or with supernatural forces acting on humans, as in "Farmer Grigg's Boggart" (Pyle—*Pepper*), "The Hungry Old Witch" (Finger), "Rumplestiltskin" (Grimm—*Household*), "The Elves and the Shoemaker" (Grimm—tr. Lucas), "Oniroku and the Carpenter" (Matsuno), or "Aladdin" (Lang—*Arabian*). Stories may be set apart when a particular locale is important, as in *The Legend of Sleepy Hollow* (Irving), "Paul Bunyan and His Blue Ox" (McCormick), *Tikta-Likta* (Houston); or when an actual historical event has been twisted almost beyond recognition, as in *Dick Whittington and His Cat* (Brown), "The Rich Widow of Stavoren" (DeLeeuw), or "Ys and Her Bells" (Cothran—*Bells*).

A vast body of stories answer how or why something happened, why some creature has a particular attribute, or why some place has a particular name, as "Why the Sea Is Salt" (Undset), "How the Robin Got His Red Breast" (Leach—*How*), "How Raven Found the Daylight" (Maher). Another group of animal stories might feature social dissatisfaction or unrest, as in the "Brer Rabbit" (Harris) tales; or they may be straight animal stories, such as "Rikki-Tikki-Tavi" (Kipling—*Jungle*), or "Lobo the Wolf" (Seton—*Wild*).

It is obvious that the above groupings—by motif, by content, or by idea—stress the subject matter of the tales involved. But it is also possible to group narrative material by its structure: for example, myths, legends, folktales, märchen, fables, pourquoi tales, noodlehead and drolls, sagas, epics, and so on. This subject will be treated in detail in a later chapter. In all of these considerations of narrative material, however, there emerge commonalities that stand out as one searches for tellable tales, rather like recognition badges. When several of these features are found in one tale, it is almost certain that that story is worth a second look; in fact, it becomes a delight to look for these specific earmarks. For instance, first look at the story introductions, which may be specific for one culture, or general for no particular group: "Once there was and was not . . ." (Spanish, Irish, and Armenian); "Wanst upon a time when pigs was swine . . ." (Irish); "Saynday was coming along . . ." (Kiowa Indian); "Once upon a time, and a long, long time ago . . ." (general).

Second, conclusions to stories may be indicative of tellable material: (1) rimes, such as "Snip, snap, snout, this tale's run out . . ." (Scandinavian); "Shoes mended, story ended"; "Come further, here's another . . ." (Spanish); (2) conjectures, such as "He married the girl, and so fer as I kin tell, they're both doin' right well . . ." (Appalachian); "If they haven't moved on, why they're still there!" (general); (3) a wish: "And so they were married and lived happily together—may we live as happily and do as well!" (general); (4) a ritual phrase, "Congratulations, congratulations" or "Sorrowful, sorrowful," depending on whether the story is sad or joyous (Japanese); "Keaspeadooksit . . . my story is done" (Micmac Indian); "And that's the way it was, and that's the way it is, until this very good day" (Kiowa Indian).

A third commonality in tellable tales is the use of rhetorical questions to catch and increase the

9

listener's interest: "Did Boots think he could fool him also? Well, we shall see about that!"

The consistent use of repetition as a technique (previously mentioned, and important) is a fourth indication:

"And is that you again, Lad?"

"Yes."

"And have you now stolen my coverlet?"

"Yes."

"And have you come for my pretty boar?"

"Yes."

"And will you come again?"

"Very likely."

Often this sort of repetition points up some particular character trait of the protagonists involved, such as the utter stupidity of the witch in "Esben and the Witch" (Manning-Sanders—*Witches*).

The fifth earmark, or commonality, may be a verselet: "With a wig, with a wag, with a long leather bag . . ." or a rime: "Flounder, flounder in the sea, prithee hearken unto me. . . ." Somewhat like this is the "run" or "point-of-rest." The "run" is often characterized by the repetition of the adjective, in its comparative forms: "If it had been dark, it was darker now, and if the sound had been loud before, it was louder now, and more horrible, and nearer. . . ."

If one had been able to listen to the old Irish shenachies, brimming with the warmth and inner delight of long known and enjoyed tales, telling their tales around the peat fires, as Seumas Mac-Manus was able to do, the characteristics of the tellable tale would be recognized at once. Mac-Manus was himself a marvellous storyteller, and his wide background of tales, his empathy and understanding of human foibles, and his wit and wisdom made his visit to the United States, many years ago, unforgettable. It is just that wit, wisdom, carefully worn-down oral patterns, and vitality of language, plus the special earmarks just mentioned, that lift a particular story out of the sea of narrative materials and set it aside as one eminently tellable.

3
Selecting Story Material

Tolkien likened the mass of narrative material growing out of human experience to a pot of soup, a "cauldron of story," in which innumerable ingredients were blended. Only occasionally is one ingredient distinguishable; it is the combination of many things that creates the flavor.

In programming, the most time-consuming and difficult aspect is the choice of material. This is far more complex than merely selecting a well-structured story or two suitable to the kind of group involved; it must take into consideration factors such as age, season, experience, special occasion, the culture of a specific group, and so on. In addition, the cauldron of folklore contains fairy tales, myths, legends, folktales, märchen, fables, tall tales, sagas, epics, drolls, formulae and chants, pourquoi, and talking beast tales. The teller must be familiar with many kinds of narrative materials in order to both select and arrange the selections within the framework of the story program, so that there is contrast, complement, and variety. Often the storyteller has to ask whether or not a story is really familiar to the children, or is only assumed to be familiar to them; whether the story should be told in the garb in which it is most recognizable (the Perrault "Cinderella," for instance) or in an interesting variant. He or she may discover a parallel story that would add spice to the planning and decide to include it in the story hour. A storyteller must decide which of two or more stories having the same action, characters, incidents, and background, is a better retelling—a better version— stylistically, a more tellable tale.

Today many single-edition, illustrated folk and fairytale books are in print; some are outstanding, some not. The storyteller considers when the use of the picture story form will add to the program and then decides where a literary fairy tale or a modern fantasy, such as *Just So Stories* (Kipling) or *Rootabaga Stories* (Sandburg) would provide contrast. Would the use of a modern fantasy like *Lion* (Du Bois) or *The Popcorn Dragon* (Thayer) serve to enrich the program? With their ubiquity, timelessness, and antiquity, their power to draw aside the curtain of the past and afford windows on the how and why of our own customs and behavior, and their capacity to give enjoyment and satisfy curiosity, folktales and fairy tales form the groundwork of a story program; however, they often need the foil of fantasy, poetry, legend, or myth, achieved through good programming.

A further examination of some rough divisions of the oral narrative is necessary here to help the reader better understand the process of selection.

This division is naturally somewhat arbitrary, and one type of material often impinges on another. The first group may be characterized by emphasis on words themselves: for example, riddles, such as "I Gave My Love a Cherry That Has No Stone" (Emrich); cumulative formula tales, such as "The Old Woman and Her Pig" (Johnson, et al.), "One Fine Day" (Hogrogian); repetitive catch phrases, including stories without an end, such as the African tale of the ant "who brought one grain of sand and added it to the pile, and another ant who brought one grain of sand and added it to the pile, and another ant . . ." ad infinitum.

Animal tales form a second group. Here, wise or foolish animals serve as protagonists in lieu of humans, and experience similar problems. Collections of such animal stories include *The Panchatantra* of India; the Anansi Spider stories of Africa (see Sherlock, *Anansi, the Spider Man*); the Rogue Reynard cycle (Norton) from the Middle Ages; the Brer Rabbit tales as written by Joel Chandler Harris, from his southern background; the tales of Kantchil, the Mouse Deer in Indonesia (see Bro, *How the Mouse Deer Became King*); fables from Aesop, La Fontaine, Krylov; and finally, the *Jataka Tales* (Babbitt) from India. This represents only a sampling from a vast body of animal lore.

Closely allied to animal stories are those which explain the how or why of some natural phenomenon, pourquoi stories such as "Why the Evergreens Keep Their Leaves" (Holbrooke), "Why the Hoofs of the Deer Are Split" (Holbrooke), "Why the Bear Has a Stumpy Tail" (Wiggin and Smith, *Laughter*), and *Why the Sun and Moon Live in the Sky* (Dayrell). Many star and constellation stories are included here, including the well-known Pleiades tales found among Native American, African, Asiatic, and Oceanic lore. Pourquoi stories are accepted by the cultural group in which they originate as plausible explanations, but are not thereby universally true.

Some pourquoi stories may also develop about natural formations, but in general such formations engender legends, in which a grain of truth may serve as the core of the material; there was such a place, action, or a person, but time and dissemination have visibly gilded the facts. Consider *The Story of King Arthur and His Knights* (Pyle), *The Legend of Sleepy Hollow* (Irving), *The Merry Adventures of Robin Hood* (Pyle), *St. George and the Dragon* (Dalgleish), "St. Francis and the Wolf of Giubbio" (Untermeyer—*Legendary*), "San Froilan of the Wilderness" (Sawyer—*Joy*), *The Legend of the Willow Plate* (Tresselt), "The Pied Piper of Hamelin" (Gibson), "The Great Bell of Peking" (Cothran—*Bells*), and countless saint legends.

The third group contains funny stories known as drolls, and these may be of various genres:

1. Completely fictitious, humorous folk tales from many nationalities: "Lazy Jack" (Jacobs—*English*), England; *The Wise Men of Helm and Their Merry Pranks* (Simon), Jewry; "Goose Hans" (Gág—*Three*), Germany; "Bouki Gets Whee-ai" (Courlander—*Piece*), West Indies; "Goody-'gainst-the-Stream" (Power—*Stories*), Scandinavia; "Mutsmag" (Chase—*Grandfather*), Appalachia.

2. Nitwit, noodlehead, or numskull stories, which may be partially developed or, on the other hand, may be complete tales: "The Horse Egg" (Jagendorf—*Noodlehead*) with many variants from many countries; "Hans Clodhopper" (Andersen—*Fairy*), Denmark; "Prudent Hans" (Grimm—*Household*), Germany.

3. Brief anecdotes or incidents surrounding one character such as the Hodja of Turkey or the Mullah of Persia.

4. The cycle of pithy, epigrammatic misadventures surrounding trickster figures like Tyll Eulenspiegel in Holland and Germany, or Baron Munchausen in Germany. These narratives are part legend, part exaggeration. American tall tales built around Paul Bunyan, Tony Beaver, Pecos Bill, and Stormalong belong to this latter group.

A fourth story group includes ballads, events, or persons celebrated in verse form and originally sung, though now often translated into prose: "Tam-Lin" (Manning-Sanders—*Tales*), "Childe Rowland" (Jacobs—*English*), "Lord Randal" (Leach, Mac.), "Robin Hood" (Picard). Related to ballads but different in form is romantic fantasy, including the märchen of Germany that are part folk, part fairy tale: "Hansel and Grethel" (Grimm—*Household*), *The Bremen Town Musicians* (Grimm), "The Frog Prince" (Grimm—*Household*); general fairy tales such as "The Twelve Dancing Princesses" (Haviland—*France*), "Bluebeard" (Perrault—*French*), "East of the Sun" (Thorne-Thomsen), *Snow White and Rose*

Red (Grimm), "Cinderella" (Lang—*Blue*); and rhymed stories partly orated, partly sung, known as contes populaires: for example, "Aucassin and Nicolette" (Jacobs—*English*). This latter form has been adapted and frequently used in many African stories. Märchen and fairy tales usually involve a prince or hero who wins, at great cost, a princess, a kingdom, or a reward. It is impossible to differentiate clearly between märchen and fairy tale, nor is it actually necessary to do so. Another variation of this romantic fantasy literature is the novella, a series tale with many parts built around a central figure or theme as a focus for the many interrelated narratives, as for example in *The Arabian Nights* (Colum), containing "Ali-Baba" (Wiggin and Smith—*Arabian*), *The Story of Aladdin* (Lewis), and "Sinbad the Sailor" (Rackham). These last named tales often appear in single editions.

Folktales comprise the fifth group. These have many of the same characteristics as fairy tales, but tend to reflect human behavior more emphatically, and usually have less of the supernatural element as a motivating factor. The folktale is actually a mirror of conduct for human beings, and is therefore funny, sad, thoughtful, or provoking, in turn: *Three Billy Goats Gruff* (Asbjornsen), "Doctor Know-All" (Gág—*Tales*), "The Flea" (Sawyer—*Picture Tales*), "Three Words of Advice" (Thompson), "The Little Rooster and the Turkish Sultan" (Gruenberg—*Favorite*), *The Bun* (Brown), "The Master Thief" (Jacobs—*European*), "The Unlucky Shoes of Ali Abou" (Carpenter—*Elephant*), and "The Hedley Kow" (Jacobs—*More English*). Folktales play strongly on emotions.

The sixth category, myths, embodies human efforts through the centuries to explain religious truth, philosophical beliefs, and phenomena which cannot be understood rationally, such as death, immortality, individual genesis, divinity, the structure of the world and the universe. Greek, Norse, Scandinavian, Egyptian, Persian, Roman, and American Indian peoples have created myths explaining, by means of gods and goddesses, such supernatural forces and/or abstract concepts as hope, curiosity, or vanity: "Pandora" (Sellew), "Persephone" (Fisher), "Narcissus" (White—*Treasury*), *The Fourth World of the Hopi* (Courlander), *Gilgamesh* (Bryson), and "Quetzalcoatle" (Purnell). Myths are difficult and require skill to both choose

and tell discriminatingly. They are quite unlike fairy tales, which often also express universal truths and enlarge on human wishes and desires; myths embody an inner yearning to logically explain the unseen, powerful forces of nature. Fairy tales reflect through fantasy and vivid imagery the cruelty and tragedy, the joy and the longing of human beings in this world, but they do not suggest a social cure or a moral except as this is incorporated in the web and woof of the tale. Howard Pyle is perhaps the exception; his retelling of fairy tales includes both proverbs and provincialisms as part of his masterful style. In programming, the storyteller must discriminate between myth and fairy tale; each reaches out to a different age group, and fulfills a different function in storytelling periods.

Another enormous body of narrative material can be designated as epic, saga, or heroic literature. In many respects the first two resemble the third, but epics involve a line or a ruling dynasty, such as *The High Deeds of Finn McCool* (Sutcliff) in Ireland; *Rama the Hero of India* (Mukerji); *The Five Sons of King Pandu* (*Mahabbarata*) (Seeger), also set in India; "Njal" in *Heroes of Iceland* (French); *The Story of Siegfried* (Baldwin), in Germany; and the Volsungs saga, *Sons of the Volsungs* (Hosford), in Scandinavia. Supernatural elements may exist, but these epics and sagas are based in fact and, in general, reveal the accretion of lore, fact, and legend which rises around a national hero or regime. They are infinitely more complex than hero tales that focus on one character—his deeds, his words, his followers, his teachings. Heroes, too, may have a supernatural aspect, but they are more often historical personages such as *Beowulf* (Sutcliff), *Roland* (Baldwin), *Charlemagne and His Knights* (Pyle, K.), "Ogier the Dane" (Hyde), *Cuchulain, the Hound of Ulster* (Hull), *[El] Cid Campeador* (Sherwood), *Rustem* (Renninger), "Jason and the Argonauts" (Jacobs—*Wonder*), "Hector" (Church—*Iliad*), and "Aeneas" (Church—*Aeneid*).

The last large category of tellable material for story programming includes the literary fairy tale and the modern imaginative story. Neither is real folklore, since they possess acknowledged authors, but many stories from this area are found in the storyteller's repertoire because they are fresh, tellable, and an indispensable part of our literary heritage: *Alice in Wonderland* (Carroll); the stories of

Hans Christian Andersen; *Pinocchio* (Collodi); the *Rootabaga Stories* (Sandburg); *Just So* and *The Jungle Book* (Kipling); *The Wind in the Willows* (Grahame); and *Winnie the Pooh* (Milne). The fairy tales written by Wilhelm Hauff, George MacDonald, Frank Stockton, Eleanor Farjeon, Rose Fyleman, and Henry Beston are inspired by and, in part, infused with folklore and folklore motifs. This material, along with recent imaginative short stories and illustrated tales, should not be overlooked in planning rich and varied story hours, although in some cases the tales or selections may need reading aloud to preserve the exact style of the author. In other cases, the storyteller may need to abridge, adapt, or retell the stories to meet individual program needs.

One final observation: though folk and fairy tales impinge upon each other, and it is not a tragic mistake to confuse them, in general folktales have a greater emotional impact on us than the more impersonal fairy tales; folktales tend to be more earthy, less sheltered in their imagery, with the stress on plot, action, brief dialogue, outline-characterization, and onomatopoetic words. We react to folk characters because they reflect our own brave, foolish, funny actions; on the other hand, fairy tales have deeper symbolism and somewhat more fanciful or mystical settings. There is, therefore, an element of contrast between the genres. Folk tales are also more usable with younger children than are fairy tales.

In considering a tale for story programming, we need to ask ourselves if this story really is familiar to the children or if we only assume that it is. They may only have heard it in a very poor version—a cartoon, or a supermarket edition perhaps. Would they enjoy it more in a better dress—or a completely new one—a variant refreshing to both listeners and storyteller? Basic plots are subject to change as they move from teller to teller, from age to age. The changes reflect differences in background, incident, customs, expressions, and characterization, yet the story still holds to the main theme and the same motivation. If only slight details are different, we recognize the story as a variation; but if everything is different except the basic motif and the general idea underlying the story, we may have a parallel. In most cases, however, as a story wanders from one culture to another, one country to another, it becomes a variant of a basic plot. Many variations of

one story can exist side by side in the same society, but this is not necessarily true of variants. For example, most American children know the Joel Chandler Harris form of "The Tar Baby." Among Navajos there is a story called "Big-Long-Man's Cornpatch" (Hogner); in Africa, among many variants, two are known as "Wakaima and the Clay Man" (Kalibala) and "All Stories Are Anansi's" (Courlander—*Dance*). But centuries before that, the people of India told an ancient tale, "The Demon with the Matted Hair" (Jacobs—*Indian*), undoubtedly a parallel of the Tar-baby story. Storytellers can find endless enrichment for programming by using variants. For example, a storyteller wishing to use *Cinderella* (Brown) might instead consider "The Girl with the Rose-red Slippers" (Green, R. L.), from ancient Egypt; "The Bear" (Lang—*Rose*), from Sicily; "A Korean Cinderella" (Carpenter—*Korean*), from Korea; "Nippit-fit and Clippit-fit" (Grierson), from Scotland; "Turkey Girl" (Leach—*Rainbow*), from the Acoma Pueblo Indians; "Little Finger" (Manning-Sanders—*Gianni*) from the Mediterranean area; "The Many-furred One" (Wiggin and Smith—*Ring*), from Germany; "Katie Woodencloak" (Thompson, S.) from Norway; "The Maiden with the Wooden Helmet" (Lang—*Violet*), from Japan; "The Little Scarred One" (Child Study Association—*Castles*), from the Canadian Micmac Indians; or "Donkey-Skin" (Perrault—*French*), from France. A storyteller should recognize, however, that not all of the hundreds of variants of Cinderella—or any other folk/fairy tale—are equally appealing, suitable for children, or right for a particular program. From an ethnological point of view, variants reflect cultural differences in mores, dress, and religion, and they are important in helping us understand the whole vast pattern of change from a sociological viewpoint. In variants, fragments of different stories may be amalgamated, multiple characters may be substituted for a single person, events may be reversed, animals may replace humans or be replaced by humans as the protagonists, as in the story of "Puss in Boots" (de la Mare—*Animal*), France; "Mighty Mikko" (Fillmore—*Nosegay*), Finland; or "The Miller King" (Tashjian), Armenia. A witch, a godmother, a magic heifer, a magic pear tree or some other such supernatural element may be introduced, and in order to make good sense and keep the context, contingent factors may then need altering. Speech patterns may color closing or opening rituals or formulae within the story, and habits of dress may illustrate costumes in widely different cultures. Consider the great differences between "Umusha-Mwaice" (Savory), from Africa, and *Mead Moon-daughter* (Boucher) from Iceland, both Cinderella variants.

With variations, it is not cultural change that is at work, but human frailty, for only details change as the story is told: general terms are substituted for particular ones—a bird replaces a sparrow; numbers change—two brothers replace three; specific characters become unspecific—the "blacksmith," for instance, is now "another person," or a "tinker" becomes "the next passer-by"; story tenses may shift from past to present; the teller may use first person rather than third person voice; the title of a character may reflect the story's society, and thus "king" may change to "tsar," "chief," or "rajah"; or a contemporary detail may take the place of an archaic one, as for instance in the Jamaican variations of some of the Anansi stories from Africa. For a storyteller, variants and variations offer endless delight and variety for programming.

Moreover, the basic stories, and variants or variations of them, may be retold in different word-patterns by different writers. These word patterns we know as versions, but this will not be confusing if we think of version as the stylistic word-arrangement used as the vehicle to convey the story. For a storyteller, it is interesting to compare the Grimm stories in the versions of E. V. Crane, Wanda Gág, Margaret Hunt, and Andrew Lang. These translators, retellers, and writers used the tool of language, each in his or her individual way, although all worked with the same raw material, the *Household Stories* of Jakob and Wilhelm Grimm. In this century, Elizabeth Shub (*Of Wise Men and Simpletons*) has given us delightful new versions of those same Grimm stories, and Thomas Whitney (*In a Certain Kingdom*) has created excellent versions from the Russian skazki. Keigwin has made an authoritative version of Andersen's tales, and Joseph Jacobs's versions of the English and Celtic stories are definitive. Flora Annie Steel wrote beautiful versions of the English and Indian tales, and Howard Pyle did the same for the King Arthur and Robin Hood legends. Sometimes commercial writers have composed versions of the works of Andersen, Hauff, Perrault, MacDonald, Grimm, and Kipling for the mass markets, but in developing their programs, storytellers should be wary of these; they are good choices for neither teller nor children, and they depreciate the quality of the storytelling program. Walter de la Mare says that tales told for centuries are apt to be worn down to the bare bones. But not all peoples, or storytellers, have equal gifts in passing on those well-worn tales as pieces of narrative literature. It takes more than plot and incidents to form a meaningful and beautiful story for children, as de la Mare's distinguished prose illustrates most emphatically. In referring to the "cauldron of story," one may speak of variants as the "spice" of the stew, and versions as the ingredients of the "basic soup stock."

Though some modern versions illustrate a desire to replace archaic terminology with more understandable language for today's readers, they are not always successful. A good version of an old tale preserves the elixir of its plot and protagonists, and keeps, as well, the viewpoint and spirit of the original storytellers. So, in translating stories into English, the translator must feel the story as a whole, identify with its culture, and make these elements discernible in the version which emerges in the translation. This is especially true of epic and heroic stories. It takes skill, empathy, and perception on the part of translator, rewriter, reteller, and storyteller to catch the flavor of, for example, Icelandic culture, or Greek, or Teutonic, or Norse civilizations—and create strong, sensitive, authentic versions of those original tales. Dealing with narrative material from a linguistic background different from one's own demands a feel for the idiomatic speech patterns and the rhythm of the sentence patterns, as well as the syntactical arrangement of verbs and nouns. The versionist must bring to his or her new creation a fitting vocabulary, spontaneous action, and appropriate description so that the characters and plot assume life and significance for the new audience. A difficult assignment, and small wonder that we turn again and again to those writers whose versions have withstood time and attack, writers such as Margaret Hunt and Joseph Jacobs. The difference that a particular version can make is illuminated when the treatment of Greek heroes by Kingsley (*The Heroes*) and Hawthorne (*Tanglewood Tales*) is compared. The events are the same, but the feeling is decidedly not.

For storytellers wishing to include illustrated editions of folk and fairy tales in their programming—and who does not!—version is exceptionally important, for although the art work may be magnificent, very often the text is poor. It may be necessary for the teller to use another version or retell the story, and then show the pictures. Marcia Brown, however, has produced works which are beautiful examples of good version and distinguished illustration: *Dick Whittington and His Cat, The Flying Carpet, Stone Soup, Cinderella, The Bun, Once a Mouse,* and *The Neighbors.*

To summarize, the storyteller's selection of stories should include variants for program contrast, as well as occasional variations and parallels. Whatever is chosen should be well written, worthy of the time and attention of both teller and listener, and contributive to the balance and mood of the story period. The bulk of programming material will be found among folk and fairy tales, but the storyteller should be aware of interesting legends, myths, riddles, hero tales, fables, noodlehead and drolls, and pourquoi tales, as well as cumulative stories, animal fantasies, and modern imaginative material. A programmer must weigh long, short, illustrated, present-day, and ancient tales, and consider the style of various stories as well, balancing flowing narratives against brief epigrammatic literature. The enormous scope of narrative literature available for the building of story programs is, in fact, amazing.

4

Sources
for Storytellers

Probably one of the greatest concerns of the beginning storyteller lies in the question, "Where can I find good material?" To find and tell stories well requires time, patience, and enthusiasm, and much can be learned from those who have been storytellers for several years. One of the best sources for stories is the general anthologies drawn up by authorities in the field of children's literature. The authors, often in several editions, have drawn representative stories from a wide field, selecting tellable tales from areas that are representative of the whole field of narrative folklore—legend, myth, and so on. Sometimes they have even indicated which stories will make the greatest appeal to a specific age group, and usually they have set aside those tales directed toward nursery and preschool groups: *Time for Fairy Tales* (Arbuthnot, all editions); *An Anthology of Children's Literature* (Johnson, Sickels, Sayers, all editions); *A Book of Children's Literature* (Hollowell); *Story and Verse for Children* (Huber); and *The Arbuthnot Anthology* (all editions). Collections such as these give an overview of the whole field of children's literature, with excellent versions of tellable tales. The older editions include basic, time-tested stories; the newer editions contain selections from recently published and well-received stories, poetry, fantasy, and individual illustrated editions of folk and fairy tales, as well as some of the older materials.

A second ready-made source is found in specific collections compiled by recognized storytellers, calling on their years of experience in children's work. The following are especially valuable:

1. *Bag o' Tales* by Effie Power, an early anthology now available in a good paperback edition. She has also written *From Umar's Pack, Stories to Shorten the Road*, and *Blue Caravan Tales*. Though out of print, these are available in large public library collections.

2. Four anthologies of easy-to-tell and familiar stories compiled by Veronica Hutchinson and carefully presented: *Chimney Corner Stories, Fireside Stories, Candlelight Stories*, and *Chimney Corner Fairy Tales*.

3. *The Golden Lynx* and *The Talking Tree*, compiled by Augusta Baker from favorite selections of children to whom she told the stories at the New York Public Library.

Another outstanding storyteller from the New York Library, Mary Gould Davis, found the children especially liked the stories she has gathered together under the title of *A Baker's Dozen*.

Long ago delightful picture stories in a tiny format were published, representing folklore from

Spain, Mexico, Holland, Russia, Japan, France, Scandinavia, Italy, and China (see series bibliography for titles). Now out of print, some of the best of these have been compiled by Eulalie Steinmetz Ross under the name of *The Buried Treasure*. More recently, additional choices from these old treasures were included in *Tricky Peik* by Baltimore storyteller Jeanne Hardendorff. Two old collections written by Howard Pyle have never lost their flavor: *The Wonder Clock* and *Pepper and Salt*. And for sheer beauty of version, master storyteller and poet Walter de la Mare has written *Animal Stories, Told Again*, and *Stories from the Bible*.

A famous English storyteller, Eileen Colwell, has listed suggestions and given practical advice, including time needed for telling, in two recent collections: *A Storyteller's Choice* and *A Second Storyteller's Choice*. These storyteller's anthologies must certainly include the works of Richard Chase, who has retold and sketched the background of European tales transplanted and rerooted in the Appalachian Mountains: *The Jack Tales* and *Grandfather Tales*, rich and rare contributions to a storytelling program. Seumas MacManus, a modern Irish shenachie, has contributed *Donegal Wonder Tales, Bold Heroes of Hungry Hill*, and *In Chimney Corners*; Jean Cothran has assembled and retold stories most effectively in *With a Wig, with a Wag* and *The Magic Calabash*.

Storytellers will find a third excellent source for stories in several series of folk and fairy tales written by Frances Carpenter, Frances Olcott, Kate Douglas Wiggin and Nora Smith, Ruth Manning-Sanders, and by Dorothy Spicer. A number of years ago Frances Olcott created *Wonder Tales from . . .* (1) *China Seas* (2) *Goblin Hills* (3) *Windmill Lands* (4) *Baltic Wizards* and (5) *Persian Genii*. Though some of the material here is fragmentary and needs retelling or amplifying, much of it cannot be found elsewhere. Olcott also compiled a valuable anthology of American Indian tales from diverse tribes, *The Red Indian Fairy Book*; although perhaps somewhat sentimental in its treatment, it provides excellent source material.

Frances Carpenter has a number of unusual tales in her *Grandmother Tales . . .* (1) *of a Korean Grandmother*, (2) *of a Russian Grandmother*, (3) *of a Basque Grandmother*, (4) *of a Chinese Grandmother*, and (5) *of a Swiss Grandmother*. She has several good *Wonder Tales* anthologies of: (1)

Ships and Seas, (2) *Dogs and Cats*, and (3) *Horses and Heroes*.

The third series, by Kate D. Wiggin and Nora Smith, is called *The Fairy Library* and contains hundreds of good stories in its four volumes: *Magic Casements, The Fairy Ring, Tales of Wonder*, and *Tales of Laughter*. These may still be found in large collections, and a recent revision of *The Fairy Ring* has been published.

Two other favorite series have appeared in the last fifteen years, one compiled by an American, Dorothy Spicer, the other the work of an English storyteller and anthologist, Ruth Manning-Sanders. Though the sources given in both series are sketchy, the tales are exhilarating, told with discrimination and flair, and representative of both familiar and unfamiliar folklore. Only a partial listing is given here, however; there are a number of others in these two series, all with the same format: Manning-Sanders's *A Book of . . .* or Spicer's *Thirteen* [13]. . . . Complete listings may be found in *Books in Print* and in the Series Bibliography. Titles from the series by Ruth Manning-Sanders include *A Book of Ghosts and Goblins; A Book of Giants; A Book of Mermaids; A Book of Witches*; and *A Book of Wizards*. Dorothy Spicer has written *13 Ghosts; 13 Goblins, 13 Giants; 13 Jolly Saints; 13 Witches*; and others.

One particular fairy tale series has proved delightful to storytellers as well as to readers because of the excellent choice of material and retelling. Developed by the head of Children's Services, Library of Congress, Virginia Haviland's *Favorite Fairy Tales Told in . . .* Germany, Spain, Sweden, England, Japan, Italy, Scotland, Denmark, Norway, France, Russia, Poland, India, and Czechoslovakia, has established itself firmly as a storytelling resource. Each volume contains four or five stories, with discriminating illustrations.

An additional series, rich and old, is the "color" library of fairy tales compiled by Andrew Lang, discussed at length later on. These are also detailed in the Series Bibliography.

A fourth source of tales for programmers may be found in several books on storytelling technique by four modern and outstanding storytellers. Stories have been included as illustrative material in these books, choice tales used by them many times over. Although not all of the stories are for the immediate use of a new storyteller, they are important stories to consider for inclusion in story hours. The books are: *The Way of the Storyteller*, by Ruth Sawyer; *The Art of the Storyteller*, by Marie Shedlock; *How to Tell Stories to Children* and *Best Stories to Tell Children*, by Sara Cone Bryant; and *The Story-Telling Hour*, by Carolyn Sherwin Bailey. Many of the stories in this last book have been republished in her *Favorite Stories for Children*.

An enormous source of program material, a fifth source, is found in the storehouse of heroic tales, myths, and legends adapted, retold, abridged, and translated by outstanding writers such as Ella Young, Padraic Colum, Thomas Malory, Walter de la Mare, James Baldwin, Alfred Church, and Babette Deutsch. These authors have provided tellable and distinguished examples of great heroic literature, and they may be located through public library folklore collections (*see* the Saga, Epic, and Hero Tales portion of the Bibliography for complete listing). It is safe to say that telling saga, epic, and hero tales is one of the most demanding and exacting of storytelling areas, not usually suitable for a beginner, and with material often not easy to work into an after-school story program. For special programming, however, hero tales are indeed choice. An excellent single source for a variety of stories from this body of literature is contained in *Hero Tales from Many Lands*, by Alice Hazeltine. In addition, the highly dramatic and very exciting stories from the Old Testament and beautiful parables from the New Testament often add to a story program. Not all versions of Bible stories are acceptable for telling, but those found in *Stories from the Bible*, by Walter de la Mare, are excellent.

Holiday anthologies form a special sixth source for storytellers. For Christmas, unquestionably the most distinguished tales are to be found in *This Way to Christmas*, *The Long Christmas*, and *Joy to the World*, all by Ruth Sawyer. These comprise beautifully retold legends, folk tales, and fantasy, all highly tellable. Elizabeth Sechrist, based on her many years of experience, has compiled *Heigh-ho for Halloween*, *It's Time for Thanksgiving*, *It's Time for Christmas*, and *It's Time for Easter*. Wilhelmina Harper has gathered stories, background material, and poetry in *Easter Chimes*, *The Harvest Feast*, *Ghosts and Goblins*, and *Merry Christmas to You*. Although there are other anthologies, these are standard on any storyteller's source list.

Anthologists and retellers who specialize in stories from specific ethnic areas form a seventh area for storytellers to examine. Natalie Carlson, calling upon her French-Canadian heritage, has written *Sashes Red and Blue* and *The Talking Cat* with subtlety and wit. Sorche Nic Leodhas (pseudonym for Le Claire Alger) retells with particular savor Scotch tales from the Highlands, eerie legends from the Lowlands and the Outer Islands, ballads and clan-hero tales from Scottish history in *By Loch and Lin*, *Heather and Broom*, *Gaelic Ghosts*, *Ghosts Go Haunting*, *Claymore and Kilt*, *Sea Spell and Moor Magic*, *Thistle and Thyme*, and *Twelve Great Black Cats*. These are invaluable for story programs.

Another most enthusiastic ethnic anthologist and folklorist is Harold Courlander, who has recorded tales from native tellers and then retold them, preserving many flavorful folk idioms and colloquialisms: *The King's Drum*, Africa; *The Hatshaking Dance*, African Anansi stories; *The Cowtail Switch*, West Africa; *Kantchil's Lime Pit*, Indonesia; *People of the Short Blue Corn*, American Hopi Indian; *Terrapin's Pot of Sense*, Afro-American; and many more. His background notes are discriminating and his sources unusually thorough. All storytellers building programs need to tap this source and discover Courlander's pungent, strong versions.

Moritz Jagendorf is another anthologizer of North and South American folklore, well documented and retold: *The New England Bean Pot*, *Up-State, Down-State*, *The Marvelous Adventures of Johnny Darling*, and *The King of the Mountain* —also only a partial list.

A final large source, perhaps the most important of all, consists of the basic folklore collected and anthologized in the nineteenth century on the European continent. At that time a mighty impulse stirred in Finland, Germany, England, and Scandinavia to unearth, investigate, and retell the folk literature of the several countries. Outstanding writers, researchers, folklorists, collectors, and translators were caught up in the wave, and a great stream of vital, hitherto unknown narrative lore became available in English translations—old tales from American Indians, Eire, Wales, Norway, Finland and Sweden, the Far East. This new "ocean of story," tapped by Jakob and Wilhelm Grimm, Henry Schoolcraft, Joseph Jacobs, George Grinnell,

Sir George Dasent, and Andrew Lang and presented in hearty, flavorful English still forms the backbone of the storyteller's collection. The stories remain as vigorous and delightful as when first published, although of course the storyteller adjusts the selections to the individual program, using the material in its familiar form or changing it slightly.

This surge of interest in folklore washed over such creative writers as Andersen, Stockton, Beston, Hauff, and inspired them to use some of the themes in their own imaginative fairy tales and fantasies, reweaving and adapting the old themes to unusual and stimulating new uses. From his years in India, Kipling produced *The Jungle Book* and *Just So Stories*, demonstrating that his long and fantastic words could enchant children. Andersen spun his stories, simple or sophisticated, first on folk themes, then around such common articles as a shirt, a broom, a top, or a tin soldier. Because the language and narrative style of such artists is unique, a good deal of the flavor depends on using their exact phraseology, and the storyteller would do well to read these stories aloud, rather than memorize or retell them—they beg for oral expression.

From this basic core of stories, perhaps we should look again at tales told repeatedly in story hours, drawn from the works of Joseph Jacobs and Andrew Lang. The retelling, adapting, collecting, and writing which these two have contributed to the field of oral literature is worthy of special recognition. Jacobs was intrigued by the faery world—the world of elves, boggarts, and changelings. He was also interested in England's heroic literature, and within these two fields he expended enormous effort to probe the legends and folklore of Ireland, Scotland, Wales, and India, rewriting the material he uncovered to retain the strength, idiomatic feeling, straightforwardness, and original quality of the story, its joyousness, sadness, wit, or beauty. Careful annotations indicate his changes and the variants or parallels he discovered—a storyteller's delight. No better sources can be tapped than *Indian Fairy Tales* (Jataka, Bidpai, and fairy lore), *English Fairy Tales, More English Fairy Tales, Celtic Fairy Tales* and *More Celtic Fairy Tales*.

At approximately the same time Andrew Lang, a Scot with gypsy blood in his veins, became entranced with the lore of the moors, fens, and lochs of his native land, and intrigued with story variants he found. His belief that folktales the world over were the outgrowth of common human experience caused him to unearth folk stories from every corner of the globe, while simultaneously making closer contact with such creative artists as Andersen and Madame D'Aulnoy. He began to compile representative tales, both known and unknown, in fresh translations (done by his wife and others) into a single volume called *The Blue Fairy Book*. This book was published over one hundred years ago; a new reprinting, celebrating that fact, attests to the soundness and popularity of his work, still widely used by both children and storytellers. Next he proceeded to collect, translate, annotate, and retell other familiar tales; then he moved on to less familiar works, and eventually to totally new and unusual narratives, publishing them in zestful, tellable versions which delighted readers and storytellers. These books form the *Color Library of Fairy Tales*, beginning with the *Blue*, and including *The Red, Green, Yellow, Olive, Grey, Lilac, Violet, Rose, Crimson, Orange, Brown* and *Pink Fairy Books*. The recent and excellent Dover reproductions, containing the original illustrations, still represent a gold mine for programmers. Not all of the stories are usable with every group, of course, nor can one storyteller tell all of the hundreds of variants the collection offers. Andrew Lang also published an excellent retelling of *The Arabian Nights Entertainments* and *Tales of Troy and Greece*.

Supplementing this basic source list are a few other older titles that should be included in the basic bibliography of any academic program in storytelling. Time-tested, they have offered much to story hours year after year: *Tales from Grimm, More Tales from Grimm*, and *Three Gay Tales from Grimm*, by Wanda Gág, drawn from childhood storytellers, warmly illustrated; *Grimm's Fairy Tales* in Margaret Hunt's definitive translation; *The Well o' the World's End*, and *Hibernian Nights*, retold by Seumas MacManus, the last of the Irish shenachies, featuring the best of the Irish heritage; *Old Peter's Russian Tales*, skillfully retold by Ransome; *Russian Tales and Legends*, by Downing, from the great treasury of Russian skazki; *True and Untrue*, by Undset; *Norwegian Folk Tales* from Asbjornsen and Moe, retold from the Dasent translation; *13 Danish Tales*, and *More Danish Tales*, retold by Mary Hatch; *Tales from a Finnish Tupa*, by Bowman; and *Perrault's Complete Fairy Tales*, as translated by Johnson. This represents a far from complete survey of old and good source material essential to any storyteller.

Epic and saga literature has been neglected here because the stories are often too long, too involved, or too complex in plot for the average story hour program. For other kinds of programming they should certainly be considered.

From the types of source material given here, how does the inexperienced storyteller go about choosing stories? Step One: Browse freely in the various collections, jotting down titles that sound inviting, or, if you have an idea in mind, look for titles that would connect with that idea. Return later to read the stories at length, discovering if they are tellable and suitable for the story period, but this initial browsing will give a feeling of some of the narrative material available.

Step Two: Check the lists of titles in the story-telling lists drawn up by experienced tellers, noting those that have appeal for the idea under consideration. One reliable storytelling list is *Stories* from the New York Public Library, edited by Augusta Baker, now in its sixth edition. Save them all. A second storytelling list is that published by the Enoch Pratt Free Library in Baltimore, edited by Jean Hardendorff, called *Stories to Tell*, 5th ed. *Stories to Tell to Children*, edited by Cathon, Hodges, Russell, is from the Pittsburgh Carnegie Library and has been extremely useful through eight editions. Annotations are given for stories on these lists, and the lists should not be discarded.

Step Three: Check through the *Eastman Fairy Tale Index* and the three supplements and jot down likely titles to identify further later on. That browsing, even without annotations, will suggest variants and stories in related areas. To a lesser degree, the *Short Story Index* (for children) is useful, though this is not directed primarily toward story hour materials. But interesting additions to the story program often emerge from just such random searches. For Indian tales, Judith Ullom's extensive, annotated *Bibliography of American Indian Folklore* points out collections which contain good stories for telling, with background information on what those collections represent.

After noting down likely titles, and their sources, locate the stories and read them to discover if they are what you wish to use in your program. Finally, after selecting the stories, make a copy of the story for a storytelling file either by hand or, if the book is ever discarded, by clipping. It is better to have the complete story in your file than an outline, and a story file is invaluable. Many stories will be told over and over, used in several different programs over the years and, if handy, easily brought into focus when needed.

It is a good thing to watch reviews for new materials, new editions of older collections, and new single editions of tales. *School Library Journal, The Horn Book*, and the *Kirkus Review Service* all point up folktales, as well as suggest bibliographies.

In summary, more stories can be found for telling than any teller can use in a lifetime. Until sure of yourself, depend on old, recognized sources for stories, using lists of stories prepared by story-telling groups and relying on the suggestions of experienced storytellers. Then, after accumulating some materials and browsing through much folklore, you will begin to have a feel for the truly tellable tale, the one that promises to be a comfortable kind of story, one you will have time to learn, that you can make your own and return to many times over.

Specific tales for planned programs will also be found. With increasing experience, branch out to explore new collections and special kinds of material—the picture-story fairy and folktales, modern fantasy, stories for special occasions and particular groups; programs for older children, and varied circumstances.

Tolkien says that now and then he came across a tale that suddenly gave him a fleeting glimpse of joy, "a lifting of the heart," and it is this kind of emotion that the storyteller setting out on the storytelling road must discover.

5

Elements
of Programming

The previous introduction was extensive because it is vital that modern storytellers realize that storytelling is an inheritance involving much more than learning stories and retelling them on various occasions. Unless they share in the spirit of the old storytellers, who felt that they were set apart as the bearers of a great tradition, modern storytellers will never bring to the recreation of their tales that "sense of story" that is so important. Few, indeed, become "storytellers" in the fullest sense of the word, yet many tell stories as part of their professional activities. Storytelling should be an ongoing experience for children, not just one scheduled activity in a busy week. The program of storytelling can provide children with something they will get in no other way, especially today. For the librarian, programming to make story times more significant is a process, not an incident, a process of choosing story materials carefully and relating them creatively.

To form a satisfying, significant whole is most important. To the selection of a story the storyteller adds his or her technique (a hidden one, to be sure) and sense of sharing in something that transcends both the teller and the group, thus catching up the children with zest and anticipation in an almost tangible web of rapport. A well-designed story hour moves from the beginning to the end with a rhythm and balance as surely as does a piece of music. There is an almost palpable texture to it and a mood which can surmount many interruptions to hold the children until the planned conclusion.

Children are not conscious of these elements, nor should they be. The preparation, the planning, the research needed to discover, put together, and create with artistry and conviction the thirty to forty-five minute story hour is the storyteller's province. During the story hour itself, the storyteller maintains a curious, three-fold inner stance as: (1) observer of the group reaction; (2) the teller, the medium for the story content; and (3) participant in an experience larger than any single element, the story itself. The story is bigger than either the telling of it or the listening to it, but it does not really come alive until the teller and child interact.

In retrospect, the storyteller goes over the story hour, reviewing (1) the telling—where could it have been improved, and how? (2) the rapport—could a better relationship have been established, a better climate for the story? (3) the program—was there too much choppiness instead of fluidity in the movement of one story into another? Did the teller demand too much serious thought, too little "funnybone," for an after-school activity? Was the reach of the stories beyond the grasp of the group? Or, was there not enough invigorating thought, enough inspiration? In finding the answers to these questions, the storyteller is investigating the important area of programming. It is true that the composition of the group (many newcomers, for instance, in an established group) can weaken the esprit de corps and make the telling more difficult, and extraneous influences such as important events or emotional disturbances have a bearing on the success of any particular story period. Some story hours leave a storyteller with an inner exhilaration, others with that feeling that nothing quite "jelled."

Careful planning, preparation, presentation, and evaluation are the tools of a storyteller who wants the most satisfying story program. It is not enough to have a well-filled pack of tales ready to tell, nor is it enough to gather children together and ask the children what they want, though there is, naturally, a place for that kind of storytelling. Because, in spite of their exposure to television, children's knowledge of the world is still limited, and they often fail to distinguish what is remote and strange from what is fantastic and unreal, what is absurd from what is, as yet, undiscovered. Nor do they really understand their deep, inner needs. The elements used in programming the story experience can answer some of these needs.

First, the storyteller must ask what he or she hopes to accomplish in the overall activity. It will surely involve creating a taste for reading on the part of the children. It will seek to stretch their horizons and to introduce them to other children and their ways of life, as revealed through our literary heritage. It seeks to demonstrate to the children the fun of words, the feel of their own language well used; perhaps the story program will help the children learn to better express themselves. A secondary objective will be to put them in touch, little by little, with the treasures of narrative literature—folklore and other kinds—in a way they will respond to, and so enjoy.

A third objective tied into a particular year's program will be the exploration of a broad theme in some depth. For example, magic, with fairies, giants, enchanted spells; animals, real and unreal, ancient, and in the future; or Indians, many tribes, many customs. This type of broad theme will stretch the children's imagination over a wide area. A fourth dimension of a good program could be the individual, smaller goals of each particular story period. For example, using the theme "Story Magic" a story program was devoted to tales about wizards; another to stories about "little people" such as "Tom Thumb" (Jacobs—*English*) ; another to mermaids. An Indian "Storytelling Fires" theme touched on Eastern Woodland Tribes one month, with each successive week featuring a different tribe to furnish the story material; in another month, Northland Indians were considered, and during the weeks of that month Canadian Indians, Eskimos, and Indians of the Northern Forests furnished the folklore and story material. In the "Story Zoo," sea creatures were the focus for one month, followed by programs for whales, seals, sharks; another for fish; another for shelled animals, and so on.

After deciding upon the objective—what is to be accomplished?—the storyteller must consider the content of the program—what material will bring this objective about?—linking together both objective and content into the design of the story period. Usually an after-school story hour is about forty-five minutes long; within this time span, the storyteller must relate the material to create balance, rhythm, and a definite mood.

First, balance in the program must be examined. A normal story hour group is mixed in experience and cultural conditioning, and ranges from the first through the fifth grades, with the largest group probably in the second through fourth grades. The attention span of the youngest is about ten minutes long, of the oldest twenty minutes. A younger listener will become involved in a story that is too difficult more readily than an older listener will with something too young. There must therefore be a balance in the length of stories—some very short, some longer. It is better, in a recreational group such as a story hour, to have several stories; two twenty-minute stories allows a short "stretcher" in between but does not allow much choice of material and is too concentrated for the younger members of the group. It is wiser to choose one long story, one very short, one of medium length, and connective material between, such as poetry, conversation, chanting, a picture, a riddle. Each selection, however, must not be chosen just as filler, but must lead from one element to another without breaking the mood of the story hour as a whole. It is possible to have four or five very short stories, if they are contrasting in content and real stories, not anecdotes. Story length, then, is one of the considerations in striking balance.

A second important element in creating balance involves variety. Variety in the type of story material within the story hour is essential. All of the stories may be on one theme, but some contrast must be present. If one tale is a short funny animal story, it should be balanced by a more serious one; if one story is matter-of-fact, it could be set off by another with an element of fantasy; if one story has the frank buoyancy of a folktale, another must have dramatic impact. The content of the story may contribute to the variety, but the style of the story also affords variety. For example, the high fantasy of the Kipling *Just So Story* "The Elephant's Child," with its wonderful flow of language, can effectively contrast with a pithy and practical Aesop fable such as "The Dog in the Manger" (Arbuthnot—*Fairy Tales*), with a variant of the animal tug-of-war story such as "Elephant and the Whale" (Bryant—*Best*), fast-moving and funny, or with an illustrated story from *The Panchatantra*, "The Elephants and the Mice" by Hirsh, for instance. Such a program would have balance of content in story length, type of story, and the rhythm of the stories used. Variety involves more than length or style, however, and more than kind of story (fable, fantasy, folktale, fairy story). Variety may be found in the background of the story, and also in the mood (humor, pathos, wonder). Variety, the objective, is attained by a judicious use of contrast and reaffirmation. An entire program of American Indian stories might be used, but they should not all be "why" stories; three fairy stories are fine if they have as much contrast as *Sleeping Beauty* (Grimm) and "Drakestail" (Manning-Sanders—*Beasts*). A final, important element in variety is the demand which the tale makes on its listeners. If they have become deeply involved in "Rikki-Tikki-Tavi" (Kipling—*Jungle*), with its intense drama, they will need to relax with something less demanding—"Goody-'gainst-the-Stream" (Jagendorf—*World*), for instance. The first element in programming, then, is to create balance through an interweaving of variety, contrast, and story length.

The consideration of rhythm in a story hour is a second important factor. This involves the quality of the individual tale and the pacing of the various stories. Quality is not the content of the story, but the feel of the story as a whole; in fact, a story hour with three stories, all humorous, could even so leave a feeling of heaviness in the story hour. The way of the story, as it moves along, and the way one story moves into another determines the rhythm of the story hour.

The third important matter for a storyteller to consider involves the placement of the stories within the time framework; as a result of this placement, the mood of the story hour is created. No unbreakable rule can be given, since each story hour is different, but in general, after an opening ritual or some other introductory factor used to focus, or settle, the group, the first story should be arresting, vivid, and not too long. Depending on the objective of that particular story hour, it can be startling, humorous, unbelievable, or very familiar, but it should "catch up" the boys and girls and kindle an esprit de corps. Some tellers use poems as connectives between stories, some conversation, some background comment, some pictures. Whatever is chosen should join the initial story to the following story smoothly without breaking the thread of anticipation for the second selection, often the pièce de résistance. This is often the most involved, the most dramatic, and the one containing the heart of this specific story hour. At its conclusion, the taste or savour of the tale will be experienced by both teller and told, if they are in tune with each other. (Never, never ask them the point, or try to reemphasize the theme.) This should be followed by a humorous, spirited, or novel selection to round out the pattern before the closing, which may be a ritual or a look-ahead. Whatever is chosen, it should be decisive, leaving a feeling of "happy ending." Stretchers—brief riddles, songs, chants, motion activities—are often used by good storytellers to keep the children from getting tired, since today's children do not have a long span of attention, due partially to the electronic media, with their incredible advertising blurbs every ten or twelve minutes. But stretchers must be skillfully interjected.

This is the pattern most commonly used, but since the objective for any particular story hour forms the background design, and the story content forms the figures against that background, variations are possible. At times a teller may plunge in with a rush, or the program may include a series of short, short stories. The placement of the stories within the story time still sets the mood of that story hour, however. Mood plays a most important part in storytelling, an indefinable quality which, like timbre in a voice, or texture in a piece of cloth, is hard to define, but vital.

Consider objectives for a moment. Many storytellers like to develop their programs one at a time. Perhaps they feel there is more spontaneity to them in this way, but this may not necessarily be true. Others prefer to set up four- or six-week story hour schedules. A longer-range program appears preferable, with a story hour running once a week from October to April (or through April) for forty-five minutes each time. This allows the storyteller to choose a big, umbrellalike theme to cover the whole story season. Within that total design, each weekly period can be developed as a distinctive part of the pattern; in turn, a distinctive pattern emerges within each weekly story hour. Behind the total story program are the ultimate goals of a storytelling program in a public library, that is, an opening window for children onto great thoughts, a pointer toward high ideals, an exposure to vivid imagination, and a sharing in high good humor as these are reflected in myth, folk and fairy tales, and other creative literature. The practical objective of whetting children's desire to explore the world through books for themselves is also an ongoing motive. One story hour of forty-five minutes is long enough to be flexible, to present several points of view, and to delight, but it will not accomplish too much toward these overall goals. But seven months of carefully designed story programs, entered into with enthusiasm and good preparation, just might. The experience is worth trying.

Children are not actually conscious of the teller's objectives, but they react obviously to the balance, rhythm, and mood of a story period. It is a help, in making them feel a part of the larger program, to give out story hour brochures which present the program for the whole season as a keepsake; this is not a necessity, only a nicety.

This discussion has focused on the recreational, after-school, volunteer story program in a public library, one that children can come to in large or small groups on a fairly regular basis. There will always be a swelling of ranks or a falling off, depending on weather, school activities, or extracur-

ricular demands, and no storyteller working with a flow of children can be guaranteed a constant group, since he or she has no captive audience. Thus there is a very real difference between this kind of story hour and a school visitation program, which may include telling stories to grades one through eight, two, three, or four times a year, each class visit lasting for twenty minutes or a bit longer. The school visit may be in a classroom, or it may be in the school library; the place has an effect on the establishment of mood. It is possible to fit a school storytelling program, with its factors of a captive, homogeneous group, into the overall theme of the library story hour quite successfully; the main theme has served as a rallying point suggesting content and choice of material for the schools. The storyteller may set aside stories for school visiting while looking for stories for the library story hour. Longer stories, and more sophisticated material, as well as selections from creative writers such as Poe, Twain, Thurber, Stockton, or Andersen, may be used for upper grade boys and girls who may not often come to the public library storyhour, because the school storyteller usually gives only one story to each of the groups reached, and all of the children are of the same age.

For example, in setting up school visitation programs we have often included, at each grade level, two traditional stories, one in the fall, and one in the spring; a holiday tale at Christmas; and finally excerpts from modern literature in June, at the end of the school year. This allows for a choice of material suited to each grade level. Of course, this takes a great deal of preparation and searching. For instance, the year that we used Story Magic for the library program, with its emphasis on the myriad magic creatures that inhabit the world of faery, we used with the sixth grades "The Contest of Vainemoinon" from the Finnish epic *Heroes of the Kalevala* in Babette Deutsch's version in October; at Christmas the story was "The Worker in Sandalwood" (Walters—*Christmas*) ; in the spring we told "The Red Shoes" (Andersen—*Complete*) ; and in June, excerpts from the science fiction trilogy by John Christopher, *City of Gold and Lead, White Mountains*, and *Pool of Fire*. The Kalevala introduces mythical personages and the power of song as a creative agent; the Christmas story stresses transformation and suprahuman resources; Andersen's story, with its apparent moral threading the fantasy, embodies magic powers; and the Christopher trilogy is a modern time-space adventure.

Because of the homegeneity of school groups, and the opportunity for a longer time for one story, a storyteller may dip into mythology, some of the Celtic and medieval hero tales, or some of the chivalric literature. Many of the children the storyteller reaches in the school program will come into the library story hour from time to time, but for others, especially in the upper grades, such a school visitation program may be the only opportunity they have to hear good storytelling. Around them on all sides are drama, television and book talks, and sometimes reading aloud, but only on rare occasions do the upper grades hear a storyteller. If a storyteller prepares carefully and is cognizant of their emerging young adult temperaments and adolescent personalities, sixth, seventh, and eighth graders do enjoy stories.

Where, using the criteria discussed, does programming extending over a long period, such as several months, and built around a basic theme, fit in? To the extent that one concentrates on a particular thematic area whose materials relate to a specific subject, it limits choice. But that should not limit the possibilities for variety. On the contrary, when imagination is used to "open up" a subject, the storyteller is likely to find that more material exists than can possibly be incorporated into one year's library story program, plus the various stories to be used in the school program. For example, in the programming described in the next section of this book, one year used a banquet theme with all of its ramifications; the theme of another year was animals of every conceivable kind; a third year featured magic and magic persons; a fourth year, journeys and how one goes on them; a fifth year the cobbler, old-time storyteller par excellence; and finally, the world of color as found in stories and story collections. A central theme thus need not limit variety; the storyteller will discover long, short, serious, and funny stories, myths, legends, fables, fantasy—the whole gamut pertaining to that theme in most unexpected ways. The only essential criterion must be that the specific story chosen will be worth telling. And therein lies a danger, that of selecting, because it fits the theme, a story unsatisfactory as a tellable narrative. Theme programming does not preclude audiovisual aids, if they are appropriate, supportive, and do not tend to push out oral presentation. It does indicate a more intensive and wider search for stories, poetry, music. A basic theme can stir imagination and creative consideration to discover how many tangential areas can be developed to an unsuspected degree.

In developing a program idea or theme, the storyteller should brainstorm all the possible related areas and list them. Jot down titles of stories found in lists, indexes, etc., whose titles or content suggest some tie to the central motif; comb the sources suggested in the previous chapters for additional tales. After reading, set aside those which are not suitable for the story hour for one reason or another, but might be serviceable in special programs. The greatest effort in story programming involves the discipline of choice as a rein for imagination. Ideas for a story theme come from every conceivable direction—a current event, some personality, a historical landmark, entertainment fields, a poem, a picture. Inspiration is everywhere. But all the ideas captured in the given time allotment cannot be used, so choose well and wisely.

This involves constantly looking over new stories, variants, and variations of old tales, searching for good versions for storytelling, staying alert to new publications. A storyteller should become familiar with a vast body of narrative literature on a continuing basis and learn to discriminate, with experience, which tales will add variety, which will appeal to specific ages, and which will make for change of pace in the story hour, always remembering the restraint of time in telling the story, as well as the time required to learn the stories and prepare for their use. Learning to build programs calls for creative skill, as surely as does learning to paint or sing. It takes analysis to enlarge upon a main idea, to see its ramifications, to snatch the initial flash of inspiration and carry it far afield, yet not so far that all of the elements cannot be interrelated and cohesive. Programming judgment is needed to discover where an illustrated picturebook format of an unfamiliar story will supplement a longer, more familiar story, or, contrariwise, a picture version of an old favorite will open up a new dimension and perhaps, by contrast, bring into focus some short, pithy new story.

Skill in creating good story hour design comes slowly and with experience, trial and error. The storyteller chooses, discards, and rearranges stories as he or she explores balance, rhythm, and place-ment in each storytelling period, in somewhat the same way that an artist considers a painting: the objectives of the total program form the back-ground, the content of each individual story hour is the subject matter; and the mood of the story-telling period that catches the children in a web of words is akin to the effect of the picture on the viewer.

6

Modifying Tales

Sooner or later, every storyteller comes across a story that, for one reason or another, he or she wants very much to use in a story hour—but cannot. If the principles discussed in programming are kept in mind, certain delimiting factors in choosing story hour materials are apparent. In brief, the story period is not long (half hour to forty-five minutes, usually); the children vary in age from the first through the fifth grade in an average group; the group is not homogeneous, so the story hour must have material that appeals to both the youngest and the oldest, the most sophisticated and the least mature; within the framework of the story hour balance, made up of variety and contrast in both content, quality of story material, and type of story materials used is necessary; yet there must be cohesiveness, harmony, and rhythm to the period as a whole so that the story hour will have atmosphere and mood. Finally, if building around a central theme, the storyteller will want that theme to be amplified and reinforced in several ways—with humor, with adventure, with interest. This is certainly not an easy bill to fill, one that takes a great deal of thought and planning. And always, of course, the storyteller must recognize that the story selected should be one he or she wants and is able to tell. So it is almost inevitable that at times a story is found that has, for example, a perfect theme but is far too long, or far too short. Or it may have just the right idea, the ideal character, and yet be poorly presented. It may be a part of a longer chronicle, with only one section containing the elements sought for. It may be right in content for the story hour, but seem a little too difficult or too complex in characterization or vocabulary.

Probably the story in question does not apply at all of these points, yet it suggests that the storyteller ask several questions: (1) Should this story be left for another occasion, when the children might be older—a school visit, perhaps? (2) Would this story be one that could be adapted—modified or changed somewhat; amplified—enriched and filled out; abridged—shortened by simplifying and condensing; or retold—keeping the theme, characters, and feel of the tale, but using other language? (3) Is it worth the time and care that any of these procedures would entail? (4) Am I capable of doing a good piece of work on this?

Adapting or retelling a story is difficult, and requires skill and background. Joseph Jacobs used the principle of identifying the root of the story, and then preserving the core of that story in all its essentials without diluting the flavor. Wanda Gág, a master at simplifying and retelling the Grimm tales,

28

worked to eliminate confusing passages, employing direct verbs wherever possible, and using the folk patterns of repetition and rhythm. Cheap versions for popular distribution often eliminate those very rhymes that contain the characteristic aural patterns of the folk tale, colloquialisms containing the spice of the tale are cut out, or worse—changed into present idioms. Perhaps so many illustrations have been created that the folktale has lost its first value —that of the aural presentation; although good illustration may add a new dimension to some folktales, many are better left without illustration, so that the child's own imagination can supply the details. For example, those folktales or fairy tales featuring widespread use of the supernatural may be more effective with only a suggestion of illustration.

Having decided that a story is indeed right for a particular purpose, the next question facing the storyteller is, "What does this story need to make it tellable and suitable for the place where I think it fits?" In most cases, it will need adapting, abridging, amplifying, or retelling. These will be discussed separately, adding examples and the reasons for their selection.

Several basic principles should be kept in mind for all of these processes. First, the essential nature of the story must be kept intact. Second, the flavor of the story, its unique taste, must be maintained. Third, the structure of the story must emerge with clarity—an engaging beginning, action that builds steadily to a recognizable climax, a satisfactory denouement, and a flavorful conclusion. An initial step in working with any story is to analyze and outline the action, to understand the reason for those actions. The main plot should be identified, and any subplot eliminated. Words should fit the theme and background of the story, and the word pattern should have both syntax and vocabulary which reflect the cultural roots of the tale. The logic of the plot, the people, and the relationships outlined in the story must be coherent and plausible, even if the story is strongly fantastic. Many times logic is indicated by verbs chosen and the flow of dialogue. Folktales and fairy tales are characterized by brief zestful description, rather than lengthy descriptive passages, but such description should include no jarring modernisms.

Although folk and fairy tales have been mentioned in discussing these procedures, the same is true for allegories, fables, myths, legends, and hero tales. Finally, the storyteller must keep in mind the difference between material for use in oral presentation and source material, or stories for silent reading.

ABRIDGING

Wide reading, experience, background, and skill with words are necessary for any storyteller wishing to change material, but an initial step in developing abilities in this field may come through abridging, since a major intent must be to preserve, insofar as possible, the words of the original while simultaneously eliminating unnecessary descriptions, tying the sequence of action more tightly, and deleting introspective and explanatory passages. The object of abridgment is to shorten and abbreviate while preserving the original words, the characteristic phrases and the sentence structure. Many times a very long story or a small book may be abridged into an excellent story to tell.

It is not always necessary to repeat a series of incidents word for word; the action may be given in detail the first time, with successive similar action summarized by saying, for example, "Again he came, and again he failed. . . ." Dialogue may be tightened by rearranging phrases and supplanting "he said," or "she replied," with direct quotes.

In abridging, the actual story structure is not reshaped for specific ends as it is in adapting. To condense, tighten, simplify, or eliminate—these are the goals for good abridgment, plus an attempt to keep the author's vocabulary and style and the mood of the story whenever possible.

In these story programs, *The Small One* (Tazewell), *Torten's Christmas Secret* (Dolbier), and "The Christmas Cuckoo" (Walters—*Christmas*) were abridged because of time and the composition of the story group.

One of these stories, "The Christmas Cuckoo," is a rather drawn out, folklike tale with a Christmas emphasis, although it can also be told at other times. Folk flavor is obvious in the choice of language, the setting, and the dialogue, and it required a great deal of condensing to let the plot stand free, uncluttered by too many words. The action and the vocabulary had extensive repetition. Yet, the tale is essentially hearty, zestful, and picturesque, and though the theme is strong, the moral need not be thrown at the listener. By eliminating some of the unnecessary words, descriptive phrases, and drawn out events, the story can be told in twenty minutes; in addition, the action flows more swiftly, the subtle satire is more evident, and the broad humor is in better focus. It is still a long story, suitable for upper elementary children, but it tells well.

The Christmas Cuckoo

Once upon a time there stood in the midst of a black moor, in the north country, a certain village; all its inhabitants were poor, for their fields were barren, and they had little trade, but poorest of them all were two brothers called Scrub and Spare, who followed the cobbler's craft, and had but one stall between them. It was a hut built of clay and wattles. The door was low and always open, for there was no window. The roof did not entirely keep out the rain, and the only thing comfortable about it was a wide hearth, for which the brothers could never find enough wood to make a sufficient fire. There they worked in most brotherly friendship, though with little encouragement.

The people in that village were not extravagant in shoes, and better cobblers than Scrub and Spare might be found. Spiteful people said that there were no shoes so bad that they would not be worse for their mending. Nevertheless Scrub and Spare managed to live between their own trade, a small barley field, and a cottage garden, till one unlucky day when a new cobbler arrived in the village. He had lived in the capital city of the kingdom, and, by his own account, cobbled for the queen and the princesses. His awls were sharp, his lasts were new; he set up his stall in a neat cottage with two windows. The villagers soon found out that one patch of his would wear two of the brothers'. In short, all the mending left Scrub and Spare, and went to the new cobbler. The season had been wet and cold, their barley did not ripen well, and the cabbages never half closed in the garden. So the brothers were poor that winter, and when Christmas came they had nothing to feast on but a barley loaf, a piece of rusty bacon, and some beer of their own brewing. Worse than that, the snow was very deep, and they could get no firewood. Their hut stood at the end of the village; beyond it stood the bleak moor, now all white and silent; but that moor had once been a forest, great roots of old trees were still to be found in it, loosened from the soil and laid bare by the winds and rains— one of these, a rough gnarled log, lay hard by

their door, the half of it above the snow, and Spare said to his brother:

"Shall we sit here cold on Christmas while the great root lies yonder? Let us chop it up for firewood, the work will make us warm."

"No," said Scrub; "it's not right to chop wood on Christmas; besides that root is too hard to be broken with any hatchet."

"Hard or not we must have a fire," replied Spare. "Come, brother, help me in with it. Poor as we are, there is nobody in the village will have such a yule log as ours."

Scrub liked a little grandeur, and in hopes of having a fine yule log, both brothers strained and strove with all their might, till, between pulling and pushing, the great old root was safe on the hearth, and beginning to crackle and blaze with the red embers. In high glee the cobblers sat down to their beer and bacon. The door was shut, for there was nothing but cold moonlight and snow outside; but the hut, strewn with fir boughs, and ornamented with holly, looked cheerful as the ruddy fire blazed up and rejoiced their hearts.

"Long life and good fortune to ourselves, brother!" said Spare. "I hope you will drink to that toast, and may we never have a worse fire on Christmas—but what was that?"

Spare set down the drinking horn, and the brothers listened astonished, for out of the blazing root they heard, "Cuckoo! Cuckoo!" as plain as ever the spring-bird's voice came over the moor on a May morning.

"It is something bad," said Scrub terribly frightened.

"Maybe not," said Spare; and out of the deep hole at the side which the fire had not reached flew a large gray cuckoo, and lit on the table before them. Much as the cobblers had been surprised, they were still more so when it said:

"Good gentlemen, what season is this?"

"It's Christmas," said Spare.

"Then a merry Christmas to you!" said the cuckoo. "I went to sleep in the hollow of that old root one winter evening last year, and never woke till the heat of your fire made me think it was summer again; but now since you have burned my lodging, let me stay in

Frances Browne, "The Christmas Cuckoo," in *A Book of Christmas Stories for Children*, ed. Maude O. Walters (New York: Dodd-Mead, 1948).

your hut till the spring comes round—I only want a hole to sleep in, and when I go on my travels next summer be assured I will bring you some present for your trouble."

"Stay, and welcome," said Spare, while Scrub sat wondering if it were something bad or not; "I'll make you a good warm hole in the thatch. But you must be hungry after that long sleep—here is a slice of barley bread. Come help us to keep Christmas!"

The cuckoo ate up the slice, drank water from the brown jug, for he would take no beer, and flew into a snug hole which Spare scooped for him in the thatch of the hut.

Scrub said he was afraid it wouldn't be lucky; but as it slept on and the days passed he forgot his fears. So the snow melted, the heavy rains came, the cold grew less, the days lengthened, and one sunny morning the brothers were awakened by the cuckoo shouting its own cry to let them know the spring had come.

"Now I'm going on my travels," said the bird, "over the world to tell men of the spring. There is no country, where trees bud or flowers bloom, that I will not cry in before the year goes round. Give me another slice of barley bread to keep me on my journey, and tell me what present I shall bring you at the twelve-months end."

Scrub would have been angry with his brother for cutting so large a slice, their store of barley meal being low; but his mind was occupied with what present would be most prudent to ask; at length a lucky thought struck him.

"Good master cuckoo," said he, "if a great traveler who sees all the world, like you, could know of any place where diamonds or pearls were to be found, one of a tolerable size brought in your beak would help such poor men as my brother and I to provide something better than barley bread for your next entertainment."

"I know nothing of diamonds or pearls," said the cuckoo. "They are in the hearts of rocks and the sands of rivers. My knowledge is only of that which grows on the earth. But there are two trees hard by the well that lies at the world's end—one of them is called the golden tree, for its leaves are all of beaten gold: every winter they fall into the well with a sound like scattered coin and I know not what becomes of them. As for the other, it is always green like a laurel. Some call it the wise, and some the merry tree. Its leaves never fall, but they that get one of them keep a blithe heart in spite of all misfortunes, and can make themselves as merry in a hut as in a palace."

"Good master cuckoo, bring me a leaf off that tree," cried Spare.

"Now, brother, don't be a fool!" said Scrub. "Think of the leaves of beaten gold. Dear master cuckoo, bring me one of them!"

Before another word could be spoken, the cuckoo had flown out of the open door, and was shouting its spring cry over moor and meadow. The brothers were poorer than ever that year; nobody would send them a single shoe to mend. The new cobbler said, in scorn, they should come to be his apprentices; and Scrub and Spare would have left the village but for their barley fields, their cabbage garden, and a certain maid called Fairfeather, whom both the cobblers had courted for seven years without even knowing which she meant to favor.

Sometimes Fairfeather seemed inclined to Scrub, sometimes she smiled on Spare; but the brothers never disputed for that. They sowed their barley, planted their cabbage, and, now that their trade was gone, worked in the rich villagers' fields to make out a scanty living. So the seasons came and passed: spring, summer, harvest and winter followed each other as they have done from the beginning. At the end of the latter, Scrub and Spare had grown so poor and ragged that Fairfeather thought them beneath her notice. Old neighbors forgot to invite them to wedding feasts or merrymaking; and they thought the cuckoo had forgotten them, too, when at daybreak, on the first of April, they heard a hard beak knocking at their door, and a voice crying:

"Cuckoo! cuckoo! Let me in with my presents." Spare ran to the door, and in came the cuckoo, carrying on one side of his bill a golden leaf larger than that of any tree in the north country; and on the other, one like that of a common laurel, only it had a fresher green.

"Here," it said, giving the gold to Scrub and the green to Spare, "it is a long carriage to the world's end. Give me a slice of barley bread, for I must tell the north country that the spring has come."

Scrub did not grudge the thickness of that slice, though it was cut from their last loaf. So much gold had never been in the cobbler's hand before, and he could not help exulting over his brother.

"See the wisdom of my choice!" he said, holding up the large leaf of gold. "As for yours, as good might be plucked from any hedge. I wonder that a sensible bird would carry the like so far."

"Good master cobbler," cried the cuckoo, finishing the slice, "your conclusions are more hasty than courteous. If your brother be disappointed this time, I go on the same journey every year, and for your hospitable entertainment will think it no trouble to bring each of you whichever leaf you desire."

"Darling cuckoo!" cried Scrub, "bring me a golden one"; and Spare, looking up from the green leaf on which he gazed as though it were a jewel said:

"Be sure to bring me one from the merry tree," and away flew the cuckoo.

"This is the Feast of All Fools, and it ought to be your birthday," said Scrub. "Did ever man fling away such an opportunity of getting rich? Much good your merry leaves will do you in the midst of rags and poverty!" So he went on, but Spare laughed at him, and answered with quaint old proverbs concerning the cares that come with gold, till Scrub, at length getting angry, vowed his brother was not fit to live with a respectable man; and, taking his lasts, his awls, and his golden leaf, he left the wattle hut, and went to tell the villagers.

They were astonished at the folly of Spare and charmed with Scrub's good sense, particularly when he showed them the golden leaf, and told that the cuckoo would bring him one every spring. The new cobbler immediately took him into partnership; the greatest people sent him their shoes to mend; Fairfeather smiled graciously upon him, and in the course of that summer they were married, with a great wedding feast, at which the whole village danced, except Spare, who was not invited, because the bride could not bear his low-mindedness, and his brother thought him a disgrace to the family.

Indeed, all who heard the story concluded that Spare must be mad, and nobody would associate with him but a lame tinker, a beggar boy, and a poor woman reputed to be a witch because she was old and ugly. As for Scrub, he established himself with Fairfeather in a cottage close by that of the new cobbler, and quite as fine. There he mended shoes to everybody's satisfaction, had a scarlet coat for holidays, and a fat goose for dinner every wedding-day. Fairfeather, too, had a crimson gown and fine blue ribands; but neither she nor Scrub were content, for to buy this grandeur the golden leaf had to be broken and parted with piece by piece, so that the last morsel was gone before the cuckoo came with another.

Spare lived on in the old hut, and worked in the cabbage garden. (Scrub had got the barley field because he was the elder.) Every day his coat grew more ragged, and the hut more weatherbeaten; but people remarked that he never looked sad or sour; and the wonder was that, from the time they began to keep company, the tinker grew kinder to the poor ass with which he traveled the country, the beggar boy kept out of mischief, and the old woman was never cross to her cat or angry with the children.

Every first of April the cuckoo came tapping at their doors with the golden leaf to Scrub and the green to Spare. Fairfeather would have entertained him nobly with wheaten bread and honey, for she had some notion of persuading him to bring two gold leaves instead of one; but the cuckoo flew away to eat barley bread with Spare, saying he was not fit company for fine people, and liked the old hut where he slept so snugly from Christmas to spring.

Scrub spent the golden leaves, and Spare kept the merry ones; and I know not how many years passed in this manner, when a certain great lord, who owned that village, came to the neighborhood. His castle stood on the moor. It was ancient and strong, with high towers and a deep moat. All the country, as far as one could see from the highest turret, belonged to its lord; but he had not been there for twenty years, and would not have come then, only he was melancholy. The cause of his grief was that he had been prime minister at court, and in high favor, till somebody told the crown prince that he had spoken disrespectfully concerning the turning out of his royal highness's toes, and the king that he did not lay on taxes enough, whereupon the north country lord was turned out of office, and banished to his own estate. There he lived for some weeks in very bad temper. The servants said nothing would please him, and the villagers put on their worst clothes lest he should raise their rents; but one day in the harvest time his lordship chanced to meet Spare gathering water-cresses at a meadow stream, and fell into talk with the cobbler.

How it was nobody could tell, but from the hour of that discourse the great lord cast away his melancholy; he forgot his lost office and his court enemies, the king's taxes and the crown prince's toes, and went about with a noble train hunting, fishing, and making merry in his hall, where all travelers were entertained and all the poor were welcome. This strange story spread through the north land, and great company came to the cobbler's hut—rich men who had lost their money, poor men who had lost their friends, beauties who had grown old, wits who had gone out of fashion, all came to talk with Spare, and whatever their troubles had been, all went home merry. The rich gave him presents; the poor gave him thanks. Spare's coat ceased to be ragged, he had bacon with his cabbage, and the villagers began to think there was some sense in him.

By this time his fame had reached the capital city, and even the court. There were a great many discontented people there besides the king, who had lately fallen into ill humor because a neighbor princess, with seven islands for her dowry, would not marry his eldest son. So a royal messenger was sent to Spare, with a velvet mantle, a diamond ring, and a command that he should repair to court immediately.

"Tomorrow is the first of April," said Spare, "and I will go with you two hours after sunrise."

The messenger lodged all night at the castle, and the cuckoo came at sunrise with the merry leaf.

"Court is a fine place," he said when the cobbler told him he was going; "but I cannot come there; they would lay snares and catch me; so be careful of the leaves I have brought you, and give me a farewell slice of barley bread."

Spare was sorry to part with the cuckoo, little as he had of his company; but he gave him a slice which would have broken Scrub's heart in former times, it was so thick and large; and, having sewed up the leaves in the lining of his leathern doublet, he set out with the messenger on his way to the court.

His coming caused great surprise there. Everybody wondered what the king could see in such a common-looking man; but scarce had his majesty conversed with him half an hour, when the princess and her seven islands were forgotten, and orders were given that a feast for all the comers should be spread in the banquet hall. The princes of the blood, the great lords and ladies, ministers of state, and judges of the land, after that, discoursed with Spare, and the more they talked the lighter grew their hearts, so that such changes had never been seen at court. The lords forgot their spites and ladies their envies, the princes and ministers made friends among themselves, and the judges showed no favor.

As for Spare, he had a chamber assigned him in the palace, and a seat at the king's table; one sent him rich robes and another costly jewels; but in the midst of all his grandeur he still wore the leathern doublet, which the palace servants thought remarkably mean. One day, the king's attention being drawn to it by the chief page, his majesty inquired why Spare didn't give it to a beggar. But the cobbler answered:

"High and mighty monarch, this doublet was with me before silk and velvet came—I find it easier to wear than the court cut; moreover, it serves to keep me humble, by recalling the days when it was my holiday garment."

The king thought this a wise speech, and commanded that no one should find fault with the leathern doublet. So things went, till tidings of his brother's good fortune reached Scrub in the moorland cottage on another first of April, when the cuckoo came with two golden leaves, because he had none to carry for Spare.

"Think of that!" said Fairfeather. "Here we are spending our lives in this humdrum place, and Spare making his fortune at court with two or three paltry green leaves! What would they say to our golden ones? Let us pack up and make our way to the king's palace;

I'm sure he will make you a lord and me a lady of honor, not to speak of all the fine clothes and presents we shall have."

Scrub thought this excellent reasoning, and their packing up began; but it was soon found that the cottage contained few things fit for carrying to court. Fairfeather could not think of her wooden bowls, spoons, and trenchers being seen there. Scrub considered his lasts and awls better left behind, as without them, he concluded, no one would suspect him of being a cobbler.

So putting on their holiday clothes, Fairfeather took her looking-glass and Scrub his drinking horn, which happened to have a very thin rim of silver, and each carrying a golden leaf carefully wrapped up that none might see it till they reached the palace, the pair set out in great expectation.

How far Scrub and Fairfeather journeyed I cannot say, but when the sun was high and warm at noon, they came into a wood, both tired and hungry.

"If I had known it was so far to court," said Scrub, "I would have brought the end of that barley loaf which we left in the cupboard."

"Husband," said Fairfeather, "you shouldn't have such mean thoughts: how could one eat barley bread on the way to a palace? Let us rest ourselves under this tree, and look at our golden leaves to see if they are safe." In looking at the leaves and talking of their fine prospects, Scrub and Fairfeather did not perceive that a very thin old woman had slipped from behind the tree, with a long staff in her hand and a great wallet by her side.

"Noble lord and lady," she said, "for I know ye are such by your voices, though my eyes are dim and my hearing none of the sharpest, will ye condescend to tell me where I may find some water to mix a bottle of mead which I carry in my wallet, because it is too strong for me?"

As the old woman spoke, she pulled out a large wooden bottle such as shepherds used in the ancient times, corked with leaves rolled together, and having a small wooden cup hanging from its handle.

"Perhaps ye will do me the favor to taste," she said. "It is only made of the best honey. I have also cream cheese, and a wheaten loaf here, if such honorable persons as you would eat the like."

Scrub and Fairfeather became very condescending after this speech. They were now sure that there must be some appearance of nobility about them; besides they were very hungry, and having hastily wrapped up the golden leaves, they assured the old woman they were not at all proud, notwithstanding the lands and castles they had left behind them in the north country, and would willingly help to lighten the wallet.

The old woman could scarcely be persuaded to sit down, for pure humility, but at length she did, and before the wallet was half empty, Scrub and Fairfeather firmly believed that there must be something remarkably noble-looking about them. This was not entirely owing to her ingenious discourse.

The old woman was a wood-witch; her name was Buttertongue; and all her time was spent in making mead, which, being boiled with curious herbs and spells, had the power of making all who drank it fall asleep and dream with their eyes open. She had two dwarfs for sons; one was named Spy, and the other Pounce. Wherever their mother went they were not far behind; and whoever tasted her mead was sure to be robbed by the dwarfs.

Scrub and Fairfeather sat leaning against the old tree. The cobbler had a lump of cheese in his hand; his wife held fast a hunch of bread. Their eyes and mouths were both open, but they were dreaming of great grandeur at court, when the old woman raised her shrill voice—

"What ho, my sons! come here and carry home the harvest."

No sooner had she spoken, than the two little dwarfs darted out of the neighboring thicket.

"Idle boys!" cried the mother, "what have ye done today to help our living?"

"I have been to the city," said Spy, "and could see nothing. These are hard times for us—everybody minds their business so contentedly since that cobbler came; but here is a leathern doublet which his page threw out of the window; it's of no use, but I brought it to let you see I was not idle." And he tossed down Spare's doublet, with the merry leaves in it, which he had carried like a bundle on his little back.

To explain how Spy came by it, I must tell you that the forest was not far from the great city where Spare lived in such high esteem. All things had gone well with the cobbler till the king thought that it was quite unbecoming to see such a worthy man without a servant. His majesty, therefore, to let all men understand his royal favor toward Spare, appointed one of his own pages to wait upon him.

The name of this youth was Tinseltoes, and, though he was the seventh of the king's pages, nobody, in all the court had grander notions. Nothing could please him that had not gold or silver about it, and his grandmother feared he would hang himself for being appointed page to a cobbler. As for Spare, if anything could have troubled him, this token of his majesty's kindness would have done it.

The honest man had been so used to serving himself that the page was always in the way, but his merry leaves came to his assistance; and, to the great surprise of his grandmother, Tinseltoes took wonderfully to the new service. Some said it was because Spare gave him nothing to do but play at bowls all day on the palace green.

Yet one thing grieved the heart of Tinseltoes, and that was his master's leathern doublet. But for it he was persuaded people would never remember that Spare had been a cobbler, and the page took a deal of pains to let him see how unfashionable it was at court; but Spare answered Tinseltoes as he had done the king, and at last, finding nothing better would do, the page got up one fine morning earlier than his master, and tossed the leathern doublet out of the back window into a certain lane where Spy found it, and brought it to his mother.

"That nasty thing!" said the old woman, "where is the good in it?"

By this time Pounce had taken everything of value from Scrub and Fairfeather—the looking-glass, the silver-rimmed horn, the husband's scarlet coat, the wife's gay mantle, and, above all, the golden leaves, which so rejoiced old Buttertongue and her sons that they threw the leathern doublet over the sleeping cobbler for a jest, and went off—to their hut in the heart of the forest.

The sun was going down when Scrub and Fairfeather awoke from dreaming that they had been made a lord and a lady, and sat clothed in silk and velvet, feasting with the king in his palace hall. It was a great disappointment to find their golden leaves and all their best things gone. Scrub tore his hair, and vowed to take the old woman's life, while Fairfeather lamented sore; but Scrub, feeling cold for want of his coat, put on the leathern doublet, without asking or caring whence it came.

Scarcely was it buttoned on when a change came over him; he addressed such merry discourse to Fairfeather that, instead of lamentations, she made the wood ring with laughter. Both busied themselves in setting up a hut of boughs, in which Scrub kindled a fire with a flint and steel, which, together with his pipe, he had brought unknown to Fairfeather, who had told him the like was never heard of at court. Then they found a pheasant's nest at the root of an old oak, made a meal of roasted eggs, and went to sleep on a heap of long green grass which they had gathered, with nightingales singing all night long in the old trees about them.

So it happened that Scrub and Fairfeather stayed day after day in the forest, making their hut larger and more comfortable against the winter, living on wild birds' eggs and berries, and never thinking of their lost golden leaves, or their journey to court.

In the meantime Spare had got up and missed his doublet. Tinseltoes, of course, said he knew nothing about it. The whole palace was searched, and every servant questioned, till all the court wondered why such a fuss was made about an old leathern doublet. Quarrels began among the lords, and jealousies among the ladies. The king said his subjects did not pay him half enough taxes, the queen wanted more jewels, the servants took to their old bickerings and got up some new ones.

Spare found himself getting wonderfully dull, and very much out of place; nobles began to ask what business a cobbler had at the king's table, and his majesty ordered the palace chronicles to be searched for a precedent. The cobbler was too wise to tell all he had lost with the doublet, but being by this time somewhat familiar with court customs, he proclaimed a reward of fifty gold pieces to any one who would bring him news concerning it.

Scarcely was this made known in the city, when the gates and outer courts of the palace were filled by men, women, and children, some bringing leathern doublets of every cut and color; some with tales of what they had heard and seen in their walks about the neighborhood; and so much news concerning all sorts of great people came out in these stories, that lords and ladies ran to the king with complaints of Spare as the speaker of slander; and his majesty, being now satisfied that there was no example in all the palace records of such a retainer, issued a decree banishing the cobbler forever from court, and confiscating all his goods in favor of Tinseltoes.

That royal edict was scarcely published before the page was in full possession of his rich chamber, his costly garments, and all the presents the courtiers had given him; while Spare, having no longer the fifty pieces of gold to give, was glad to make his escape out of the back window, for fear of the nobles, who vowed to be revenged on him, and the crowd, who were prepared to stone him for cheating them about his doublet.

The window from which Spare let himself down with a strong rope, was that from which Tinseltoes had tossed the doublet, and as the cobbler came down late in the twilight, a poor woodman, with a heavy load of fagots, stopped and stared at him in great astonishment.

"What's the matter, friend?" said Spare. "Did you never see a man coming down from a back window before?"

"Why," said the woodman, "the last morning I passed here a leathern doublet came out of that very window, and I'll be bound you are the owner of it."

"That I am, friend," said the cobbler. "Can you tell me which way that doublet went?"

"As I walked on," said the woodman, "a dwarf, called Spy, bundled it up and ran off to his mother in the forest."

"Honest friend," said Spare, taking off the last of his fine clothes (a grass-green mantle edged with gold). "I'll give you this if you will follow the dwarf, and bring me back my doublet."

"It would not be good to carry fagots in," said the woodman. "But if you want back your doublet, the road to the forest lies at the end of this lane," and he trudged away.

Determined to find his doublet, and sure that neither crowd nor courtiers could catch him in the forest, Spare went on his way, and was soon among the tall trees; but neither hut nor dwarf could he see. Moreover, the night came on; the wood was dark and tangled, but here and there the moon shone through its alleys, the great owls flitted about, and the nightingales sang. So he went on, hoping to find some place of shelter.

At last the red light of fire, gleaming through a thicket, led him to the door of a low hut. It stood half open, as if there was nothing to fear, and within he saw his brother, Scrub, snoring loudly on a bed of grass, at the foot of which lay his own leathern doublet; while Fairfeather, in a kirtle made of plaited rushes, sat roasting pheasants' eggs by the fire.

"Good evening, mistress," said Spare, stepping in.

The blaze shone on him, but so changed was her brother-in-law with his court life, that Fairfeather did not know him, and she answered far more courteously than was her wont.

"Good evening, master. Whence come ye so late? But speak low, for my good man has sorely tired himself cleaving wood, and is taking a sleep, as you see, before supper."

"A good rest to him," said Spare, perceiving he was not known. "I come from the court for a day's hunting, and have lost my way in the forest."

"Sit down and have a share of our supper," said Fairfeather. "I will put some more eggs in the ashes; and tell me the news of court—I used to think of it long ago when I was young and foolish."

"Did you never go there?" said the cobbler. "So fair a dame as you would make the ladies marvel."

"You are pleased to flatter," said Fairfeather; "but my husband has a brother there, and we left our moorland village to try our fortune also. An old woman enticed us with fair words and strong drink at the entrance of this forest, where we fell asleep and dreamt of great things; but when we woke everything had been robbed from us—my looking-glass, my scarlet cloak, my husband's Sunday coat; and, in place of all, the robbers left him that old leathern doublet, which he has worn ever since, and never was so merry in all his life, though we live in this poor hut."

"It is a shabby doublet, that," said Spare, taking up the garment, and seeing that it was his own, for the merry leaves were still sewed in its lining. "It would be good for hunting in, however—your husband would be glad to part with it, I dare say, in exchange for this handsome cloak"; and he pulled off the green mantle and buttoned on the doublet, much to Fairfeather's delight, who ran and shook Scrub, crying—

"Husband! husband! rise and see what a good bargain I have made."

Scrub gave one closing snore, and muttered something about the root being hard, but he rubbed his eyes, gazed up at his brother, and said—

"Spare, is that really you? How did you like the court, and have you made your fortune?"

"That I have, brother," said Spare, "in getting back my own good leathern doublet. Come, let us eat eggs, and rest ourselves here this night. In the morning we will return to our own old hut, at the end of the moorland village where the Christmas Cuckoo will come and bring us leaves."

Scrub and Fairfeather agreed. So in the morning they all returned, and found the old hut little the worse for wear and weather. The neighbors came about

them to ask the news of the court, and see if they had made their fortunes. Everybody was astonished to find the three poorer than ever, but somehow they liked to go back to the hut. Spare brought out the lasts and awls he had hidden in a corner; Scrub and he began their old trade, and the whole north country found out that there never were such cobblers.

They mended the shoes of lords and ladies as well as the common people; everybody was satisfied. Their custom increased from day to day, and all that were disappointed, discontended, or unlucky, came to the hut as in old times, before Spare went to court.

The rich brought them presents, the poor did them service. The hut itself changed, no one knew how. Flowering honeysuckle grew over its roof; red and white roses grew thick about its door. Moreover, the Christmas Cuckoo always came on the first of April, bringing three leaves of the merry tree—for Scrub and Fairfeather would have no more golden ones. So it was with them when I last heard the news of the north country.

The Christmas Cuckoo

Once upon a time there stood in the midst of a bleak moor in the north country, a certain village; all its inhabitants were poor, but the poorest of them all were two cobbler brothers called Scrub and Spare. Their hut was of clay and wattles, the door was low and always open, the roof did not entirely keep out the rain, but it had a wide hearth for which the brothers could never find wood enough to make a good fire. Better cobblers than Scrub and Spare might be found, but they managed to live, what with their small barley field and a cabbage patch, until the day a new cobbler arrived. He had lived in the capital city of the kingdom, by his own account, and cobbled for royalty; his awls were sharp, his lasts new, his stall in a neat cottage, with two windows. One of his patches outwore two of the brothers'.

The season being wet and cold, the barley did not ripen, nor the cabbages head, so when Christmas came, Scrub and Spare had nothing on which to feast but a barley loaf, some rusty bacon, and their own beer. And the snow was too heavy to get firewood.

Beyond their hut at the edge of the village spread the bleak moor, once a great forest. Great roots, loosened from the soil by the wind and rain, were

sometimes to be found, and one of these, a rough, gnarled log, lay hard by their door. Said Spare, "Shall we sit here cold on Christmas, while the great root lies yonder? Let us chop it for firewood!" And though Spare would rather have not chopped wood on Christmas, they did, with pulling and pushing, at last bring the old root safely to the hearth where it began to crackle and burn into red embers. "Long life and good fortune to us both!" said Scrub. "Why, what is that now?" For out of the blazing root they heard, "Cuckoo! Cuckoo!" as plain as on a May morning.

"Bad!" said Scrub, terribly frightened. "Perhaps not," was Spare's answer, and as they watched, out of a hole at the side which the fire had not reached, there flew a large grey cuckoo who lit on the table before them. "Good gentlemen, what season is this?"

" 'Tis Christmas," said Spare.

"I went to sleep in the hollow of that old root one evening last summer, and did not wake till your fire made me think it was summer again. You have burned my lodging, so let me stay with you till spring comes. When I go traveling again, I shall bring you a present for your trouble."

"Stay, and welcome," and Spare gave him a barley slice to keep Christmas. The cuckoo ate the slice, drank a bit of water, and found a snug hole in the thatch of the hut. For days he slept, but one sunny morning he wakened the brothers shouting his song. "I'm on my

Abridged from Frances Browne, *The Christmas Cuckoo*, in *A Book of Christmas Stories for Children*, ed. Maude O. Walters (New York: Dodd-Mead, 1948).

travels," he said. "No country of flowers but I will cry there before the year is up! A slice of barley bread for the journey, then, and what shall I bring you?" Scrub thought, "If a great traveller like you, Cuckoo, could know of any place where jewels of tolerable size might be found, that would help such poor men as Spare and me!"

"I know of no pearls or diamonds," replied the cuckoo, "but there are two trees hard by the well that lies at the world's end—one with leaves of gold, the other a merry tree with leaves that never fall. He who has such a leaf will have a blithe heart whatever comes."

"Good master Cuckoo, bring me a leaf off that tree," cried Spare. But Scrub called him a fool! *He* would have a leaf of pure, beaten gold! Before they could say another word, the cuckoo flew out of sight shouting its song.

Poorer than ever were the brothers that year. But for their barley field, the cabbage patch, and a certain maid named Fairfeather, Scrub and Spare would have left the village. To eke out a scanty living the brothers worked for rich villagers now and again; Fairfeather thought the two cobblers beneath her notice! The villagers forgot them, until the first of April, when a hard beak knocked at their door. "Cuckoo . . . let me in with my gifts!" In came the cuckoo, a golden leaf on one side of its bill, a fresh green leaf like laurel on the other side. "Take them—it is a long trek from the world's end! I am hungry for barley bread." And a thick slice from the last loaf he got, nor did Scrub grudge it, for the gold leaf was more than he had ever had in his hand in his life. "Bah, Spare, yours is like any hedge leaf!" he taunted. The cuckoo finished the slice, and said Spare could have a different leaf another year if he would, for the cuckoo was willing to give them each, for their hospitality, a second leaf. "For me, the gold!" said Scrub; but Spare would still have the merry one. So away flew the cuckoo.

Scrub vowed his brother too foolish to live with, having made such a choice, and taking his lasts and awls, he left the wattle hut for the village. The villagers agreed, when he showed them his gold leaf; the new cobbler took him at once into partnership; Fairfeather smiled on him; and in the course of the summer a grand wedding was held to which Spare was not invited, for he was a disgrace to such a company! Only a lame tinker, a beggar boy, and a poor woman thought to be a witch remained Spare's friends. As for Scrub, he had a scarlet coat for holidays and a fat goose, for feasting!

Spare lived in the old hut, worked the cabbage patch, and grew more shabby daily in his old coat, but he never looked sour. Even the tinker was kinder, the beggar boy less mischievous, and the old woman more good-natured. And the first of April, the cuckoo came tapping at his door with another gold leaf for Scrub, a green one for Spare. But the cuckoo stayed the long winter in the old hut of Spare and not the hut of Lady Fairfeather! Scrub spent the gold leaves. Spare saved the merry ones. And so it went.

One day a great lord, the owner of the village, came to the neighborhood. He was melancholy, for he had been prime minister, in high favor, until he lost office and was banished to his own estate. On a day his lordship met Spare water-cressing at a near-by stream; from the hour of that discourse on, the lord lost his sad demean and made merry fishing, hunting, and feasting in his hall. The strange story spread throughout the north country. Rich men, poor men, beauties whose youth was gone, wits who had run out of fashion came to bring Spare their troubles, and returned happy. The rich left presents, the poor thanks—and Spare had bacon with his cabbage and fewer ragged clothes. "Perhaps," said the villagers, "there is yet some sense to Spare. . . ." So his fame reached the court and the king, who sent a royal messenger, with a mantle of velvet, a ring of diamonds, and a command to repair at once to court. "Tomorrow, at two hours after sunrise will I come," said Spare. Well he remembered that tomorrow was the first of April!

After the cuckoo delivered the leaf, he said sadly, "I shall not come to court for they lay snares for me. Be careful of your leaves, and give me a farewell barley slice, Spare!" Spare did so and sorrowfully sewed his leaves into the lining of his old doublet, thereafter setting out for court. But once at court, despite his common look and shabby jacket, the king conversed with him an hour, and gave orders for a merry feast for all at once, the lords forgot their spites, the ladies their envy, the ministers greeted each other, and the judge was fair. As for Spare, though he had his own chamber, a seat at the king's table, royal robes and jewels, he wore his old jacket, saying: "Sire, this old doublet was with me before I came to court, and it agrees with me," and the king commanded all the court to allow Spare his way. So time moved on, and word came to Scrub of his brother's fortune at court. "And all because of three green leaves!" Scrub exclaimed. "Why should we not fare as well with three gold leaves?" With no further ado, leaving all their humble furnishings behind them, they donned their best attire, picked up Fairfeather's looking-glass and Scrub's drinking horn, and set forth with great expectations. The three gold leaves were wrapped and hidden away carefully on their persons.

At noon, the sun being hot, they rested awhile under a tree, looked to the safety of their gold leaves, and scarcely noticed the old, thin dame bearing a long staff and a wallet, who suddenly appeared before them.

"A bit of water that I may mix with my mead—can ye tell me where to find it, great lord and lady?" she asked. "Mayhap ye will grant the favor of sharing a bit of bread and mead with so poor an old woman?" So Scrub and Fairfeather both ate and drank, and fell sound asleep with their eyes wide open, for the woman was the wood-witch, Buttertongue, and her potion was magic; her sons Spy and Pounce were never far away, and they were always in mischief. "Ha, sons of mine, come and carry home a harvest," called Buttertongue. Out came the two dwarfs, bearing with them the treasure they had found for the day in the city of the king. It was nought to look at, being only the old leathern doublet of Spare, which his new and haughty page Tinseltoes had thrown out the window in great disdain one early morn while Spare still slept. For though Spare had long served himself, and was not ashamed of his cobbler's past, his young page was. To Tinseltoes the old doublet was a sad reminder of his lord's humble past—it were better thrown out!

Old Buttertongue, Spy, and Pounce, having relieved Fairfeather of her looking-glass, and Scrub of his silver-rimmed goblet, and rejoicing over the three gold leaves, went on their merry way, casting the old doublet over the still-sleeping Scrub and his wife. So the sun was setting when Scrub and Fairfeather woke from their courtly dreams to find themselves possessed of only a shabby jacket, and cold and hungry to boot! But scarcely was it buttoned on Scrub than he began to talk merrily to his wife, brought firewood, and struck a flint to it. In secret old Scrub had carried his flint and pipe with him, and the fire burned rosily. Luck was with them, for a cuckoo's nest in a near-by oak yielded a meal of eggs to roast. So it was with Scrub and Fairfeather that they remained for many days, happy as larks in the green forest, building a small greenwood hut, finding eggs and berries, and never once missing their golden leaves—not ever guessing the secret of their new happiness!

As for Spare, when he missed his jacket, he set the whole court to seek it, and quarrels broke out everywhere. The king wanted more taxes, the queen more jewels, and the servants bickered constantly. Nobles now began to wonder how a cobbler had gotten to the king's court, and set the king to searching through the chronicles of the kingdom to see if such a thing had ever been done before! A reward of fifty gold pieces was offered to anyone who would return the lost doublet. From every corner of the realm folk came bringing every sort of old leather coat, and tales and gossip as well, so that it was reported to the king that Spare himself had slandered the king! No help for it

then, for since the chronicles had yielded no light on court cobblers such as Spare, he was at once banished and Tinseltoes settled in his chambers at court. Secretly Spare let himself, by a strong rope, down from a castle window, nearly toppling over a woodcutter with a load of fagots who stared in amazement. "Did you never see a fellow coming down from a window then?" asked Spare. "Aye, that I did. The last time I came by this very window a fellow leaned out and threw on me a shabby leather jacket! I'll be bound, but I'm thinking that was the very jacket of the cobbler at court. Are you not he?" "That I am," replied Spare. "Tell me at once which way it went."

"As I walked on," said the woodcutter, "a dwarf ran up, bundled it up and ran off to the woods with it. It was the dwarf, Spy, I think."

"Honest friend, my thanks to you. The mantle I wear is yours if you will follow the dwarf and return me my doublet!" But the woodcutter had no use for a green velvet mantle, and only pointed out the forest way at the end of the lane. With no further delay, Spare took to the road, but he found neither dwarf nor jacket nor hut for shelter, and it was only at long last that he glimpsed a rosy fire gleaming through the thickets. A low hut was there, and crouched by the fire, roasting eggs, was Fairfeather, garbed in a kirtle of plaited rushes. Within the hut snored Scrub, clad in the shabby coat. So changed was Spare, that Fairfeather did not know him, and offered him a share of the simple meal. Spare explained. "I have but come from court for a day in the forest, and lost my way. How is it that so fair a dame as you has never been to court?" Then Fairfeather poured out the tale of the old woman and the dwarf and the robbery. "Yet never before has my man been so merry!" she added. "Though we have nought to our name but the shabby jacket he is wearing."

"It is shabby indeed," Spare nodded. "I would gladly exchange this court mantle for it, for your kindness," and he threw off the green velvet cloak, and buttoned on the leather doublet. Startled into wakefulness, Scrub sat up and rubbed his eyes. "Is it really you, my brother Spare? Is your fortune now made?" he exclaimed.

"It is indeed," Spare answered. "Come, let us eat the eggs and rest, and tomorrow we shall return to our old village where the cuckoo comes so merrily every first of April!"

Early the next day, they took their way to their childhood home, where they found the small hut little worse for wear and weather. Spare found the awls and lasts he had hidden in the far corner, and the neighbors began to bring in their shoes. Never were such cobblers as Scrub and Spare, now! From near and far people came with gifts, the poor did them service, and the hut itself flowered with honeysuckle and roses. Every year the Christmas Cuckoo came with his offer of gold leaves, but Scrub and Fairfeather and Spare would have no more of them, and chose only the merry green leaves. So it was with them when last I heard the news of the north country!

ADAPTING

In many ways, adapting stories is the most difficult of all the techniques used to rework oral narrative for a children's story hour. Modern civilization has few traditional storytellers, and since most of the lore of our own country has come through the printed page, it is therefore at least second hand. This is even more true of stories from Asia, Europe, and Africa, since they were first collected in the original language, translated at length into English, and finally adapted for children; most oral narratives were intended for adults, with children forming only a fringe audience. This has often meant that adult references and insinuations clung to the texts, that explicit procreation and mating practices were described; or that adult ethics were implied in the narrative. At times strong language, violence, strange idioms or dialects, or crude terminology pervaded the stories. In order to make such tales meaningful to children, a child's frame of reference must be substituted for the adult one. A brief glance at adult folklore or recently translated material from unfamiliar African languages or native American Indian tongues will quickly illustrate this point. And even an excellent translator may not necessarily have a facility for storytelling, especially storytelling for young ears. Recognizing these factors leads to deeper appreciation of such adapters and writers as Joseph Jacobs.

When a story already translated into English and written for children is discovered, adapting will not pose such a herculean task, although the material may need some altering to make it more suitable for a specific program. It may be too long, too short, too difficult, too wordy, too introspective, too involved, too fragmentary, or awkward in style. Adaptation must keep as much of the feeling, language, and structure of the original as possible, and yet incorporate needed changes. Such a framework limits the adapter, and challenges his or her ability and skill. Description must be graphic, but elaborate phrases can be eliminated, paragraphs can be clarified to bring out meaning, minor plots or characters can be deleted, scenes of violence can be softened, but not eradicated, since the inclusion of such action may be vital to the development of the plot. Similes, metaphors, provincial expressions, and idioms that are included in the original story must be kept, but modified to maintain flavor.

Though some changes in vocabulary may be necessary, children are capable of recognizing, and enjoying, unusual and different words if the context makes the meaning clear. However, if language, plot, characters, theme, and background demand major changes, perhaps the story is better saved for older listeners.

The original story must be recognizable in the adaptation; changes that emphasize the appeal, the suitability, and the interest must be incorporated into the web and woof of the original tale with skill.

The Ebony Horse (White), *The Carpet of Solomon* (Ish-Kishor), *The Fox, the Dog, and the Griffin* (Anderson), and "Compair Taureau" (Field—*American*) were adapted for our programs because of length, complexity, detail, or thematic material.

The Ebony Horse is one of a long series of stories compiled in *The Arabian Nights*, and its roots lie in those adult romances. It is one of two retold by Anne Terry White and included under one title in this edition. As the story stands, it is somewhat involved, rather wordy, overfull of description, complex in action, with flashbacks to different scenes, and too many characters interweaving in the action. It was necessary, for our purposes, to shorten and simplify it for children in the fourth through sixth grades, deleting some of the descriptions and some of the action, and compressing the action of the plot so that it did not ramble. Yet we wanted to keep the same narrative flow of an Arabian Nights story, some of the feeling of the East in its phrasing and idioms, and much of Anne White's own form and language. Descriptive passages, where possible, were made part of the dialogue, time adjectives were used for phrases that stretched out events and, although divisions by chapter and headings were kept, they were shortened.

The story as adapted takes about twenty minutes and is vivid and action filled. The children have responded well to the telling of it.

Sinbad the Seaman—The Ebony Horse

1. GIFTS FOR A KING

Long ago in ages past there was in Persia a great and powerful King, Sabur by name. He was the richest and wisest of all kings. Moreover, he was generous. He gave to all who asked, loved the poor, and did justice to all. The King had three daughters, fair as flower gardens blooming bright, and a son handsome as the full moon.

Twice in the year the King kept festival. At those times he threw his palaces open and distributed money to the poor. People came to him from far and near to wish him joy and bring him gifts.

Now on one such holiday, as Sabur sat on his kingly throne, three wise men came to him. One was a Hindi or Indian. The second was a Greek. The third was a Persian. Knowing that the King loved science, each had brought him something he had devised and had made with his own hands.

The Indian came forward first and laid before him a present fit for a great king. It was a man of gold, set with precious gems and costly jewels. In its hand the figure held a golden trumpet.

Sabur asked, "O Sage, what is the virtue of the figure?"

"O my Lord," the wise man answered, "if this figure be set at the gate of your city, it will be guardian over it. If an enemy should enter the place, it will blow the trumpet at him and he will drop down dead."

The King marvelled. "By Allah, O Sage," he cried, "if your word be true, I will grant you your wish and your desire."

Then the Greek came forward and presented his gift. It was a basin of silver in which there was a peacock of gold, surrounded by four and twenty chicks.

Sabur asked, "O Sage, what is the virtue of the peacock?"

"O my Lord," answered he, "as often as an hour of the day or night passes, the peacock pecks one of the chicks, and cries and flaps its wings. And when the month comes to an end, the peacock will open its mouth, and there you will see the crescent moon."

"If you speak the truth," Sabur said, "I will grant you your wish and your desire."

Then the Persian Sage came forward and presented Sabur with a horse of blackest wood, ebony inlaid with gold and jewels, and harnessed with a saddle, bridle, and stirrups such as befit a king.

Sabur was amazed at the horse's beauty. "What is the use of this horse of wood?" he asked.

"Oh my Lord," the Persian answered, "if one mounts this horse, it will carry the rider wherever he wishes to go. It will go through the air and will travel in a single day the space of a year."

"By Allah," said the King, "if your words are true, I will surely grant your wish and your desire."

Then each man took what he had made and showed the King the mystery of its movement. The trumpeter blew his horn. The peacock pecked its chicks. And when the Persian Sage mounted the ebony horse, it soared with him high in the air and came down again.

Seeing all this, the King rejoiced. "Now that I am sure you have told the truth," he said to the three wise men, "I must keep my promise. Ask what you will, therefore, and I will give it to you."

Now the report of the King's three beautiful daughters had reached the sages. So they answered, "If the King is pleased with our gifts, we beg him to give us his daughters in marriage."

Said the King, "I grant you your wishes and desires. You, O Hindi Sage, shall have my eldest daughter. You, O Greek, shall have my middle daughter. And you, O Persian, shall have my youngest daughter." And he bade his servants prepare everything for the ceremonies.

Now it happened that the Princesses were behind a curtain looking on. When they heard this, the youngest fastened her eyes on her husband to be, and her heart sank. The Persian Sage was a hundred years old, with goggle eyes, hollow cheeks, a nose like an eggplant, slit ears, overlapping teeth, and lips like a camel's, loose and hanging. In brief, he was a horror, a frightful monster.

As for the girl, she was the fairest and most graceful of her time, all made for love. So when she saw her suitor, she went to her chamber and wept and wailed.

The Prince, her brother, Kamar al-Akmar, had just returned from a journey. Now he was very fond of his youngest sister, and hearing her weep, he went to her.

Anne Terry White, *Sinbad the Seaman—The Ebony Horse: Two Arabian Tales* (Champaign, Ill.: Garrard, 1969).

"What ails you?" he asked. "Tell me and hide nothing."

So she smote her breast and answered: "O my brother, my dear one! Know that my father has promised me in marriage to a magician who brought him as a gift a horse of black wood. He has bewitched my father with his craft. But as for me, I want none of him. Because of him I wish I had never come into the world."

Her brother comforted her and then went to his father.

"Who is this wizard to whom you have promised my youngest sister in marriage?" the Prince said. "And what is the present he has brought you, for the sake of which you have killed my sister with grief?"

Now the Persian was standing by, and when he heard the Prince's words, he was filled with fury.

But the King said, "O my son, if you saw this horse, you would be amazed." Then he bade the slaves bring the horse before him.

When the Prince saw it, it pleased him. Being a good horseman, he mounted it at once and struck its sides with the stirrup irons. But the horse did not stir. At that the King said to the Sage, "Go show him its movement that he also may help you win your wish."

The Persian bore the Prince a grudge and saw a way to get even with him. So showing the Prince a pin on the horse's right shoulder, "Turn this," he said, and left him.

Thereupon the Prince turned the pin, and lo! the horse soared with him into the air like a bird. In a twinkling it carried the Prince out of sight. At this, the King said to the Persian, "O Sage, now make him descend." But the Sage replied, "O my Lord, I can do nothing. You will never see him again, for he never asked me how to make the horse descend, and I forgot to tell him."

When the King heard this, he was enraged. He bade his men beat the Sage and put him in jail. Then the King cast the crown from his head and beat his face and smote his breast. Moreover, he shut the doors of the palaces and gave himself up to weeping and lamenting, he and his wife and daughters and all the folk of the city.

2. PRINCE AND PRINCESS

The horse carrying the Prince did not stop soaring with him till it drew near the sun. At this the young man gave himself up for lost.

But soon, being a man of wit and knowledge, he bethought him that there must also be a pin to make the horse come down. So he began feeling all the parts of the horse and felt a pin on the left shoulder like the one on the right. He turned it and at once the horse began to descend little by little to the face of the earth. When the Prince saw this, he began to turn the horse's head wherever he wanted to go, making it rise and fall at his pleasure. Then he rode through the air, viewing the earth and seeing cities and countries he had never seen.

Among the rest he saw the fairest of cities set in the midst of a green and smiling land, rich in trees and streams, with gazelles pacing daintily over the plains. He circled above it, looking right and left. By this time the sun was near setting. So he looked about for a place where he might safely stay so that none should see him or his horse.

Now in the midst of the city was a palace, rising high and surrounded by walls. He turned the descent pin. Then like a weary bird the horse sank down and alighted gently on the terrace roof of the palace.

The Prince dismounted and began to go around about the horse and examine it. By this time night had come. He was both hungry and thirsty, for he had not tasted food or drink since he left his father. Surely, he thought, a palace like this will not lack food.

He sat on the roof till he was certain that all in the palace slept. Then leaving the horse above, he went in search of something to eat. Soon he came to a staircase. Descending to the bottom, he found himself in a court, but he did not know where to go next.

He had almost made up his mind to return to the horse when he saw a light in the palace. He made toward it and found that it came from a candle that stood by the head of a huge guard who lay sleeping in front of a door. He was like one of the jinni, broader than a bench. He lay before the door with the hilt of his sword gleaming in the flame of the candle. At his head was a leather bag hanging from a column of granite.

The Prince put his hand on the bag, took it aside, and opened it. It contained food of the best. He ate his fill and refreshed himself. After this he hung up the provision bag in its place. Then he drew the guard's sword from its sheath, and, sword in hand, went forward into the palace.

He did not stop till he came to a second door, with a curtain drawn before it. He raised the curtain little by little, and behold! there stood a couch of whitest ivory, inlaid with pearls and jewels, and four slave girls slept around it. He went up to the couch to see what was thereon and found a young lady asleep. Her hair lay like a garment about her, and she herself was like the full moon rising over the eastern horizon.

He stood gazing at her as she lay in her beauty and loveliness. Then, trembling in every limb, he went up to her and kissed her on the right cheek.

At this she awoke. She opened her eyes and saw the Prince standing beside her.

"Who are you and where do you come from?" she asked.

Said he, "I am your slave and your lover."

"Who brought you here?"

"My Lord and my fortune."

Then the Princess Shama al-Nahar—for such was her name—said: "Doubtless you are the son of the King of Hind who asked for me in marriage yesterday. My father rejected you, pretending you were ugly. By Allah, my sire lied in his throat when he said this thing, for you are no other than beautiful."

Love took hold of her heart like a flaming fire, and they began to talk together. Suddenly her waiting women awoke. Seeing the Prince with their mistress, they said to her, "O my lady, who is this with you?"

Said she: "I know not! I found him sitting by me when I woke up. Doubtless it is he who seeks me in marriage from my father."

"O my lady," they said, "by Allah this is not he who seeks you in marriage, for he is hideous, and this man is handsome. Indeed, the other is not fit to be his servant."

Then the maidens went out to the guard. Finding him asleep, they awoke him.

"How happens it that you are on guard at the palace," they said, "and yet men come in to us while we are asleep?"

When the guard heard this, he reached in haste for his sword and found it gone. Fear took hold of him. Trembling, he went in to his mistress and saw the Prince sitting at talk with her.

"O my lord, are you man or jinni?" the guard cried.

Then the Prince was like a raging lion. He took the sword in his hand and said to the slave, "I am the King's son-in-law, and he has married me to his daughter and bidden me go to her."

At this the guard ran shrieking to the King.

3. SINGLE COMBAT

"What has happened to you?" said the King. "Speak quickly and be brief, for you have fluttered my heart."

"O King," cried the guard, "come to your daughter's help! A devil of the jinni, in the likeness of a king's son, has got possession of your daughter. So up and at him!"

"How come you to be so careless of my daughter as to let this demon come at her?" the King cried.

Not waiting for an answer, the King betook himself to the Princess' quarters, where he found her slave women waiting for him.

"What has happened to my daughter?" he demanded.

"O King," they answered, "sleep overcame us, and when we awoke, we found a young man sitting upon her couch. Never did we see any more handsome. We questioned him and he told us you had given him your daughter in marriage. More than this we know not. But he is modest and does nothing which leads to disgrace."

The King's wrath cooled when he heard this. Then he raised the curtain little by little, and looking in, saw the Prince sitting by his daughter. At this sight he rushed in upon them, drawn sword in hand.

The Prince leaped up. Seizing his sword, he sprang toward the King with so terrible a cry that the King paused. Seeing that the Prince was stronger than he, he sheathed his sword and stood still till the young man came up to him.

"O youth, are you man or jinni?" he asked.

The Prince answered: "If I did not respect you as this lady's father and my host, I would spill your blood! How dare you pair me with the devils, I who am a prince of the royal house of Khosru?"

The King was struck with awe and fear. "If you are indeed of the kings as you pretend," he said, "how comes it that you enter my palace without my permission? How comes it that you dishonor me by entering my daughter's chamber? You know right well that I have not given her to you in marriage. And now, who will save you from my might and majesty? If I cried out to my slaves and servants to put you to the vilest of deaths, they would slay you at once."

"Verily," answered the Prince, "I wonder at you! Can you wish for your daughter a mate handsomer than myself or one better fitted to rule?"

"Nay, by Allah," the King returned. "But I would have had you act after the custom of kings. You have dishonored me."

"You are right, O King," the Prince answered. "But if you call your slaves and servants and they fell upon me and slay me, you would only let all know of your disgrace. Therefore, I would counsel you otherwise."

Said the King, "Let me hear what you have to advise."

The Prince said: "Either you meet me in single combat and he who is victor shall rule the kingdom;

or you send out against me all your horsemen and footmen and servants and let me engage them in single combat. If I overcome them, I shall be your son-in-law."

The King was amazed at the Prince's boldness. But being at heart sure that the Prince would be slain, he accepted his idea. He called the guard and bade him go to his chief minister, his Wazier, and tell him to assemble his forty thousand horsemen and have them arm and mount their steeds.

As for the King himself, he sat a long time conversing with the young Prince, being pleased with his wise speech and good sense and fine breeding.

Now when it was daybreak, the King returned to his palace and sat on his throne. Then he commanded that one of the best of the royal steeds be saddled for the Prince.

But the youth said, "O King, I will not mount horse till I come in sight of the troops."

"Be it as you will," replied the King.

Then the two went to the parade ground, where the troops were drawn up.

"Ho, all you men," the King cried, "a youth has come to me who seeks my daughter in marriage. A man of stouter heart than he I have never seen. No, nor a man of stouter arm, for he claims that he can overcome you single-handed and force you to flee. So when he charges down upon you, receive him on point of pike and edge of saber." Then turning to the Prince, he said, "Up, O my son, and do your duty on them."

"O King," answered he, "you do not deal fairly with me. How shall I go forth against them, seeing that I am on foot and the men are mounted?"

The King answered him: "I bade you mount and you refused. But choose whichever of my horses you like."

Then the Prince said, "I will ride no horse but that on which I came."

"And where is your horse?"

"On the roof of your palace."

When the King heard these words, he cried: "This is the first sign you have given me of madness. How can the horse be on the roof? But we shall see at once if you speak truth or lies."

Then the King said to one of his chief officers, "Go to my palace and bring me what you find on the roof."

So the officer and his men mounted to the roof. There they found a horse standing. But when they drew near, they saw that it was made of ebony and ivory. So they laughed and said: "Was it of this horse the youth spoke? He must be mad. However, we shall soon see."

Then they lifted the horse and carried it to the King.

All the lords flocked round to look at it. They marveled at its beauty and the richness of its saddle and bridle. The King also admired it and wondered with great wonder.

"O youth, is this your horse?" he asked.

"Yes, O King," the Prince answered. "This is my horse, and you will soon see what a marvel it is."

"Then take and mount it," said the King.

But the Prince said, "I will not mount till the troops withdraw afar from it."

So the King bade them retire a bowshot from the horse. At this its owner said: "O King, look now! I am about to mount my horse and charge upon your troops and scatter them right and left and split their hearts apart!"

"Do as you will," the King answered. "Do not spare their lives, for they will not spare yours."

Then the Prince mounted, settled himself in the saddle, and turned the pin of ascent. All eyes were strained toward the horse. They saw it begin to heave and rock and sway to and fro. It made the strangest movements a steed ever made, and suddenly it soared high into the sky.

When the King saw this, he cried out to his men, "Catch him, catch him!"

But the Wazier said to him: "O King, can a man overtake the flying bird? This is surely a mighty magician or jinni or devil. Praise Allah for delivering you and your troops from his hand."

The King returned to the palace, went straight to his daughter, and told her all. But the Princess no sooner heard what had happened than she fell violently sick and took to her pillow.

"By Allah," she moaned, "I will neither eat nor drink till Allah brings him back."

Her father was greatly concerned and mourned greatly, but he could do nothing to soothe her. Her love and longing only increased.

4. WON AND LOST

Prince Kamar al-Akmar, when he had risen high in the air, turned his horse's head from the city of Sana'a to his native land. When he drew near the capital, he circled about over the city. Then he alighted on the roof of the King's palace, where he left his horse and descended.

He was surprised to see the threshold of the palace strewn with ashes and feared that one of his family was dead. Then he entered and found his parents and his sisters all in mourning, pale and sad. When his father made sure that this was indeed his son, he cried out with joy and gladness. His mother and sisters also fell upon him, kissing him and weeping with joy. Then they questioned him, and he told them all that had happened from first to last.

"Praised be Allah for your safety, O coolness of my eyes and core of my heart!" his father exclaimed.

With this the King ordered a festival, and the glad news flew through the palace and the city. The people beat drums and cymbals and put on gay garments and decorated the streets and markets. The King made great feasts for the people, and for seven days and nights all creatures were glad.

After a while the Prince asked about the maker of the horse. "Tell me, O my father," the young man said, "what has happened to the Sage?"

The King answered: "May Allah never bless him! He was the cause of your leaving us, O my son, and since the day you disappeared he has been in jail."

The Prince then urged his father to release the Sage from prison. So the King did. He sent for the Persian and gave him new clothing and treated him with all favor. But the King refused to give him his youngest daughter in marriage.

Now the King had told his son not to go near the ebony horse. But the rejoicing was no sooner over than the Prince's mind turned to the lovely daughter of the King of Sana'a. His heart was filled with love and longing. So early in the morning he went out of the palace to the horse and, mounting it, turned the pin of ascent. At once the horse flew up like a bird and soared with him into the sky. The Prince flew on and on till he came to the city of Sana'a and alighted on the palace roof as before.

Quietly he crept down. The guard was asleep again. So the Prince raised the curtain and went in until he came to the alcove chamber of the Princess. He stopped to listen. And lo! he heard her weeping, while her women sought to comfort her.

"O our mistress," he heard them say, "why will you mourn for one who does not mourn for you?"

Said she, "O you foolish ones, is he for whom I mourn one of those who forget or are forgotten?" And she wept again.

The Prince's heart swelled when he heard the Princess' words. So he came in and took her hand in his. "Why all this weeping and mourning?" he said.

When she recognized the Prince, the Princess threw herself upon him and took him round the neck and kissed him.

"For your sake I weep," she said, "because of my separation from you. If you had tarried longer, I would surely have died. How could you leave me?"

"Do not think about what has been," he said. "I too have grieved through all this time. But now I am hungry and thirsty."

At this the Princess bade her maidens bring food and drink, and they sat talking till night ended.

Now when day broke, he rose to take leave of her, saying he would come to her once every week. But she wept and said: "I pray you, by Allah Almighty, take me with you wherever you go. I cannot bear to be separated from you."

"Will you indeed go with me?" he asked.

"Yes."

"Then," said he, "arise and we will depart."

So she rose at once and put on what was richest and dearest to her of her trinkets of gold and jewels. Then they went up to the roof of the palace. He mounted the ebony horse and took her up behind and made her fast to himself, tying her with strong bonds. After this he turned the shoulder pin, and the horse rose high in the air.

When her slave women saw this, they shrieked aloud and ran and told her father and mother. In hot haste they mounted to the palace roof, and looking up, saw the magic horse flying away with the Prince and Princess.

"O King's son," the King cried out, "I pray you, do not take our daughter from us!"

The Prince made him no reply. But thinking that the Princess might repent, he asked her, "Would you have me restore you to your mother and father?"

"By Allah, O my lord," she answered, "my only wish is to be with you, wherever you are."

Hearing these words, the Prince rejoiced, and they rode till they came in sight of his father's capital.

Now the Prince wished to bring the Princess into the city with due honor. So he set her down in one of the King's gardens and taking her into a summer house left the ebony horse at the door.

"Sit here," he said, "till my messenger comes to you. I will now go to my father to make ready a palace for you and show you my royal estate."

She was delighted. "Do as you will," she said.

Then the Prince left her and went to his father, who rejoiced in his return. Then the Prince said to him: "Know that I have brought with me the King's daughter of whom I told you. I have left her in a garden outside the city and have come to tell you that you may go forth to meet her in royal procession."

"With joy and gladness," the King answered.

Straightway he gave orders that the town be decorated. Then he mounted his horse and rode out in all his majesty, he and his army and high officers of the household. Drums and kettledrums, fifes and clarinets, and all manner of instruments accompanied them.

The Prince meantime got ready for the Princess a litter of brocades—green, red, and yellow. In this litter he set Indian and Greek slave girls to be the Princess' attendants. Then he left the litter and went on ahead to the summerhouse where he had set the Princess down. But when he came there, he found nothing—neither Princess nor horse.

At first the Prince beat his face and tore his garments and wandered round about the garden as if he had lost his wits. Then he came to his senses and said to himself: How could she have come at the secret of the horse, seeing I told her nothing of it? Maybe the Persian Sage who made the horse has stolen her away in revenge for my father's treatment of him.

Then he sought the guardians of the garden and asked them if they had seen anyone come in.

"Only the Persian Sage," they said. "He came to gather healing herbs."

The Prince knew then that it was indeed he who had taken the Princess away. When the people came, he was much abashed before them. Turning to his father, he told him what had happened and said: "Take the troops and march them back to the city. As for me, I will never return till I find my Princess."

5. THE SAGE AND THE LADY

After the Prince left the Princess in the summerhouse, the Persian entered the garden to pluck certain herbs. As he approached the summerhouse, he smelled the sweet perfumes that came from the Princess. He followed the sweet smell to the door of the summerhouse—and there he saw the horse. He went up to it and examined it and found it whole and sound. He was about to mount it and ride away. Then he thought, first I will see what the Prince has brought and left here with the horse.

So he went inside and saw the Princess. He knew at once that she was a highborn lady and guessed why the Prince had left her. So he went up to her and kissed the ground before her. At this she raised her eyes to him, and finding him very ugly, she asked, "Who are you?"

He answered: "O my lady, I am a messenger sent by the Prince. He has bidden me bring you to another garden nearer to the city, for my lady the Queen cannot walk so far.

"Where is the Prince?" asked the Princess.

"He is in the city with his father and will come for you in great state."

Said she, "Tell me, could he find none handsomer to send to me?"

The Sage laughed loudly. "O my lady, let not the foulness of my face and form deceive you," he said. "Indeed the Prince has chosen me, in his jealousy and love of you, because I am so ugly."

When she heard this, it seemed reasonable to her. So she rose and put her hand in his. "O my father," she said, "what did you bring me to ride on?"

He replied, "O my lady, you shall ride the horse you came on."

Said she, "But I cannot ride it by myself."

So he mounted, and taking her up behind him, bound her to himself with firm bonds. Then he turned the ascent pin. The horse rose high in the air. Nor did it slacken in its flight till it was out of sight of the city. Now when Shama al-Nahar saw this, she asked him, "Where are you taking me? No, you! Where is the garden and my Prince?"

Answered the Sage: "Curse the Prince! He is a mean and witless knave!"

She cried: "Woe to you! How dare you disobey your lord's command?"

"He is no lord of mine," replied the Persian. "Know you who I am?"

"I know nothing of you save what you told me," answered the Princess.

"What I told you," said he, "was a trick of mine against you and the King's son. I have long lamented the loss of this horse which is under me, and which I made myself. But now I have got firm hold of it and of you, and I will burn his heart as he has burned mine."

When she heard this, she slapped his face and wept over what had befallen her. But the Sage rode on and on without stopping till he came to the land of the Greeks. There he alighted in a green meadow.

Now this meadow lay near the city of a powerful King. It chanced that the King went forth that day to hunt and amuse himself. As he passed by that meadow, he saw the Persian standing there with the lady and the horse. Before the Sage was aware, the King's slaves fell upon him and carried him and the lady and the horse to their master.

The King was amazed at the difference between the man and the maid. "O my lady," he asked, "what kin is this old man to you?"

The Persian made haste to reply. "She is my wife," he said.

But the lady at once denied it. "O King," she said, "by Allah, I know him not nor is he my husband. Nay, he is a wicked magician who has stolen me away by force and fraud."

Thereupon the King bade his servants beat the Persian, and they beat him till he was well-nigh dead. After this the King commanded that he be taken to the city and cast into jail.

As for the Princess, the King put her in his harem, where she lived with his wives and their servants. And as for the horse, the King set it among his treasures, though he did not know its secret.

6. THE RESCUE OF SHAMA AL-NAHAR

The Prince, meantime, had taken what he needed of money and set out to trail the Sage and the Princess. He journeyed from country to country and city to city. Everywhere he asked about the Princess and the ebony horse, and all who heard him thought him mad. Thus he continued to do for a long time, but he could find no news of the Princess.

At last he came to the land of the Greeks, and as chance would have it, he stopped at a certain inn where he saw a company of merchants sitting at talk.

"O my friends," he heard one of them say, "I lately heard a wonder of wonders."

"What was that?" the others asked.

He answered: "I was visiting a certain district in a certain city and I heard its people chatting of a strange thing that had lately happened. Their King went out hunting with a company of his courtiers one day and they came to a green meadow. Here they saw an old man standing and a woman sitting beside a horse of ebony. The man was foul of face and form, but the woman was a marvel of beauty and loveliness and perfect grace. As for the horse, it was a miracle. Never did eyes see anything more goodly."

"And what did the King do with them?" asked the others.

The merchant answered: "As for the man, the King questioned him. He pretended that the woman was his wife, but she declared he was an enchanter and a villain. So the King took her from the old man and had him beaten and cast in jail. As for the ebony horse, I know not what became of it."

At this the Prince drew near the merchant and began questioning him. When he knew the name of the city, he was filled with joy, and as soon as day dawned, he set out and never stopped traveling till he reached that city.

But when he wanted to enter, the gatekeepers laid hands on him to bring him before the King. For it was that King's custom to question each stranger as to his craft and why he came to the city. But it was supper time and too late for the King to see the stranger that day. So the guards took the Prince to the jail for the night. But when the warders saw his handsomeness and grace of bearing, they could not find it in their hearts to imprison him. They made him sit with them outside the walls. And when food was brought to them, he ate with them.

"What countryman are you?" they asked the Prince.

"I come from Fars," he answered, "the land of the Khosru."

When they heard this, they laughed, and one of them said: "We have a man from Fars here in the jail with us. Never saw I a bigger liar than he."

"And never did I see any fouler of face and uglier than he," said another.

"What have you seen of his lying?" asked the Prince.

Answered they: "He pretends that he is one of the wise doctors. If he is so wise, why does he not cure the beautiful woman he brought here? She is mad. The King is in love with her and does his utmost to discover a cure for her. For a year past he has spent treasures on doctors on her account. But none can cure her."

When the Prince heard this, he quickly devised a plan whereby he might come to his love and rescue her.

As soon as morning came, the warders took the Prince before the King. The King at once questioned him what and where and why.

"As to my name," the Prince replied, "I am called in Persian Harjah. As to my country, I come from the land of Fars. And I am of the men of the art of medicine, healing the sick and those whom the jinni drive mad. Whenever I see a patient, I heal him. This is my craft."

The King rejoiced with great joy on hearing this.

"O excellent Sage, you have indeed come to us at a time when we need you," he said.

Then he told the Prince about the madness of the Princess and how he had found her and the Sage and the horse. "If you can cure her, you shall have everything you ask of me," he ended.

"Allah save the King," said the Prince. "Tell me about her madness. Also tell me this, O King. What have you done with the horse?"

"O learned youth, it is with me yet, laid up in one of my treasure chambers."

At this the Prince thought, the best thing I can do is first to see the horse and see if it is whole and sound. If not, I must find some other way of saving my beloved.

So he turned to the King and said: "O King, I must see this horse. Perhaps I can find in it something that will serve me for the curing of the lady."

"With all my heart," replied the King. And taking him by the hand, he showed him into the place where the horse was.

The Prince went round about it, examining its condition. He found it whole and sound. At this he said to the King: "Now I would go in to the lady that I may see how it is with her."

So the King took him to the Princess' apartment, where they found her wringing her hands and beating herself against the ground. But this was not from any madness caused by the jinni. She acted this way so that none might approach her.

When the Prince saw her thus, he said to her, "No harm shall befall you, O delight of the three worlds."

Then he went nearer to her till he managed to whisper, "I am Kamar al-Akmar."

At this she looked up from the floor and saw him and cried out with a loud cry and fell down fainting from too much joy. But the King thought that this was a yet worse madness brought on by her fear of him, so he went out.

Then the Prince put his mouth to the Princess' ear and said to her: "O Shama al-Nahar, skill is needed to save us from this King. My first move will be to go out now and tell him you are possessed by an evil spirit and that is why you are mad. I will promise to heal you and drive away the evil spirit. So when he comes in, speak smooth words to him so that he will think I have cured you."

"I hear and obey," she said.

So he went out to the King in gladness and said to him, "O King, I have cured her for you. So now go in and speak softly to her."

Thereupon the King went in. She rose when she saw him and kissed the ground before him, and bade him welcome.

He was ready to fly for joy at her words. He bade the women attend her and take her to the baths and make ready dresses and adornments for her.

So they went in to her and greeted her. She returned their greetings in the pleasantest fashion. At that they put royal dress upon her, and a collar of jewels about her neck. They took her to the baths, and when they brought her out, she was like the full moon.

The King joyed in her with great joy and said to the Prince, "O Sage, all this is your doing."

The Prince replied: "O King, her cure is not yet complete. To complete it you must go forth, you and all your troops and guards, and bring her to the place where you found her. Nor must you forget to bring the beast of black wood which was with her. There is a devil inside it. Unless I get him out by a spell, he

will return at the beginning of every month and make the lady mad."

The King cried, "With love and gladness, O you most learned of all who see the light of day!"

Then he ordered the ebony horse to be taken to the meadow and he rode there with all his troops, bringing the Princess.

Now when they came to the appointed place, the Prince bade them set the Princess and the steed as far away from the King and his troops as eye could reach.

"With your leave," the Prince said, "I will now proceed to work the spell and imprison the evil spirit that he may never more return to her. After this I shall mount this wooden horse and take the lady up behind me. At that the horse will shake and sway to and fro and move forward till it comes to you. Then the affair will be at an end. After that you may do with her as you will."

When the King heard these words, he rejoiced with great joy. So the Prince mounted the horse and took the Princess up behind him. The King and his troops watched him while he bound her fast to him. Then he turned the ascent pin, and the horse soared with them high in the air till they disappeared from view.

The King stayed there half the day awaiting their return, but they did not return. Then he went back to the city, shut himself up in the palace, and grieved a long time. But at last he was comforted.

"Verily," his officers said to him, "he who took the lady from you is an enchanter. Praised be Allah who has delivered you from his craft."

The Prince continued toward his father's capital in joy and cheer. At last he alighted on his own palace, where he set the lady down in safety. Then he went in to his father and mother and greeted them and told them of her coming, and they were filled with gladness.

The King spread great feasts for the townsfolk. For a whole month they held high festival. After this the Prince and the Princess were married.

King Sabur broke the ebony horse in pieces, lest it bring his son to harm. As for the Prince, he wrote a letter to the Princess' father, telling him all that had befallen her, and sent the letter by a messenger, together with costly presents. The King of Sana'a rejoiced greatly when he received the letter and the presents and by the same messenger sent back rich gifts to his son-in-law.

In course of time King Sabur died. Then his son took the throne. He ruled so justly that all the people praised him. And Kamar al-Akmar and his wife Shama al-Nahar lived in all joy and satisfaction.

The Ebony Horse

In ages past there lived in Persia a rich and powerful King, Sabur by name, who had three daughters, very fair, and a handsome son. Twice in the year the King kept festival, and threw his palaces open to all, distributing gifts to the poor. From far and near people came to bring him gifts. On one such holiday, three wise men came to visit him—a Hindu, a Greek, and a Persian. Knowing that the King loved science, each had brought him a gift he had devised himself.

The Hindu came first, and presented the King a man made of gold, set with costly jewels, bearing a golden trumpet in its hand. King Sabur asked, "O Sage, what is the virtue of this figure?"

"My Lord, set this figure at the gate of your city as guardian. If an enemy should enter the place, the trumpet will sound and he will drop dead."

"By Allah, Sage, if your word is true, I will grant your dearest wish."

Then came the Greek, bearing as gift a basin of silver in which a peacock stood surrounded by four and twenty chicks. Then asked the King the virtue of this gift, to which the Greek replied, "O Sire, at the passing of each hour, the peacock crows, flaps his wings, and pecks one of the chicks. At month's end, his mouth is opened and shows therein a crescent moon."

"Well said," answered King Sabur. "Your wish is granted."

Then came forward the Persian sage, leading a horse of ebony inlaid with gold and jewels, harnessed with a royal saddle. Sabur was amazed at the beauty of the horse, and inquired its virtue.

"My Lord, but mount this horse and it will carry the rider through the air, traveling in one day a year's journey!" responded the Persian.

"Your wish, too, shall be granted." And with the words the gold man blew his trumpet, the peacock pecked its chicks, and the ebony horse soared aloft. And King Sabur rejoiced in his gifts.

The three sages bowed before the King, and asked that each might receive one of his lovely daughters as wife, to which the King agreed. "For you, O Hindu, my eldest; to you, Greek sage, my second; and for you from far-off Persia, my loveliest and youngest daughter." And he bade his servants go and prepare the wedding feasts.

Now the Princesses had seen everything from behind a silken curtain, and the youngest one despaired, for the Persian was a hundred years old, goggle-eyed, hollow-cheeked, loose of lip and large of nose! A fright, indeed! She fled to her chamber weeping, but not before her brother, the Prince Kamar al-Akmar, had seen her. On learning of her father's promise to the giver of the horse, he sought his father, demanding the reason for such action.

"She will surely die of grief," said the Prince, not knowing the old Persian stood near and overheard. He was greatly angered. But the King ordered the servants to bring forth the ebony horse, and on seeing it, the Prince, a fine horseman, must forthwith mount. "Show him, Sage, the working of this creature; perhaps it will help you in your wish." The Persian, however, still angered, motioned toward a pin in the shoulder of the horse, and as the Prince mounted into the air, stepped back with an evil smile. "You will not see him again, O Sire! He did not inquire, and I did not show him, the pin to bring the horse again to earth." At this the King was enraged, and had the Sage thrown into jail, while he and all his court gave themselves to weeping.

PRINCE AND PRINCESS

The ebony horse soared into the air, nearer and nearer to the sun, and the Prince, who could do nothing, thought himself doomed. But nevertheless, he felt over the horse seeking a pin like the one he had touched to ascend. His fingers found it, and pulled; at once he began to descend. Before him was the fairest of cities with trees, gardens, and streams around, and a palace rising in front of him in the midst of the city. Like a weary bird, the ebony horse sank and alighted gently on the terraced roof of that palace; the Prince dismounted, and looked around. He was hungry, and after assuring himself that everyone slept, he walked

toward a staircase, descended, and found himself in a court where a light burned. A mighty guard lay sleeping there, his sword gleaming and a bag hanging on a nearby column. The Prince examined the bag, found food and ate; then, carefully taking the guard's sword, went toward a second door, covered with a curtain. Raising the curtain, he beheld four slave girls sleeping around a couch of ivory on which lay the fairest of women. Long he gazed, then bent and kissed her, at which she opened her eyes. "Who are you?" she murmured. "A Prince, and one who loves you," he answered. "Doubtless, then, you are the suitor my father just yesterday rejected for his sheer ugliness." Then suddenly the slave girls wakened; they were alarmed, seeing the stranger, and asked from whence he had come. But when the Princess replied that it was the

Adapted from Anne Terry White, *Sinbad the Seaman—The Ebony Horse: Two Arabian Tales* (Champaign, Ill.: Garrard, 1969).

suitor her father had rejected, they shook their heads . . . he had been hideous . . . but this one, ah, this one was handsome indeed! And they ran to the guard and upbraided him for sleeping, while a stranger had taken his sword and come into the room of the Princess. Then the guard ran to the Princess and accused the Prince, who was angered. "I have done nothing," he said. "Go and bring the King to the Princess in all haste."

Then did the guard run and bring the King, who would have leaped upon the Prince with drawn sword, but seeing that the Prince was the stronger, he sheathed it and asked who, and from whence the stranger had come.

"I am a Prince of the royal house of Khosru. Could you wish for your daughter a younger or more handsome husband, or one more fitted to rule?" The King was not entirely pleased, and said, "Your manner of coming is not in keeping with the custom of kings! You have dishonored me!" To this the Prince agreed.

"You are right, O King," he said. "And if you will meet me in single combat, we shall let the winner decide who will hereafter rule. Or, be it to your pleasure, send out to me all your horsemen and footmen and servants and let me engage them in a single combat. If I overcome them, I shall be your son-in-law." To this the King gave assent, being sure the Prince would fail; but then, he stayed to converse longer with the young man, and was further pleased with his manner and his breeding, so that when daybreak had come and the

forty thousand troops of the King had assembled at his command, the King himself ordered a royal steed to be brought for the young Prince. "No," replied the Prince. "Until I stand before your troops, I will not mount; nay, and then I will mount no horse except that one on which I came." Then the King was puzzled indeed. "Since you will take no horse of mine, and I see no horse of yours, how then will you confront all these armed men to claim the Princess?"

"O Sire, send your servants to bring forth the horse that is on the roof of your palace, and make haste." The servants ascended to the roof, but when they saw only an ebony horse bejeweled and ivory-decorated, they laughed aloud; then, bearing it on their shoulders, they brought it to the Prince. The King marveled at its beauty, and, at the request of the Prince, commanded his troops to withdraw apace. "See now, O Sire! I mount my horse, and I will charge your troops!" With a cry, the Prince jumped to the saddle, pressed the ascent pin in the shoulder of the horse, and with a heaving and rocking and swaying, suddenly he soared into the sky, leaving the troops below, and the King, crying out for him to return! "He will never return, your highness, for this is of some jinni or devil!" said his chief vizier. The King found that he must agree, and went to tell the Princess, who wept and became violently ill. "Never shall I eat or drink till my beloved returns," said she, nor could her father comfort her.

WON AND LOST

Prince Kamar al-Akmar turned his horse's head from the city of Sana'a to his native land, and when he drew near, circled and alighted on the roof. The palace was strewn with ashes of mourning, and his family was wrapped in weeping. When his father saw that the Prince had in very truth returned, he cried aloud in joy. From the palace the good news spread to every part of the city, drums and cymbals were beaten, and a great feast was held. "And the maker of the ebony horse—where is he?" asked the Prince. On learning that he was yet imprisoned, he begged that he be released, and brought into the King's favor, though the King would not give the youngest daughter to him as wife, at any cost. And the Persian Sage was still angered at this.

Now when the festivities of welcome were over, the Prince remembered the lovely daughter of the King of Sana'a. Early in the morning he went to the horse, mounted it, and flew like a bird to the city of Sana'a where he again alighted on the roof of the palace. Quietly he crept down to the door of the Princess' room, raised the curtain, and came upon the princess

weeping. "Must you so weep?" he said softly, taking the Princess' hand in his, and at his voice, the Princess threw herself upon him. "Because you were gone, and I did not think to see you again, I weep! I pray you, do not leave again—or take me with you, if you go, for I cannot bear to be separated from you." At her words, the Prince was glad. Then the Princess donned her finest robe and most precious jewels, and with the Prince went to the ebony horse on the roof. He mounted, made sure she was fast behind him, and they soared away. Nor did the cries of the King or her maidens stop their flight.

To the city of the Prince they flew, and the Prince, wishing to bring her into the city in a fitting state, set her down in one of the King's gardens, in a summerhouse, with the ebony horse near by. "I go now to my father to make all ready for you, only wait here for a while." So saying, he left her and went to the King.

"I have brought with me a King's daughter, of whom I spoke earlier. She waits for us in a garden outside the city, that we may go forth to meet her in royal procession," said the Prince. "With great joy!" exclaimed the King, and gave orders that the town be decorated and that the army come forth, and drums and fifes, and clarinets accompany the procession. In the meantime, the Prince made ready a litter of brocades, scarlet and gold and emerald, with slave girls as attendants, and so he went forth to meet his Princess. But when he arrived, he found neither Princess nor ebony horse. The Prince was distraught and tore his garments. Then he wondered to himself: "The Persian Sage—could he have found the ebony horse and stolen the girl? Perhaps he has revenged my father's broken word!" And he sought the guards of the garden, and found that the Persian Sage had indeed come into the garden to gather healing herbs. Then the Prince knew that the Princess was gone in truth.

THE SAGE AND THE LADY

When the Prince had left, the Princess waited in the summerhouse. Not long thereafter, an old man gathering herbs came and looked in at her. It was the Persian Sage, and seeing the ebony horse standing there near her, he realized that she had come with the Prince. "Oh my lady, I am sent by the Prince to bring you to a garden nearer the city," he said, bowing himself. "Indeed, can that be true, with one so old and ugly?" the Princess wondered, but being assured that it was precisely because of that, lest jealousy enter in, that the Prince had chosen him, he mounted the ebony horse taking the lady behind him, and the horse rose high in the air. No cry from the Princess hindered him, nor did he stop till he came to the land of the Greeks, where he alighted in a green meadow, which lay near the city of a great King. By chance the King himself was passing near, and seeing the old sage and the lovely Princess, he stopped, wondering at the difference between them. "She is my wife," the magician exclaimed, but the Princess wept and cried aloud, "Not so! He is a wicked magician who has taken me by force!" Whereupon the King commanded his servants to beat the Persian and throw him in jail. The Princess he put into his harem, and the ebony horse he stored among his treasures.

THE RESCUE OF SHAMA AL-NAHAR

Meantime the Prince had set out to trail the Sage. From country to country he journeyed, from city to city, asking always about an ebony horse and a lovely Princess, but none could give him answer to his questions. At last he came to the land of the Greeks, and stopping at an inn with some merchants, he heard the story of the King, the old man, and the lovely Princess in the green meadow, with a horse of ebony standing near at hand. The Prince could scarcely contain himself and questioned the speaker as to the very city and where it might be. By daybreak he was on his way, nor did he stop until he reached the walls of the city. It was yet early in the day and the guards would not let him enter, but made him eat with them, as he waited without. "Whence do you come?" they asked of him. And when he said he was from Fars, the land of the Khosru, they laughed. "We have also a man from Fars here," they said. "He is a bigger liar than ever we have seen! So foul, and so full of words that mean nothing! He says he is a wise doctor. But if he is wise, why can he not cure the lady he brought with him to this place? She is mad, and though the King has tried this whole past year, no one can cure her. The King would gladly marry her if she were healed."

When the Prince heard this, he thought of a plan. The guards took him to the King for questioning, as was their custom, and the Prince gave answer to the King, telling him he was a man of medicine, from the land of Fars, and was wont to cure all manner of sickness, especially those whom others called mad. On hearing this, the King rejoiced. "I have a lady here who has been mad more than a year, and I would give you whatever you desire if you should cure her." Then he told the Prince how he had found her, and the horse of ebony which he had put among his treasures. The Prince determined to see first the horse, to be sure it would still soar, and this he asked of the King, saying perhaps there was something on the horse that would help him understand the lady's madness. The King showed him first the treasure, then took him to the lady's chamber, where they found her wringing her hands and beating her head against the ground. When she saw the Prince, and heard him say her name, she fainted from the joy of it, but the King thought it was from fear of him, and he left hastily. Then the Prince spoke in the ear of the Princess, telling her to be calm, and listen carefully, for he had come to rescue her. She must pretend to be recovering, for he would drive out the evil spirit which possessed her, and therefore she must meet the King gently and bid him welcome. The lady promised to do so, and when the slave maids came in she greeted them with graciousness, so that they ran to the King with the news that the foreign medic had indeed cured her! With the greatest joy the King commanded that she be perfumed and bathed and oiled, with all manner of flowers, and garbed in silks and jewels.

Upon seeing her in all her beauty the King was elated and promised the strange young doctor his heart's desire. But that Prince replied to him that the cure was not quite complete. Yet one more thing must be done, or else the madness would return at the beginning of each month. "You must bring the ebony horse to the meadow where you first found him, for he is possessed of an evil spirit. Bring also the maid, and all the troops and guards to that same place. Arrange yourselves as far as eye can see on one side of the meadow. I will go to the other side, and take the lady with me. We shall mount the ebony horse, and I will exorcise him of the evil spirit within, that he may never more return. You will see him shake, and sway, and then move slowly toward you. After that you may do with the lady as you will, for she will be cured."

So the King did as he was bade, and the soldiers and the guards also; and they watched as the Prince mounted the ebony horse, with the lady behind him.

The horse did indeed shiver, and sway, and started forward, and then it mounted to the sky and disappeared from sight. Half the day the King waited for their return, and when he saw that he had been mistreated, he grieved and returned to his palace. But at length he recovered.

And the Prince soared through the sky to his own city, and to the palace of his father, where they were received with rejoicing and great feasts and ceremonies for thirty days. The Prince sent a message to the father of the Princess, and he rejoiced also and returned rich presents to the bridal couple. The ebony horse was broken in pieces, and Kamar al-Akmar and his lovely wife, the Princess of Sana'a, lived in joy and satisfaction many years.

AMPLIFYING

The question of when to enlarge a fragment of story, a short fable, or an incident, depends upon the use planned for the story, and whether or not it is worth the amount of creative imagination and research necessary. If the basic structure of a story is present in the material, so that a real story—although perhaps a short one—can be built up, and if the material possesses a freshness, an unusual angle, a rare spark of humor, or some other special sort of quality, it is probably worth the attempt. Amplifying requires skill; while fleshing out the bare bones with description and adding background and insights into the plot to emphasize the motivation for actions, the storyteller must remember that legends, folktales, fairy tales, and fables in their very nature are not introspective, heavy with morals, didacticism, or description. Yet amplification can bring vitality to what otherwise might be dull, or never usable because it is so fragmentary. The myths of Bullfinch are a good example of this process; all of the necessary facts are there, but nothing else, and to make them tellable requires that they be recreated in more appealing guise.

"The Beast with the Single Horn" (Jacobson) was discovered while looking for a story about the unicorn to fit into the Story Hour Zoo program. In its original form, it was a fragment of legend from China. As it was reworked, it evolved into a "why" story explaining Chinese written language, brief but structured.

"The Squonk" (Stoutenberg—*Tall Tale*) comes from a series of anecdotes gathered from the tall tale lore of our early frontier days. Adrien Stoutenberg delightfully amplified some of this lore into animal tall tale stories, but left some of the material in a fragmentary state. The silly Squonk was appealing as a tall tale animal suitable for the Story Hour Zoo; the author's phraseology was retained wherever possible, but stretched into a plot with a climax and a real denouement. As it now stands, it takes about eight to ten minutes and elicits appreciative giggles. A hint of folk speech has been incorporated.

"The Cock and the Cats Who Bore His Litter" (Cooper) is a brief ironic fable from Greece. As translated by Cooper, the fable is five or six lines long. Amplified, with color and some reflection on the culture, it is short, but complete and spicy.

"October 25, St. Crispin's Day" (Belting—*Eve*) is a brief vignette of a medieval pageant held every year. This short word-picture was part of The Cobbler's Bench story program, and fitted into the section of stories on cobblers and saints. It is based on a brief prose poem, with brilliant illustration, of the celebration of St. Crispin, missioner to the Gauls, a shoemaker by trade. Shown with the illustration, this was a sketch that laid the scene for the stories which followed. As such, it held the interest of the children, and lasted about two minutes.

The Cock and the Cats Who Bore His Litter

A cock once employed several cats to carry his litter when he appeared in public. When the fox saw him, proudly borne along, she murmured to herself, "I warn you, friend cock, to be on your guard. For if you study the faces of those cats, they look as though they were carrying off a captured prey, and not an unwelcome burden."

Before long, the cats becoming hungry, made short work of their master, and divided the object of their crime among them.

A false sense of security often leads to danger.

Frederick T. Cooper, "The Cock and the Cats Who Bore His Litter," *Argosy of Fables*, from Phaedrus, *Fables*, Appendix II, no. 16 (New York: Frederick A. Stokes, 1921).

The Cock and the Cats Who Bore His Litter

In some far-off time there once lived in the East a magnificent cock. His comb was curly and scarlet, and he thrust his head high and shook it at all the foolish hens who admired him. His tail feathers were bronze and green and blue, and they shone like polished copper. All told, he was a haughty and beautiful fellow, and well he knew it! Not only was he handsome, but fate had blessed him with wealth, and so he lived in style, with servants and footmen to carry his litter, when he deigned to appear in public. Not just one footman in front of the velvet curtained litter, and one behind! Ah no, for him he must have several, that he might be raised high for all to see.

Now the footmen the cock employed to carry his litter were not from his own kind. Indeed, that would have been very ordinary. His footmen were sleek, supple cats who moved with such grace that there was scarcely a jiggle, in perfect rhythm with each other. The cock drew his litter curtains apart only slightly, just enough to see that the passers-by were noticing his company, and he did not often look down at the cats who shouldered him, for they were servants and he was the master. And so the days passed, and the cock grew lazy, and more proud, and more indifferent to the commonplace things around him.

Now there was a fox who stood among the people lining the streets as the litter passed by. Perhaps she had a special interest in the cock, for she was known to have a special fondness for fowl of any sort; or perhaps she envied him his wealth and his position. Although she kept her distance, her beady eyes sparkled and she waved her bushy tail thoughtfully, as only a fox may when she is contemplating a situation. She watched the proud cock lolling on his silken cushions and noted the scornful glance he cast at his litter-bearers now and then. Every so often her eyes lighted on the cats, swinging along under the litter, their velvet paws making no sound, and their long tails curled in graceful arches behind them. Not a sound did the cats make, not a turn of their heads did they give, nor a blink of their yellow eyes. Yet the fox felt a shiver run down her spine as they swung along, and she slipped back into the crowd of watchers. "Aha, my fine sir! You should have a care over those litter-bearers! They are not all that they seem, I am afraid!" Many times the fox watched the lofty litter with its arrogant cock, and always she felt uneasy when she observed the cats. They were too perfect and too assured as they carried the master's litter. But she did not say anything to them, and though once she hinted at this to the cock, he tossed his scarlet comb disdainfully and did not listen.

So time passed, with the cock becoming more high and mighty, and the cats more crafty and sleek. One day a festival was held, with flags and food, and parades everywhere. Everyone went around laughing and celebrating. The litter of the cock was borne proudly through the streets, as usual, but when the cat-bearers had carried their lord to his mansion, instead of depositing him before the great entrance, they kept moving along. "Stop, I tell you! I would descend!" commanded the cock, but the cats marched on. "You will be punished for this," crowed the irate master, but the cats swung along in perfect rhythm.

At last, in a lonely place, far from the great mansion, they set the litter down, and ringed around it licking their mouths and waving their tails. The cock was suddenly terribly afraid, and pulled the heavy curtains close. But it was too late! Carefully, and quickly, the hungry cats pulled the gaudy cock out of the litter, snatched off his gorgeous jewels and threw them aside—and made fast work of the heavy, well-fleshed rooster! When they had scattered the feathers here and there, and divided every last shred of skin and bone, they sat in the sun beside the litter and licked their fur. And what they did after that, nobody knows, but that was the last time the cats bore the cock's litter!

Amplified from Frederick T. Cooper, "The Cock and the Cats Who Bore His Litter," *Argosy of Fables*, from Phaedrus, *Fables*, Appendix II, no. 16 (New York: Frederick A. Stokes, 1921).

RETELLING

The art of retelling stories so that they take on fresh appeal and new form is one of the most demanding and yet one of the most satisfying areas for a storyteller. To some extent, everyone who tells stories is a reteller, recreating legends, folktales, or other oral narratives. But retelling refers to a deliberate search into sources, either ancient or modern, to create a tale in a new form with only basic plotline, theme, and characters carried over. No effort is made to maintain another's style or to shorten or lengthen an original work toward a specific end. In a sense, retelling a story partakes a little of all the techniques discussed: the storyteller may abridge and adapt to fit in a particular insight, or may add to the plot creatively. However, a storyteller should attempt to retain the intent and mood of the material. The best retellers of folk material have always respected their sources and used them with honesty. Walter de la Mare is one of the most loved of retellers, as are Wanda Gág, Flora Annie Steel, George Dasent, and others previously mentioned.

"The Ride on the Gravestone" (Ralston) is a fragment of a Russian legend found in an adult source. It had no color, only a stark recounting of events. Dialogue was developed, some background color provided, and the plot clearly defined through a steady progression of events. The result: a spooky story, excellent for ghostly programs.

Also retold for various programs were *Thirty Gilt Pennies* (Kelsey) and "Unda Marina's Footprints" (Topelius). The former is a series of legends; the latter a fragmentary vignette changed into a pourquoi tale.

The Ride on the Gravestone

Late one evening a certain artisan happened to be returning home from a jovial fest in a distant village. There met him on the way an old friend, one who had been dead some ten years.

"Good health to you!" said the dead man.

"I wish you good health," replied the reveller, and straightway forgot that his friend had ever so long ago bidded the world farewell.

"Let's go to my house. We'll quaff a cup or two once more."

"Come along. On such a happy occasion as this meeting of ours, we may well have a drink." They arrived at a dwelling, and there they drank and revelled.

"Now then, goodbye! It is time for me to go home," said the artisan.

"Stay a bit. Where do you want to go now? Come and spend the night with me."

"Ah no, brother! Don't ask me; it cannot be. I've a business to do tomorrow, so I must get home as soon as possible."

"Well, goodbye. But why should you walk? Better get on my horse, it will carry you home quickly."

"Thanks, and let's have it." He got on its back, and was carried off—just as a whirlwind flies. All of a sudden, a cock crew. It was awful! All around were graves, and the rider found he had a gravestone under him!

W. R. Sheddon Ralston, "The Ride on the Gravestone," *Russian Fairy Tales* (London: Smith-Elder, 1873).

The Ride on the Gravestone

Across seven kingdoms and across seven seas, there lived many years ago a jovial young peasant about to be married. On the night before his wedding he set out from his own village where he had feasted and made merry, to journey to the village of his bride-to-be. Gifts and good wishes he had in store, and a light heart, so when he met a traveler on the road he hailed him and wished him good evening. The traveler pulled up to a stop, and the bridegroom saw with a start that it was an old friend who had been dead for some ten years.

"My good fellow, long life to you and health!" greeted the traveler, and though the bridegroom was taken aback indeed, he waved his hand.

"A very good health to you in return! Where have you been these long years?" he questioned, forgetting that as far as he knew, his friend had been safely buried for some time.

"Come, stop and share a cup with me, and I shall tell you all that has happened," replied the traveler, and seeing that the bridegroom was willing, they turned and sought a near-by tavern. The hours passed, and the bridegroom grew more merry with each cup, and his tongue recounted all the delights awaiting him on the morrow when he should meet his promised

Retold from W. R. Sheddon Ralston, "The Ride on the Gravestone," *Russian Fairy Tales* (London: Smith-Elder, 1873).

bride, and share in the festivities that had been planned. The bridegroom was a craftsman and an artisan, and he had spent many days decorating and preparing the new home.

"You must visit us in our little house," he said, again not thinking that his friend would find that somewhat difficult! "Now, alas, it grows late and I must be on my way, or tomorrow will be here before I arrive!"

But the friend laid his hand on the bridegroom's arm, pleading that they share a bit more time, that, perhaps, the young man would come to his house—or even spend the night? "Quite impossible!" answered the young artisan. "My promised bride is waiting for me, and I must hurry."

"Then let me loan you my horse, for it will surely speed you on your way," and the traveler jumped from his horse and helped his friend to mount.

"Thanks, and Godspeed to you, my friend," called the bridegroom, and away he flew, with the speed of a whirlwind!

But suddenly, a cock crowed! The rider heard a shriek, he felt a shudder, and when he looked down at his horse—there was nothing there! He found to his horror that he was perched atop a huge gravestone, in a lonely cemetery, with tombstones all around him, and yawning at his feet, was a deep empty grave!

Years later, the villagers still spoke in whispers about the bridegroom who had disappeared and never afterwards been seen!

7

Tips
for Tellers

The folktales, fairy tales, legends, and hero stories of the past were meant to be listened to; printing was a secondary consideration. It is regrettable that most people become acquainted with folklore through books rather than through live storytelling, since a real "storyteller"—one of the grand species—comes only now and then, and is unforgettable. However, most of us can learn something about telling stories; often we begin with something in our own backgrounds, or some remembered tale from our childhood. All of us, as tellers, can give our listeners something to remember and take away with them, something more important than the storyteller. We can be enthusiastic, can delight in our materials, and can continue to grow in our ability as storytellers—purveyors of the oral tradition. Why, then, do we tell stories?

Stories are told for the sheer delight of the words and images they conjure up; to arouse an emotional response in a child; to call up in that child a recognition of the joy, disappointment, grief, and laughter held in common with children everywhere; to stretch the child's horizon, to show new vistas, to give new insights into some particular situation. Perhaps the storyteller hopes to strengthen the child's sense of security, to underline the worthiness of living, to undergird faith in life, or to give an appreciation of people and places encountered. It is therefore important to choose good stories, to tell them well, and to become channels for the story, so that it takes on new life. Learning to select stories means learning to hear them with an inner ear; some stories, when read silently, seem inadequate but, when used orally, sparkle and blossom out. Sandburg's *Rootabaga Tales* are good examples of this. Other stories may also need oral interpretation, but always in the author's exact words because of his or her individuality and unique style, such as the tales of Farjeon, Grahame, Kipling, and Milne. Such stories should be memorized (somewhat dangerous) or read aloud; some picture books also need the exact words of the author, either through memorization or through "upside down reading" because of the close interweaving of text and illustration; some selections taken from books or longer works, because of the close construction of the whole, should also be presented in the author's language, such as those of Hauff, Stockton, and Housman.

After isolating some stories to consider for a storytelling program, try to relate to them before beginning to consciously learn them. Analyzing the story first, to discover those elements in it that make it particularly appealing, often helps the storyteller mentally fix the structure of the story. Was it an innovative plot? Some amusing incident? Some redoubtable, memorable character? A mood that clings? Exploring the story in this way often points out the hinges of action in the tale and sets forth the sequence of events more clearly, so that the steps of action can be seen. All of the great storytellers stress the importance of being able to envision the tale on the screen of the mind as a series of pictures, framed with an introduction and tied up with a definite conclusion. A real relationship exists between the clarity with which the story is seen inwardly, and the vividness with which it is audibly presented. Also, merely memorizing the story leaves the storyteller vulnerable to a sudden interruption, an emotional strain, or a physical disability, such as a headache, often with disastrous consequences.

If a story has been carefully prepared and used, but the group response was unsatisfactory, ask some questions: Was the story a misfit for this group? Some Eastern and African stories are very sophisticated and subtle, requiring an older age group than the more obvious European tales. Was the theme of the story too difficult for the group to appreciate? Was the style of the story too difficult or too unusual? Was the weather too muggy, or the situation around too busy, or was there an important event or some other excitement at hand? In evaluating these diverse factors, the teller learns to examine both the stories and the presentation more carefully.

Perhaps the story was well prepared and personally satisfying, but still did not receive the envisioned results. This is not an uncommon experience; perhaps this is a story that is "congenitally impossible" to tell, at least at this time. If this same material is repeatedly tried, always with the same reaction, even though used for different groups and with a refined telling, it is best put aside, perhaps forever. Possibly it would be usable if read aloud, and could be attempted once or twice. But it is also possible that an error in judgment was made, that the story selected was not as good as at first thought. Everyone can make such a mistake, and there are, after all, hundreds of other stories to discover.

However, perhaps the preparation left out background material that should have been given before the narrative, or an essential word was unfamiliar to the listeners. Even though context usu-

ally supplies the meaning, if the story concerns an exotic time or place or custom, some clarification may be called for. Or perhaps the title spoiled the suspense of the tale; if it was not a good title, it could even have stirred up a negative feeling. A title may be given later, and illustrations shown afterwards, if necessary; for instance, we have found with older boys that many of the stories of James Houston, with their stark Arctic background and strong graphic art, are well-received in this way.

Each teller has a unique potential and individual limitations, and it is wise to discover early in the game what these are. If some built-in limitation that cannot be changed is found, it must be accepted and the storytelling art built around it— for example, if the teller simply cannot remember sequences, cumulative stories are to be avoided. If tall tale humor does not seem amusing, leave tall tales out of the repertoire. Storytellers must in many ways match their personality to their stories; and eventually the feeling should be one of: "*My story . . . I feel it.*"

Thus, when beginning the search for stories to use in a specific story program, jot down the sources of those which look promising, and those with titles that suggest further investigation. Put them aside, then, for future reference and continue the search. One of the considerations a new teller must be aware of, beyond the content of the story and its tellability, is the amount of time it will take to learn the story, the energy involved, and the deadline for its use. He or she will also be governed in the search by the resources at hand and by a reflection on the time, place, and group involved. Stories for the playground are not necessarily the kind of stories to use in a sheltered corner; suburban children may need time to become attuned to African stories; and tall tales do not fit every kind of group. In most cases, however, a well-prepared storyteller, one who speaks zestfully and quickly establishes rapport with the group, will find a good response whatever the story and in spite of handicaps.

While all of these suggestions are not suitable to every person, since each of us learns in an individual way, some specific helps may have value. If a story is found, type, copy, or clip it and put it in a story file. Such a file is invaluable for a new teller just testing his or her "story strength." Read the story through quickly all at once, to get an overall

Children's Faces Looking Up

Program building for the storyteller

BY DOROTHY DE WIT

effect, and then reread it again just for the fun of it. Next, read and note the sequence of events. Another reading will bring out the special phrasing, the characteristic flavor, or the rhymes or particular expressions that will preserve the individuality of the story. Then put it aside for a while, and let it lay fallow. If your reading background is wide and touches on many different areas, you will probably be able to retell the story in words similar to those in the written version, using the significant phrases previously noted. This will provide more poise and self-confidence, and more enthusiasm in the retelling, than if the story were memorized. In addition, any feelings of self-consciousness will be lessened.

Read the story again with an emphasis on characterization, to savor the different personalities and, if necessary, to imprint them more vividly on your mind by looking at their interpretation through illustration. Small details will sharpen and set the characters apart one by one; in a good folktale or fairy tale, there will be no long and involved description: "She was a witch, she was very old, . . . and she was always hungry!" or "There was a soldier marching along the road—left, right, left, right! He had been to the war for five years so that he was very brave. . . ." or "A king had two sons— they were a reckless pair of fellows who always had something foolish to do. . . ." or "There was once a merchant so rich that he could have paved the whole street, and perhaps even a little side-street besides, with silver!"

After the story has "rested" for a bit, it is useful to take out the text and underline sentences that constitute the sequence of events. Try to reconstruct the plot in outline form, writing down the hinges of action, even numbering them if that helps. Doing this fixes the character associated with that event in mind and helps the story "stick." Sometimes taping a story helps you to hear your interpretation of the tale and to better gauge its effect on a listener. Finally, in odd moments—bus riding, waiting for a crossing, or an elevator—go over the story mentally, making it a part of you. In this type of learning, the story speaks for itself, and the teller becomes vividly aware of the variety and interest in its content. The storyteller becomes the channel for the tale, much as an artist uses technique to reproduce accurately pictures seen from within.

No one can estimate how long it should take to learn a story, since this is conditioned by how rapidly the material is absorbed, how much time is required for it to "jell," how much time is available before the deadline of sharing it, and the extent of the teller's previous experience. The wider the experience, the more surely the teller proceeds in learning stories. The other side of the coin, however, is that the more experience that is gained, the higher the standards for selecting and telling!

Understanding the "why" of story action helps to fix the logic and sequence of the plot in mind. A knowledge of place and people in the tale will give some feeling for the way that words would be used, and for any special word that would be vital to an understanding of the story: for example, the word *chattee-maker* (an Indic pot-maker) in *The Valiant Chattee-maker* (Price). In telling the story, such a word should be defined and any explanations given ahead of time. Proper names or strange names must be pronounced the same way each time, and learned by writing them out if they are difficult, as is the case with many Indian, African, Eskimo, and Mexican names.

The beginning and the ending are important, and the storyteller should fix these in mind, even memorizing them if necessary. However, remember that the teller, as the keeper of the content, does not have to let anyone know if something was forgotten. Pick up the forgotten phrase, or word, or action inconspicuously, if it is essential to the thread of the story: "You remember I told you . . ." or "Ah, but something had happened a long time ago . . ." or some such catch-up to smoothly reverse the time of action. If the forgotten material is not essential, but belongs to the story, there will always be another time. And if an interruption occurs during the story, accept it with a smile and incorporate it into the woof of the story so skillfully that the listeners are not at loose ends at all. Even ringing bells and falling screens can be overcome!

Remember that the introduction sets the stage and whets the appetite; that incidents coalesce around specific characters, and mount to a "show down," a climax; that some solution is thereby discovered; and that thereafter all the details are folded up together, and learning stories will be easier. It is the story that is too long, too involved, or too full of interests and ideas that is difficult to master. Russian and American Indian stories often have such qualities, and may need tightening or abridging to eliminate some of the unnecessary descriptions, events, or characters, or to make the dialogue more succinct, or the wording more economical. Experience tells.

This is the time to consider what pacing and timing means to a storyteller. A sense of timing causes the storyteller to speak deliberately, in a relaxed manner, matter-of-factly, neither holding back nor pushing the words ahead. When conflict enters the story, and the teller quickens the flow of the words and leaves fewer pauses between them, timing is being utilized. When a sense of urgency can be noted in the words and the movement of the story as one sentence is built upon another, perhaps toward a climax, again timing is present.

Perhaps the teller pauses before the story peaks, or hesitates almost imperceptibly before a phrase—all of these have to do with the delivery of the story, with the method in which the story becomes an oral narrative. This can be felt, and is one of the difficult parts of the fine art of storytelling. Pacing, on the other hand, is concerned with the tempo in which the story is written, with the way in which the paragraphs are put together; the pacing of a story can be discerned in silent, as well as in oral reading; and although a good storyteller can make some difference in the pacing of a story through a judicious use of timing, he or she cannot really change it without changing the structure of the tale itself. Timing is a tool of the storyteller, used to interpret what is being told; pacing is concerned with the flow of the narrative. Thus *The Bun*, by Marcia Brown, is briskly paced; "Why the Bear Is Stumpy-tailed" (Haviland—*Norway*), is gently paced. "The Day Tuk Became a Hunter" (Melzack), Eskimo, starts with a feeling of urgency and builds steadily in intensity; "Cinderella" (Lang—*Blue*), runs smoothly, sliding one event into the next carefully and without much tension. The feeling that one story is "well-paced" or that another "moves too slowly" comes gradually, after browsing at length among folktales and creative narratives. However, the storyteller learns the skill of timing only through practice and concentration.

Recordings and tapes made by such renowned storytellers as Ruth Sawyer, Gudrun Thorne-Thomsen, Claire Bloom, Frances Sayers, and Augusta Baker are worthy of careful listening for the method of their separate deliveries and their use of timing. Maurice Evans, Boris Karloff, Laurence Olivier, and Christine Price are noted for their articulation and for the way in which they infuse their readings with a sense of drama. Weigh the choice of selection (monologue, story, or poetry) with the delivery each of these artists has given to each genre. Pearl Primus, Ed Begley, Harold Courlander, and Richard Chase have taped distinctive regional stories with unusual backgrounds and flavorful language that gives a different focus to each particular kind of story. *The Jack Tales* (Chase), European folktales adapted by the mountain people of Appalachia, are wonderful examples of very relaxed and deliberate pacing; the West African story "Talk" (Courlander—*Switch*) moves with an almost staccato rhythm. Irish stories move with a lilt, and their inverted syntax gives them a distinctive rhythm, as in "Hudden, Dudden and Donald O'Neary" (Jacobs—*Celtic*). Catch the no-nonsense approach of the Norse tales "Gudbrand on the Hillside" (Dasent) or "Three Billy Goats Gruff" (Dasent). The Scotch twist their phrases and make use of terminology like that of no other people—"lass" (girl), "bonnie" (pretty), "kirk" (church); Norwegians say "Old Goody" rather than "old woman." Words and phrases such as these, rather than dialect, add cadence and flavor to speech patterns and rhythm to the stories as a whole. If pacing refers to sentence patterns and paragraph framework, rhythm refers to the word patterns, and both of these factors are determinants in choosing stories for contrast and variety in program balancing. French-Canadian speech has a different cadence from that of the West Indies, and the cadence of Spanish, even in English translation, is not at all like German. A storyteller will develop an ear for these differences, and use them.

The stance or pose of the storyteller is important in presenting the story. If telling a funny story, a droll—"Lazy Jack" (Jacobs—*English*) or "The Horse Egg" (Jagendorf—*Noodlehead*)—try to feel the rollicking humor and enjoy it with the children, not by going into gales of laughter but by a special glint in the eye, the quirk of a smile, or a lifted eyebrow, and pause to give the children time to laugh. If the humor is sly, such as that in the Hodja stories "Money from Heaven" (Kelsey), "Three Fridays" (Kelsey), or the French-Canadian tales "The Skunk in Tante Odette's Oven" (Carlson—*Cat*), and "Little Nichet" (Carlson—*Sashes*), the teller should give the children the feeling that he or she is laughing inside, as they are. But with tall stories, the teller must maintain the straightest kind of face, even while saying the most outrageous things; this is one reason why younger children do not identify readily with tall tale humor—they are too literal. Also, stories which point up the illogical, ludicrous side of adult conduct—"Anansi Goes Fishing" (Courlander—*Switch*), or "The Gift That Came Back" (Kelsey—*Hodja*)—may not seem funny to very young children, who are not yet sure how adults are supposed to act. All of which is to suggest that the storyteller must take the story seriously, especially if—and even though—it is humorous; the humorous story is one of the hardest to tell.

Obviously, vocabulary is an important tool for a storyteller. Nothing replaces picturesque, well-chosen words drawn from a rich word bank. It takes conscious effort to enlarge a horde of words, but it is the one tool the storyteller uses constantly; nothing is more distracting or in poorer taste than the interjection of some local colloquialism or provincialism dropped into a story, such as "O.K.," "gosh," or "you know."

Another essential tool is the voice of the teller. Involved here is the pitch, articulation, voice texture, control and breath support, and the clarity of word production. It is difficult to do justice to a story's cast of characters whose temperaments constantly undergo change, with only one voice; and when that single voice must also indicate the dramatic development, the plot, while simultaneously opening a door to a hidden world that touches on things of the spirit, evoking a mood, the vital role played by the voice in a storyteller's technique is apparent. In drama, several voices interact with each other, and lights, sets, and costumes augment the power of speech. But storytelling is a narrative art, and part of the artistry is to remain within the dimensions of straight narrative. The verbal framework must express vitality, pathos, abandon, restraint, emotion, or humor without a stage, without excessive action or gesture, with both composure and intensity. What a difficult challenge! May Hill Arbuthnot says that a voice continually used in the service of beauty will grow in depth and richness; if the development of buoyancy and vitality in the voice, rather than despair or whininess, is cultivated, the teller's voice will soon become a good

medium for storytelling. A low voice is more pleasant than a high one, a rich voice more effective than a thin voice. Flexibility in the voice allows for the expression of those nuances of feeling conveyed by words and defines separate characters by changes in voice timbre alone rather than through use of volume or dramatic fervor, as in "The Three Bears" (Hutchinson—*Fairy*) and "The Three Little Pigs" (Power—*Bag*). Learning to support the breath from the diaphragm, rather than from the throat, gives control needed for long passages without strain; and breath support is necessary for good timing—increasing the speed of words, hinging them together smoothly and rapidly in quick succession, or pausing. Good breath control is also a factor in enunciating words clearly, so that all the letters are well articulated, the vowels full and round, the consonants sharp and well formed. Good breath support prevents a person from wanting to swallow the words or letting the ends of words slip down the throat. Most important, the secret of being heard clearly to the farthest part of a room comes through projecting the voice onto the air waves by well-controlled breathing, not by raising the voice and shouting.

Speech and voice texts suggest exercises to develop breath control, and practice, taping, or cupping a hand around one ear and closing the other, will help the storyteller to listen to his or her own voice, to work on any deficiencies. Posture is also important when speaking, but the situation determines whether the teller should sit or stand. Good posture underscores good breath control; to feel alert yet relaxed is part of the secret of being alert and relaxed.

A regional accent is not necessarily bad, unless it is so decided as to cloud the meaning of a story, or unless it has developed into a twang or a nasal quality. A storyteller who has either of these latter traits should try to develop a more conventional pronunciation and a richer, better modulated voice. If an accent is small, forget it, and others will too; the same counsel is true for nervousness. In essence, then, the storyteller must know how to say the right thing, in the right way, to the right people, at the right time.

If gestures with the face or hands are used in normal speech, use them naturally in storytelling; mirrors will reveal whether facial expressions are mobile or not. But overdramatization can be a hindrance to eloquent storytelling and is really not necessary if the storyteller knows the material and has a good rapport with the audience. Hands should neither hang like shovels, be waved aimlessly, hooked into pockets, draped across the face, propped under the chin, nor twined into jewelry or ties. Anything which detracts from the words of the story is out of place. Two things are very much in place, however—an inconspicuous handkerchief for emergencies, and dentures, if necessary, that fit firmly.

Perhaps this is the place to suggest that children should be in place, too. Not sitting so close to each other or the storyteller that their necks and heads will be under strain, not looking into the sun, not feeling that they must sit in straight jackets. The teller should be able to catch each child's eye and draw him or her individually into the story-weaving web. If discipline is needed during the story, drop the child's name into the story, or pause, take a long look, or lift an eyebrow. The best way, however, is to catch up their interest so completely that they cannot help giving themselves to the story. A good storyteller builds eye contact and rapport with each individual child and with the group as a whole, thus engendering an almost tangible esprit de corps in the storytelling group.

In-depth storytelling techniques are discussed in *The Way of the Storyteller* (Ruth Sawyer), *The Art of the Storyteller* (Marie Shedlock), *How to Tell Stories to Children* (S. C. Bryant), and *Children and Books* (May Hill Arbuthnot, all editions).

One of the essentials of a good storyteller, and of the librarian-storyteller in particular, is a blotter-like capacity to soak up ideas from old and new storytelling literature. Consistently become familiar with the experiences of other compatriots in the storytelling world to discover old source materials and review and evaluate new approaches; be aware of new materials as they appear in articles, books, pamphlets, bibliographies; watch for publications of new story anthologies and new editions of old ones; and look into tapes, cassettes, and other audio-visual aids. And then, spongelike, try to squeeze out all that has been absorbed to enrich the storytelling role.

Part 2

DEMONSTRATION PROGRAMS

8

Problems Encountered

Where can themes for creative story programs be found? Actually, almost anywhere. Perhaps a phrase from a story or poem brings an idea into focus; perhaps someone drops a suggestion that begins to grow; perhaps a current problem is confronted, or perhaps a child says "That was a good story! Do you got any more like that?" and a spark is ignited, an idea set winging its way. An old and large book collection is a blessing, a gold mine for unearthing fascinating narrative material for a storyteller. A diversity of sources is necessary because children need all kinds of nourishment for their questing minds and growing spirits, and storytelling is such an exceptional way to provide both tender and tough fare through fairy and folk narratives without moralizing, depreciating society's ills, or harping on the bitter and the sweet in life. Children do not look for great truths, hidden symbolism, or obscure meaning in stories, but they do sense them and identify with them.

Gathering stories around a central theme and extending that basic idea in many ways over several months can be very creative. With much to choose from, the temptation to include something just because it carries the germinal idea in its title or in its content may emerge. It is always wiser to choose material fundamentally sound in structure and appealing in character and plot rather than that which is designed to teach some specific attitude or written for some express purpose. Whether developing a long-range program for several months or just a six-week story plan—the principles are the same.

The story season for the following story programs is October through April, or approximately 26 story programs, including special Easter, Halloween, and Christmas weeks; each story hour varies from thirty minutes in the first three programs to forty-five minutes in the later three, and is directed toward children from the first through the fifth grades. Early in the spring, before the current school year ends, the storyteller should begin to jot down ideas for next year's story program, including a tentative theme. The programmer then divides the theme finally chosen into months and weeks: October, 4 or 5 periods; November, 4; December, 3—possibly 4 to allow for special Christmas events; January, 4; February, 4; March, 4 or 5; and April, 4—the last of which may be a closing program or party. This schedule allows for one story session each week, on the same day, at the same time, to parallel the school schedule with its Christmas and spring recesses. Special holidays may call for family story hours or other particular ways of observance, or the storyteller may choose not to have special events, but include some story relevant to the holiday on the nearest story day. If the story season is approximately 26 weeks long, and each program includes 3, possibly 4 tales, the storyteller would be selecting between 78 and 104 different narratives. That is admittedly a large number for each story season, but not at all an impossible task; there are scores of worthwhile stories to choose from representing a great variety in type, genre, and source.

The theme finally selected should be both general and broad enough to allow for many subdivisions and many interpretations. For example, "Indians" might be picked as an umbrella theme; this theme is big enough for all kinds of stories. Indian narrative literature has, however, a structural and stylistic framework, at least in North American Indian literature, that is distinctive: one tale resembles another in the use of language, the sentence patterns, the metaphor, and the basic view of life. Would a program of 78 to 94 North American tales prove to be somewhat monotonous for a whole season, in spite of the vast differences in tribal customs, religions, festivals, and so on? Perhaps. It might, then, be well to include representative pourquoi, epic, and animal stories from South American Indian peoples, from the Arctic Indians, or the Indians of the Caribbean and Central American regions; each of these has a different cultural influence acting upon the oral heritage, and each reflects a different national flavor, created as the Indian peoples have related to non-Indians around them. Perhaps the theme should even be broadened to cover storytelling around the fires of other primitive peoples of long ago—the Eskimos, the Oceanic islanders, the natives of Australia. Such a change would allow for greater variety and better balance in programming, while simultaneously serving to enrich the oral heritage of the story children. In a six-week story program, an all-Indian repertoire chosen from the North American Indians is plausible; but a longer story program necessitates more flexibility, more room for choice. Whatever the theme chosen, such considerations must enter in.

Within a theme such as "Animals," the storyteller must be sure to include pourquoi stories; folktales of foolish and wise animals like those found in India's *Panchatantra*, the *Jataka Tales* (Babbitt), or the Russian animal fables; fairy tales

of enchanted animals; legends; realistic stories; stories of real animals such as "Lobo, the Wolf" (Seton—*Wild*); and fantasy like *The Country Bunny and the Little Gold Shoes* (Heyward).

With these specific ideas and a calendar, the storyteller can begin to arrange each individual story hour, remembering that an after-school story program is a recreational, rather than an academic, undertaking. Use a light hand in planning the objectives, educational though they may be; whatever ulterior motivation is inherent in a choice of theme, keep it somewhat covert. This is not intended to denigrate any basic objectives; these should remain clearly in mind, with the constant reminder that a story hour is primarily for fun, not instruction.

One of the most enjoyable aspects of programming is to mentally brainstorm an idea, suggesting related areas and unusual angles of that subject theme. Creativity is stimulated by browsing through the dictionary for definitions and connotations of a key word. For instance, when the Cobbler's Bench program was developed, every aspect of the word "cobbler" was checked in the dictionary, and an encyclopedia and a thesaurus were consulted for information on what cobblers did, when and how they worked, the tools used, and their historical relationship to the community. The storyteller browsed among nonfiction books to discover facts about the shoemakers in Europe, in colonial America, and on the frontier. References to shoes or footwear as they appeared in mythology, proverbs, and poetry were noted, using indexes to poetry, guides to proverbs, and dictionaries of mythology. (Recall the winged sandals of Hermes? "Let us walk in the white snow. . . ." "The shoe is on the other foot now?") The *Subject and Title Index to Short Stories for Children* (ALA) suggested material other than folklore; costume books portrayed styles of footwear both weird and fascinating; and the *Index to Fairy Tales* (Eastman) listed stories in subject areas associated with feet, legs, shoes, jumping, running, leather, sewing, dancing! As fast as usable ideas were discovered, they were jotted down. Then the programmer began to recall specific stories which might fit in— *Puss in Boots* (Brown), *Cinderella* (Brown) and *Abu Kassim's Slippers* (Green). Others flocked to mind—*The Twelve Dancing Princesses* (Grimm), *Down, Down the Mountain* (Credle) (squeaky shoes), and "Hop o' My Thumb" (Rackham).

Whenever a title was found that might fit under one or another area of the theme, it was written under that heading. Later the teller would check those titles under the sources included, to see if the stories suggested were tellable and suitable for a story hour program, whether they should be allocated for a special kind of storytelling in schools or on other occasions, or whether they should be disregarded as story material. If suitable, the story was set aside for copying and putting into the year's story depository or file.

This brainstorming was followed by a search through the storyteller's existing file of stories (used and unused) to discover any relevant tales there—Ah! That one! The last time it was used, it had been well liked, so into this year's program it went! Usually a storyteller can find many stories to carry over from previous years, a help in programming, since these will only need to be refreshed.

From general indexes, dictionaries, and encyclopedias to the storytelling lists of stories, the indexes of the large folklore anthologies, the collections of tales compiled by well-known storytellers—thus the search continues, with the teller jotting down titles and sources, however provocative or whimsical, and then locating and evaluating them. The wonder is that there is so much at hand.

In going through individual stories later to choose those to be related to specific parts of the story theme, many will be discarded for obvious reasons—too long, too short, too fragmentary, too complex for an after-school group, or perhaps too time-consuming to learn in the given period. Some stories may be discarded because they would not tell well, some others might need too much time to adapt or retell for this specific program, but perhaps could later be made a part of the story file. However, eventually a core of tales will emerge; it is from these, then, that the storyteller begins to build each individual story program. Incidentally, remember the library catalog of fiction; this may suggest illustrated single editions of fantasy, or picture books which might add spice and color to the folklore.

And now to consider how to create each story hour so that it will have variety in content, unity, rhythm, and mood while simultaneously providing expression to specific ideas that can simmer in the minds of the story hour listeners. The most important of all story hour materials are the stories themselves—funny, sad, dramatic, action-filled, informative, illustrated, traditional, modern—but the programmer should also be aware of such related material as poetry, pictures, filmstrips, realia, puppets, records, and films. In addition, such special features as food, a visitor, or some other unusual item may be included at times.

Now the selected stories are rearranged, reread, regrouped for each week's program until finally the whole season's story hours are completed. Then the storyteller should type up the whole program, to see it in its entirety. A story brochure, to be given to each child, can prove to be both attractive and interesting as a keepsake and as a means of publicizing the story program. It is not a necessity, but can help to focus the whole story program for the children. When brochures are to be used, the dummy should be carefully checked for spelling, sources, bibliographic references, design for pages and cover.

Plan any publicity to attend the storytelling program for the year, how this information will be given to the children, and when. If there is to be a special story hour bulletin board for display of weekly items associated with the story hour, plan this, too, and gather the necessary materials. In the programs included in this book, the displays included puppets, book jackets, papier-mâché animals, collage designs, realia, pictures, and so on. Finally, work out any news releases or publicity for newspapers, bulletins, or the schools. Then check everything through for the umpteenth time, and start learning the stories for the first story session!

In general, then, this is a feasible plan to follow for programming. One further word should be added, however. At times it has been difficult to find an appropriate story in line with a specific theme. If a story whose specific content fits the needs cannot be found, it is better to choose another good but slightly unrelated story, and relate it to the story program through contrast or rhythmic pattern. In programming on a specific theme, it is not necessary to have the entire story content about food, for example, or shoes. It may be enough to have a term or a relevant word included in the title, such as "Donkey Lettuce" (Manning-Sanders—*Witches*), for instance, in the Feast O' Fun program. This story is a delightful fairy tale, and it was placed on the program because of content, but the title makes it appropriate to a story menu, as well. Contrariwise, some tales have exactly the content needed for the theme, but do not indicate this in their titles; this content instead emerges as the stories are read through in preparation for selecting material for the programs. It is always the content, genre, style, of the narrative material which contributes the balance, rhythm, and mood of the story hour, not necessarily the title.

Finally, other stories that might fit into a chosen theme are constantly to be found, especially after that particular story hour has already gone by, or a brochure has been printed. Should such a story be found in time to learn it for the desired program, use it. Otherwise, add it to the story file for future reference. It is amazing what is discovered on a story treasure hunt, and it is a remarkable way of enlarging one's acquaintance with a vast store of oral and written literature of every description. Good hunting, then!

9

Six Story Programs

FEAST O' FUN

HUNGRY? AH, FOOD! LET'S HAVE A FEAST! WHO'S THE HOST? WHERE'S THE FEAST? WHEN WILL IT BE?

THE TABLE IS SET . . . and THE FEAST WILL HONOR . . . and now, WHAT'S ON THE MENU? SPECIALTY OF THE HOUSE and FOR DESSERT . . . THE GUESTS INCLUDED . . . and THE GUESTS WERE DRESSED IN . . .

FOR ENTERTAINMENT THERE WAS . . . and the GIFTS PRESENTED WERE . . . GUESTS ARRIVED ON . . . AND EVERYONE SAID OF THE FEAST O' FUN . . .

This running commentary of headings, similar to ones used for each story period, provided both the story titles and a skeleton script for a series of puppets made by the children for different stories. Made on their own time, each week featured a different child's figurine; all were arranged around the story board. Construction of the puppets was entirely volitional, and they included every sort of material from every age level. At the conclusion of the year's program individual puppets were briefly brought into a puppet stage frame, as the headings and titles were read, forming a well-received dramatic summary presentation. The story periods for this particular season were each one-half-hour, so less material was included than in the longer story programs. In addition, this story season began on Halloween, rather than the first week in October, also shortening the season.

Hungry?: Since Halloween coincided with the first story hour, the room was darkened and a jack-o'-lantern was placed in front, lighted with a flashlight; "The Hungry Old Witch," with its beautiful opening phrases, was a natural opener. This story is dramatic and must be timed well, and at its conclusion the children will need something to laugh at; but of course at Halloween they must also shiver a bit, so "Mr. Miacca," the boy-eating ogre, made a good foil, and the brilliant illustrations in this single edition helped. "Chunk o' Meat" is very abrupt, very repetitive, and builds steadily to an obnoxious "You did!" as a shock ending. This was the successful beginning of the Feast o' Fun story program.

Ah, Food!: This second story hour emphasized seasonal food with "The Pumpkin Giant," followed by a funny animal story, "Fill-to-the-brim-and-eat," and finished with a riddle tale about a fox and an armadillo. The first choice was somewhat involved, in contrast to the other, shorter pieces.

Let's Have a Feast!: In this third program, "The Feast of Lanterns," a short Oriental variant on the Rip Van Winkle theme, was followed by a modern fantasy on the motif of overeating, "The Kingdom of the Greedy." The last story, "Stolen Turnips and the Magic Tablecloth," an old Russian fairy tale, must be abridged when used with younger children. It is akin to "East of the Sun," but is not a variant.

Who's the Host?: "The Miller King" moves fast and with much wit; it was nicely offset by "Esben and the Witch," a nonchalant, cumulative witch story. Both of these contrasted with the rollicking character of a Japanese folktale, "The Old Woman Who Lost Her Dumpling."

Where's the Feast?: The mood of this program is set first with "East of the Sun," a long, traditional Scandinavian fairy tale, romantic and flowing. This leads into "Beyond the Clapping Mountains," a lively, down-to-earth animal story from Alaska, that contrasted with the legend of "The Sunken City," somewhat sad.

When Will It Be?: This program began with "The Winter of the Blue Snow," a tall tale of Paul Bunyan abridged for use here, a story both matter of fact and appealing to the older boys; this in turn was balanced by "The Lost Half Hour," a symbolic fairy tale of time mysteriously missing; and a pourquoi tale of April's lost day, "March and the Shepherd."

The Table Is Set: "Pies of the Princess," a pourquoi story that bounces along like its little heroine, opened this program; then the pace changed with a romantic fairy tale of a knight's bravery, "The Enchanted Knife." The lilting "Dancing Kettle," a folktale from Japan, finished this gay story hour.

The Feast Will Honor: This was the Christmas story hour, and "The Three Young Kings" started it off, followed by the brief and lovely fable of why angel hair is used on Christmas trees, "The Christmas Spider." The last story, "Schnitzle, Schnotzle, and Schnootzle," based on a Tyrolean folktale, is the epitome of the Christmas spirit; the story left a glow of laughter as well as delight.

What's on the Menu?: "Donkey Lettuce," an enchanting fairy tale, not too long, opened the hour; "The Perambulatin' Pumpkin" rambled along with high good humor, Appalachian style, and the program was completed with a dramatic fairy tale, "The Magic Apples."

Specialty of the House: In "The Magic Dumplings," a Chinese pourquoi story, the listeners heard why dogs hate cats; then followed an English variant of the stone soup motif, "Stone Stew"—very digestible, however! "Pepper for Parsnips" is brief and pithy—a good conclusion.

And for Dessert: This program jumped with a vengeance into nitwit humor with "The Horse Egg," rolled along with the ridiculous antics of the villagers in "The King's Rijstepap," and ended with giggles at the salty humor of "The Pudding That Broke Up the Preachin'," a long story from Appalachia. This program emphasized that laughter is indeed a good dessert for anyone.

The Guests Included: First came "Hop o' My Thumb," a familiar fairy tale; then "The Coconut Thieves," an African trickster tale with animal protagonists. Both of these counterbalanced "Hans in Luck," clever folktale humor.

The Guests Were Dressed in: "The Shoemaker's Apron," a legendlike story of a wily cobbler, somewhat subtle for very young listeners, began the hour; then came the balance-wheel of a merry Japanese folktale, "The Magic Listening Cap," and a delightful variant on the Cinderella theme, "The Many-furred Coat."

For Entertainment There Was: This program started with a complete change of scene, "The Hat-shaking Dance," an Anansi droll, followed by "The Dancing Yellow Crane," a brief cautionary tale from China. The ending story was "The Harp, the Mouse, and the Bum Clock," an old tale with a marvelous Irish lilt and rhythm.

The Gifts Presented Were: "The Blue Rose," a romantic fairy tale especially suitable for older girls, opened; in "Pumpkin Trees and Walnut Vines," the witty old Hodja appears in one of his pungent epigrams; finally, "A Gift from the Heart," a thought-provoking, short folktale, finished the program.

The Guests Arrived on: "A Short Horse," an animal droll from the Blue Ridge, started this program, while "The Bear," another unfamiliar, charming variant on the Cinderella motif, Sicilian style, followed. "The Landship," filled with magic, moved briskly along, well-told in this edition but without the glowing illustrations that later appeared in the Caldecott winner *The Fool of the World*.

And Everyone Said: The closing program began with "A Costly Feast," a Hodja story, followed by "Eat, and Like It," a witty, moral tale. These two stories were in preparation for the puppet presentation described in the opening paragraph, and the final story, "The Way of the Master," was followed by a story cake, the closing treat. Actually, the content of the story programs for this year was fairly traditional, with no ulterior motive except good programming and hearty enjoyment planned about the thing the children most enjoy—good food.

Themes and Stories
Hungry?
"The Hungry Old Witch" in Finger, Charles, *Tales from Silver Lands*

"She was a witch . . . she was very old . . . and she was always hungry. . . ." Atmospheric, and scary; wonderful for older children. See also Holiday Stories, page 116.

Mr. Miacca. Ness, Evaline.

Wherein a clever little boy outwits a hungry ogre. Short and easy. See also Holiday Stories, page 116.

"Chunk o' Meat" in Chase, Richard, *Grandfather Tales*

From the Appalachian hills, the story of a lad who found a haunted piece of meat to go with his runner beans. Scary—surprising.

Ah, Food!
"The Pumpkin Giant" in Harper, Wilhelmina, *The Harvest Feast*

A giant from an enormous pumpkin—the father of all pumpkin pies! See also Holiday Stories, page 116.

"Fill-to-the-brim-and-eat" in Sleigh, Barbara, *North of Nowhere*

Greedy Anansi finds a bowl that never empties, and reaps the reward of his greed. Good African flavor, easy to tell.

"The Lazy Fox" in Barlow, Genevieve, *Latin American Tales*

South American variant on the familiar motif of choosing tops or bottoms of the crops; the protagonists are a smart armadillo and a lazy fox. Pithy and amusing.

Let's Have a Feast!
"The Feast of Lanterns" in Wiggin, Kate D., and Smith, Nora, *Tales of Wonder*

A Chinese variant on the Rip van Winkle theme, with good local color.

"The Kingdom of the Greedy" in Harper, Wilhelmina, *The Harvest Feast*

What kind of kingdom thinks that the most important thing in the world is to eat, eat, eat? May be used as a holiday or a general story.

"Stolen Turnips and the Magic Tablecloth" in Ransome, Arthur, *Old Peter's Russian Tales*

The old Russian planted turnips on the roof of the dovecote, but his shrewish wife would not be satisfied, especially when the forest children stole them! Abridge this for story hour use.

Who's the Host?
"The Miller King" in Tashjian, Virginia, *Once There Was and Was Not*

Sly fox and poverty-stricken miller's son conspire to find a fortune and marry a princess—a la Puss in Boots.

"Esben and the Witch" in Manning-Sanders, Ruth, *A Book of Witches*

This story features repetition, rhythm, and tongue-in-cheek humor of Little Fool Esben, who proved to have more brains than anyone else!

"The Old Woman Who Lost Her Dumpling" in Hearn, Lafcadio, *The Boy Who Drew Cats*

A merry old woman chases her rice dumpling on its runaway flight and outwits the ferocious Oni. Delightful to tell.

Where's the Feast?
"East of the Sun and West of the Moon" in Asbjornsen, Peter, and Moe, Jorgen, *East of the Sun and West of the Moon*

Norwegian variant on the beauty and the beast theme, but with a less subtle flavor, featuring a lass and a white bear. Long, romantic.

"Beyond the Clapping Mountains" in Gillham, Charles, *Beyond the Clapping Mountains*

Animal Eskimo story about two young geese, brief and easy to tell.

"The Sunken City" in McNeil, Edwin, *The Sunken City*

The Dutch legend of the rich widow of Stavoren whose greed brought about the demise of the harbor and buried the city.

When Will It Be?

"The Winter of the Blue Snow" in McCormick, Dell, *Paul Bunyan Swings His Ax*

> A chapter on the phenomenon of weather never before known until Paul Bunyan stepped into the picture. Straight-faced, tall tale humor.

"The Lost Half Hour" in Ross, Eulalie S., *The Lost Half Hour*

> Everyone thought Bobo was a simpleton, until he killed the dragon and rescued the princess by his wit. Romantic and fun to tell.

"March and the Shepherd" in Arbuthnot, May Hill, *Time for Fairy Tales*

> An Italian story of how April got short-changed and March overendowed with days. Different and easy.

The Table Is Set ...

"The Pies of the Princess" in Power, Effie, *Bag o' Tales*

> (Originally in Chrisman, Arthur, *Shen of the Sea*.) A merry Chinese princess creates the first chinaware.

"The Enchanted Knife" in Lang, Andrew, *The Violet Fairy Book*

> If the daring young man could tame in three days three horses who had never felt a bridle—well and good, the princess was his. Ah, but could he?

"The Dancing Kettle" in Uchida, Yoshiko, *The Dancing Kettle*

> Whoever saw a kettle grow sharp little ears, and dancing feet? But the old priest did, and he did very well thereby. Fun to tell.

The Feast Will Honor ...
(Christmas program)

"The Three Young Kings" by Albee, George S., in Wernecke *Christmas Stories from Many Lands*

> See Holiday Stories, page 115.

"The Christmas Spider" in Eaton, Anne, *The Animals' Christmas*

> See Holiday Stories, page 118.

"Schnitzle, Schnotzle, Schnootzle" in Sawyer, Ruth, *The Long Christmas*

> See Holiday Stories, page 118.

What's on the Menu?

"Donkey Lettuce" in Manning-Sanders, Ruth, *A Book of Witches*

> A magic wishing cape and a gold coin under his pillow each morning—with such fortune, who could go wrong?

"The Perambulatin' Pumpkin" in Credle, Ellis, *Tall Tales from the High Hills*

> A Blue Ridge tall tale of the pumpkin that demonstrated that even a vegetable has a remarkable will of its own. Very funny.

"The Magic Apples" in Baker, Augusta, *The Talking Tree*

> A cap, a magic purse, and a tablecloth that had endless resources; why should the lad not have the haughty princess also? Easy and well liked.

Specialty of the House

"The Magic Dumplings" in Wiggin, Kate D., and Smith, Nora, *Tales of Laughter*

> A Chinese story of why dogs and cats fight each other.

"Stone Stew" in Edmonds, I. G., *Trickster Tales*

> "Stone Soup," in British dress, with two tramps and a gullible, cross housewife. Amusing variant of an old favorite.

"Pepper for Parsnips" in Campbell, Alfred S., *The Wizard and His Magic Powder*

> A tale from the Channel Islands, showing the power of a sneeze. Unusual, pithy, funny.

And for Dessert ...

"The Horse Egg" in Jagendorf, Moritz, *Noodlehead Stories*

> Every country has had them—the foolish ones who believe a watermelon is a potential baby horse! Very short.

"The King's Rijstepap" in Hart, Johan, *Picture Tales from Holland*

> A flavorful Dutch rice pudding, hilarious to tell, wherein the villagers perpetuate their leader's blunder, to honor royalty!

"The Pudding That Broke Up the Preachin'" in Credle, Ellis, *Tall Tales from the High Hills*

> Unbeknownst to each other, everyone dropped a pinch of salt in the pudding, sooooooo! Long, but hilarious.

The Guests Included ...

"Hop o' My Thumb" in Rackham, Arthur, *Arthur Rackham's Fairy Book*

> A thumbful of familiar delights, with Rack-

ham's illustrations to show for a plus! Long, and imaginative.

"The Coconut Thieves" in Fournier, Catherine, *The Coconut Thieves*

Stunning, stylized illustrations by Domanska in a lively and exotic animal tale from Africa; a somewhat long single edition.

"Hans in Luck" in Wiggin, Kate D., and Smith, Nora, *Tales of Laughter*

Hans, in true blunderbuss fashion, manages to win out.

The Guests Were Dressed in . . .

"The Shoemaker's Apron" in Fillmore, Parker, *The Shepherd's Nosegay*

See Cobbler's Bench for annotation, page 90.

"The Magic Listening Cap" in Uchida, Yoshiko, *The Magic Listening Cap*

Delightful tale of the old man who received, for his goodness, a cap that enabled him to understand the birds. Short, good.

"The Many-furred Coat" in Wiggin, Kate D., and Smith, Nora, *The Fairy Ring*

From the fur of every creature, a disguise for the outcast princess, who won the prince. Cinderella in furs; a good variant on that theme.

For Entertainment There Was . . .

"The Hat-shaking Dance" in Courlander, Harold, *The Hat-shaking Dance*

Poor Anansi—always in trouble, always endearing! Here's why he has no hair on his bald spider-head. An African droll.

"The Dancing Yellow Crane" in Lim, Sian-Tek, *More Folk Tales from China*

The China-that-was, a young student, and a remarkable helper. Very short, pithy; a cautionary tale. Good for older children.

"The Harp, the Mouse, and the Bum Clock" in Haviland, Virginia, *Favorite Fairy Tales Told in Ireland*

An old Irish folk tale scintillating with humor, featuring a remarkable cockroach.

The Gifts Presented Were . . .

"The Blue Rose" in Frost, Frances, *Legends of the United Nations*

(Also in Eulalie Ross's book of the same title.) A frankly romantic but perceptive

fairy tale from China, wherein the princess must make an impossible choice, unless love is the deciding factor. Allegorical, somewhat wistful.

"Pumpkin Trees and Walnut Vines" in Kelsey, Alice, *Once the Hodja*

The irrepressible Turkish Hodja, teacher, trickster, and short-end recipient of many pranks, questions nature's ways. Short, easy to tell, wry humor.

"A Gift from the Heart" in Pridham, Radost, *A Gift from the Heart*

Rare and choice Bulgarian folk tale, with a lad making a choice: for all his months of labor, should he take a piece of gold or three small walnuts?

The Guests Arrived on . . .

"A Short Horse" in Credle, Ellis, *Tall Tales from the High Hills*

Tall tale par excellence from the Blue Ridge, explaining why mountain horses are peculiar.

"The Bear" in Lang, Andrew, *The Rose Fairy Book*

Sicilian fairy tale, a variant of Cinderella. Unusual twist.

"The Landship" in McNeil, Edwin, *The Sunken City*

A Canadian author's distinguished version of the traditional fairy tale, "The Ship That Went by Land and Air," filled with adventure.

And Everyone Said of the Feast o' Fun . . .

"A Costly Feast" in Jagendorf, Moritz, *Noodlehead Stories*

(Also in Alice Kelsey's *Once the Hodja*.) The tricky teacher tries out some absurd logic on gullible fellows who have set out to trick the Hodja—to their sorrow. Very funny, and easy to tell.

"Eat, and Like It!" in Jagendorf, Moritz, *The Priceless Cats*

Italian folk tale of peasants who turn up their noses at their humble fare, until hunger and a wise old priest force them to reconsider.

"The Way of the Master" in Edmonds, I. G., *Trickster Tales*

If the Master should make a faux pas, so would all of his followers—but that was not in his plan!

STORY HOUR ZOO

The intent behind this story hour was to stretch the children's imagination as far as it would go when thinking of the whole animal kingdom—not just real animals, but all of the implications of the word. Therefore, at the initial story hour the brief film *ANIMULES* on papier-mâché craft was shown; this demonstrated in a colorful and humorous way the things that can come out of rolled paper, a bit of paste, some dabs of paint, a button, some yarn, and a strong imagination. During the story months, the children brought in animals they made of papier-mâché, bags, cloth, or any other media; these were gathered in a display collection around the story board. Each week saw new additions to the menagerie, and at the end they created an animal parade and an exhibit.

Pachyderms and Such: Storytelling began with the biggest land animals of all with "The Elephant's Bathtub," wry and witty folktale with an East Indian flavor; this was followed by the wonderful Kipling fantasy of "How the Camel Got His Hump."

Horses, Horses, Horses: In the succeeding week horses galloped in, first with a long fairy tale, full of magic, "Dapplegrim." "The Smoke Horse" is much shorter, and has a subtle humor which contrasts with the legend of "The Horse That Liked to Play Tricks" from old French sources. The latter, however, had to be tightened and abridged, as it was rather broken in its printed form.

Cats: This theme came on Halloween, so of course there was a scary story; but first the drama was heightened with a fairy tale, "The Golden Lynx," followed by a rhythmic Jamaican Anansi story, "Ticky-picky-boom-boom," full of alliteration and rhyming. Storytelling ended with the eerie "The Boy Who Drew Cats" from Japan.

Monsters: Here the pompous, short dragon story, "My-Lord-Bag-of-Rice" was contrasted with a traditional monster tale, "Alberto and the Monster," then finished with a dramatic why-story about the creation of the Indian tribes in Montana and Idaho, "The Kamiah Monster."

Dogs and Wild Dogs: Since dogs are so well-loved, the climate was already created when this story hour began, and the funny folktale "The Dog That Learned to Read" was a natural. Variety came in with the trickster tale, "How Saynday Ran a Foot-race with Coyote," whose rhythm and picturesque language made a good foil for the Uncle Remus story of "Mr. Wolf Makes a Failure." As always in the Uncle Remus stories, the children appreciate the wit and wisdom; the dialect should be modified.

Make-believe Critters: These stories involved animals who live only in story. The tiny Kappa of Japan plays tug-of-war with a big brown horse in Dorothy Baruch's story of the same name; this was followed by a fearsome creature, "The Bored Tengu," an unusual Oriental figure; finally, the repetitive nonsense of "The Hobyahs," which in the Story Zoo program brought the children to the Thanksgiving session.

Thanksgiving Tales: "How Turkey Got His White Tail Feathers" was brief and succinct, followed by "The Pumpkin Child," a long fairy story from Persia. "The Ballad of the Pilgrim Cat," a long prose poem, was introduced with background remarks and some of the opening verse, then narrated in prose, finishing with the last rhymed stanza.

Barnyard Fowls and Animals: "When Rooster Was King of the Cats," a bit long, very clever, and with a sardonic flavor, opened the program; it needed the silly sort of humor of "Goose Hans" as contrast. If the nitwit tale of Hans is typical Grimm droll-fare, "Señor Billy Goat" is full of Puerto Rican color and wit.

Hoofs and Horns: A national spirit is also embodied in "Kantchil Grows Strong at the Welling-Well"; the small mouse-deer is a para-type of the American Brer Rabbit figure, with the same wit, but Indonesian characteristics. The same is true of "Victory of the Buffalo," but this story is strong and heroic, explaining the importance of the water buffalo in Indonesia. Finally, for contrast, came a brief but dramatic pourquoi story from the American Indians, "Why the Hoofs of the Deer Are Split."

Animals at Christmas: Here animals were much in evidence, as in an illustrated medieval legend,

"The Lamb and the Child"; this was followed by a folklike imaginative story, "The Christmas Cuckoo," that must be abridged for telling in most story periods. The third story, "The Small One," a modern tale, was excellent for telling but needed abridgment; care must be taken to preserve the distinctive Mexican syntax and flavor.

Animals in Legend: "The Thunderbird," a long, very dramatic legend, was in sharp contrast to the Scotch shape-changer tale of "The Seal-catcher and the Merman." "Yanni and the Dragon" was blustery, boastful, and brief.

Snakes and Slithery Creatures: "The Frog That Swallowed the Ocean" revealed some of the mythology of the Pacific peoples. This was a far cry from the delightful fairy story, "The White Snake." "The Legend of the Lizard" was pithy, a nature story from Oceania, short and unusual.

Bird House: The program opened with "King Stork," one of Howard Pyle's delightful fairy stories, rather long, completely absorbing. There is now an illustrated version by Trina Shart Hymen that will add to the enjoyment if a single edition is called for. "Robin Redbreast" is easy and short, and "Rusty Jack" is witty and homespun, with a lilt to the words.

Seashore and Deep-sea Dwellers: "The Whale That Smoked a Pipe," a Glooscap Indian tale with simple, subdued humor, opened. It was set off by a dramatic and involved fairy story, "The Golden Crab." Finally, "The Wonderful Tree" followed, a trickster tale about Sungura, the hare from Africa, a word play on an old folk theme, introducing Kamba the tortoise, as well.

Mythological Animals: "The Fox, the Dog, and the Griffin" was adapted from a modern imaginative story; an abridged version of the Frank Stockton story "The Griffin and the Minor Canon," found in his *Ting-a-ling Tales*, is similar in feeling, and has some of the same serious undertone. Used in contrast was the fairy story "The Golden Phoenix," in the version of Canadian folklorist Barbeau. This particular story hour concluded with a retelling of the epigrammatic story "The Beast with the Single Horn." Check for any recent, better unicorn tales to replace this latter story.

Monkey Island: "The Green Monkey," really a prince in disguise, flowed smoothly and was very different from the animal story from Africa that followed it, "Grandmother and the Apes." "Why Monkeys Live in Trees" is a pourquoi story, also African, wry and witty.

Bears, Badgers, and Diggers: Badger, mischievous compatriot of Glooscap, appeared in "Badger and the Green Giant"; this has something of a fairy tale quality, and is well-paced. "Kunikdjuaq," a tender and vivid Eskimo tale of the love between an old woman and her adopted bear-son, was a rather short story, and "Little Nichet's Baby Sister" featured the irrepressible French-Canadian folk character, who bubbles into trouble with the best of intentions, as ever.

Rabbits, Rodents, and Sly Ones: In "The Race between the Hare and the Hedgehog" we found a variant of a well-known fable—pleasant and easy to tell, followed by a longer, beautiful fairy tale of devotion, "The Mouse Princess." To close, a funny Spanish variant of an old favorite, "The King of the Leaves," was used.

Creepers and Crawlers: An age-old droll based on the misinterpretation of words was used in a witty French variant, "Little Cricket"; this was balanced by the obvious Anansi trickster story, "How Spider Got a Thin Waist"; and this, in turn, was set against another funny tale, also based on misunderstanding of meaning but this time with a strong Latin flavor, "Juan Bobo and the Veiled Ladies."

Tall Tale Critters: Eventually in a story hour zoo the unbelievable tall tale animals of North America must be confronted, especially "The Squonk, the Goofus Bird, and the Whiffle-poofle." This material is anecdotal but was retold as a brief animal story, so that the play on the ridiculous onomatopoeic names would come through. And then followed the never-to-be-underestimated "The Fast Sooner Hound," which was contrasted with a marvelous turkey tall tale. "Saved by a Turkey" must be told with a straight face and exaggerated drama, but it appeals to older children.

People Who Became Animals: Finally, of course, no Story Zoo would be complete without human metamorphosis stories, as in "The Enchanted Mule," a surprisingly difficult story to tell, but funny; this was followed by the sad and lovely "The Gull"; and an adapted version of the Louisiana Creole tall tale, "Compair Taureau and Jean Malin."

Animals Who Turned into People: Animals, too, can undergo metamorphosis—like "The Hedgehog Who Became a Prince," tart and brisk; the strange "The Giant Okab" from Persia; and the long and merry Pyle story of "Peterkin and the Little Gray Hare."

At the closing program, a stuffed animal parade followed the exhibit of "animules" the children had made, and animal crackers made the program very satisfying! At a program shortly thereafter, the public-relations speaker from the zoo brought live animals and small mounted mammals just to put everything into focus.

Themes and Stories

Animules
Animules, 16mm film, color, 11 min. Distributed International Film Foundation, 475 Fifth Ave. Dept. 916, New York, N.Y. 10017

> A very brief film demonstrating children making papier-mâché animals.

Pachyderms and Such
"The Elephant's Bathtub" in Carpenter, Frances, *The Elephant's Bathtub*

> The envious pot-maker told the king that the washerman could wash one of the king's grey elephants into a white one . . . but he must have a special bathtub to do it!

"How the Camel Got His Hump" in Kipling, Rudyard, *Just So Stories*

> Unduplicatable humor and high fantasy, but Kipling's words must be used. The lazy camel who only said "Hummph!" was fittingly rewarded.

Horses, Horses, Horses
"Dapplegrim" in Wiggin, Kate D., and Smith, Nora, *The Fairy Ring*

> Scandinavian fairy tale, somewhat reminiscent of "East of the Sun," and just as romantic and long—the story of the lad who trained his foal, and through it found his fortune and a princess. In the best of the fairy tale tradition.

"The Smoke Horse" in Carpenter, Frances, *Wonder Tales of Horses and Heroes*

> Crafty fellow who fell into his own trap when he suggested that he should deliver the king's message to his deceased father in the heavens. Implicit Oriental humor and a practical joke which boomerangs.

"The Horse That Liked to Play Tricks" in Carpenter, Frances, *Wonder Tales of Horses and Heroes*

> Bewitched horse, a tailor with big shears, and French villagers make an unusual legend. One must limit the telling to only one section from this otherwise rather rambling, but interesting, narrative.

Cats
"The Golden Lynx" in Baker, Augusta, *The Golden Lynx*

> When the prince and his coachman switched identities, it was the golden lynx who brought affairs to rights again.

"Ticky-picky-boom-boom" in Sherlock, Philip, *Anansi, the Spider Man*

> Down the road they came, the yams running with their insistent, alliterative rhythm, funny and fearsome both! Delightful to tell.

"The Boy Who Drew Cats" in Hearn, Lafcadio, *The Boy Who Drew Cats*

> An old Japanese tale of cats painted on canvas, and the artist who woke to find one painted cat dripping blood. Spooky, dramatic.

Monsters
"My Lord-Bag-of-Rice" in Manning-Sanders, Ruth, *Book of Dragons*

> Hidesato, a fearless man, stepped over the Dragon King, and came face to face with a monster centipede. Dramatic and yet humorous, and easy to tell.

"Alberto and the Monster" in Sechrist, Elizabeth, *Once in the First Times*

> Tagalog tale, from the Philippines, with formula of three princes, three magic charms, three dragons to slay, and a threefold reward. European influence; interesting to tell.

"The Kamiah Monster" in Martin, Frances, *Nine Tales of Coyote*

> Full of action, talking animals, and a cunning twist, as explanation of the dispersion of the Blackfeet, Flathead, Sioux, and Nimipu Plains Indians.

Dogs and Wild Dogs
"The Dog That Learned to Read" in Carpenter, Frances, *Wonder Tales of Dogs and Cats*

> The credulous Arabian weaver brought his

dog to the village teacher that he might learn to read, thus setting up an absurd chain of events. Funny, easy to tell, but must be well-timed. For older children.

"How Saynday Ran a Foot-race with Coyote" in Marriott, Alice, *Winter-Telling Stories*

Saynday, Kiowa Indian trickster, gets his just desserts from Coyote who turns the tables on him. Brisk, tongue-in-cheek humor.

"Mr. Wolf Makes a Failure" in Harris, Joel Chandler, *Brer Rabbit*

"All is not dead that seems dead!" A variant of "Heyo, House!" Short, funny, careful retelling of Harris's Uncle Remus as "Br'er Rabbit" by Margaret Wise Brown—sly commentary on human nature.

Make-believe Critters

"Kappa's Tug-of-war with Big Brown Horse" in Baruch, Dorothy, *Kappa's Tug-of-war with Big Brown Horse*

See Story Hour Canvas, page 109, for annotation.

"The Bored Tengu" in Palmer, Robin, *Dragons, Unicorns and Mythical Beasts*

Unusual, funny folk tale from Japan, about the fierce Tengu who kidnaps a fearless boy to keep him a captive storyteller for his family.

"The Hobyahs" in Fenner, Phyllis, *Giants and Witches and a Dragon or Two*

See Holiday Stories, Halloween, page 116.

Thanksgiving Tales

"How Turkey Got His White Tail Feathers" in Belting, Natalia, *The Long-tailed Bear*

Delightful Tewa pourquoi story of the flood and the fleeing creatures, one of whom didn't quite make it. Suitable for Thanksgiving, or in general. See also Holiday Stories, page 118.

"The Pumpkin Child" in Mehdevi, Ann S., *Persian Folk and Fairy Tales*

See Holiday Stories, page 118.

"Ballad of the Pilgrim Cat" in Wibberley, Leonard, *The Ballad of the Pilgrim Cat*

A ballad, long and whimsical, of the first cats in this country. May be adapted for prose retelling, and is useful at Thanksgiving. See also Holiday Stories, page 118.

Barnyard Fowls and Animals

"When Rooster Was King of the Cats" in Belting, Natalia, *Cat Tales*

Wry humor, of a domineering rooster who threatened his cat followers with the fire he kept in his scarlet comb . . . until he was exposed by one wily female!

"Goose Hans" in Gág, Wanda, *Three Gay Tales from Grimm*

A Lazy Jack tale, with Wanda Gág's inimitable twist and illustration. A droll, not so easy to tell, but very good.

"Señor Billy Goat" in Belpré, Pura, *The Tiger and the Rabbit*

Folk tale from Puerto Rico, in which the greedy billy goat is ousted by the ant-friend of an unduly polite old couple. A hint of Spanish dialect, as colorful as the Caribbean from which it comes.

Hoofs and Horns

"Kantchil Grows Strong at the Welling-Well" in Bro, Marguerite H., *How the Mouse Deer Became King*

By sheer wit tiny Kantchil, the Indonesian trickster, vanquishes mighty Harimu, the terrible tiger. The situation is funny, but the story is not humorous. Harold Courlander also has this story in *Kantchil's Lime Pit*, written more briskly.

"Victory of the Buffalo" in Courlander, Harold, *Kantchil's Lime Pit*

The people of West Sumatra build their houses to resemble the horns of a water buffalo, remembering that it was the water buffalo's courage which preserved their republic.

"Why the Hoofs of the Deer Are Split" in Holbrooke, Florence, *A Book of Nature Myths*

A pourquoi Indian story of cruelty punished. Short and effective.

Animals at Christmas

"The Lamb and the Child" in Frye, Dean, *The Lamb and the Child*

An illustrated legend from the medieval Christmas season, concerned with the shepherds and a trick played on them at the time of the birth of Christ. See also Holiday Stories, page 118.

"The Christmas Cuckoo" in Walters, Maude A., *A Book of Christmas Stories*

> Very long, but a good story. See Holiday annotations, page 118, and section on modifying, page 36.

"The Small One" in Tazewell, Charles, *The Small One*

> A beautiful story that must be abridged about the small donkey that carried Mary to Bethlehem.

Animals in Legend

"The Thunderbird" in Chafetz, Harold, *Thunderbird*

> Strong and dramatic, the story of how the thunderbird was created from the giant Nasan. Striking illustrations and dignified Indian style. Good for older children.

"The Seal-catcher and the Merman" in Grierson, Elizabeth, *The Scottish Fairy Book*

> Unusual transformation story, with a touch of Gaelic mysticism, appropriate for ecology-minded older children. Good story, rather stark, and straightforward.

"Yanni and the Dragon" in Manning-Sanders, Ruth, *A Book of Dragons*

> "Good morning, Yanni, my Yanni, my dinner! I am hungry, my Yanni, my dinner!" But Yanni's sweetheart defied the dragon by saying coyly, "Go and meet the dragon, my love, my Yanni. *I have eaten nine dragons and I do not want this one!*" Very funny, tongue-in-cheek, and short.

Snakes and Slithery Creatures

"The Frog That Swallowed the Ocean" in Carpenter, Frances, *Wonder Tales of Ships and Seas*

> A myth of the Pacific peoples, unusual and brief.

"The White Snake" in Tashjian, Virginia, *Once There Was and Was Not*

> The king had a white snake, in a covered dish, brought to him before each meal; by eating a bit of it, he was able to understand the birds. An Armenian fairy tale, very smooth and imaginative.

"The Legend of the Lizard" in Beckley, René, *Folklore of the World: Australia*

> Short pourquoi story of why the mountain-devil-lizard of Australia is so fierce looking. Pointed, interesting.

The Bird House

"King Stork" in Pyle, Howard, *The Wonder Clock*

> A long, involved story with a magic whistle, cap of darkness, flying feather, and a riddle contest. The teller must identify with Pyle's style to make the story ring dramatically. Also published in a new single illustrated edition by Trina Shart Hymen and in Phyllis Fenner's *Giants and Witches and a Dragon or Two*.

"Robin Redbreast" in Fisher, Agnes, *Once upon a Time*

> When the world was dark and cold, robin found fire; holding it against his breast, which it scorched, he brought it to the animals. An ancient pourquoi story.

"Rusty Jack" in Cothran, Jean, *With a Wig, with a Wag*

> With a tame, rusty crow, Jack finds wife, fortune and castle. An American parallel to Puss in Boots, easy and funny.

Seashore and Deep-sea Dwellers

"The Whale That Smoked a Pipe" in Carpenter, Frances, *Wonder Tales of Ships and Seas*

> Glooscap story of the lovable culture figure of the Micmac Indians, fresh and zestful, which explains the whale's spouting.

"The Golden Crab" in Lang, Andrew, *The Yellow Fairy Book*

> Long, romantic fairy story about a prince enchanted into the shape of a crab, caught by a fisherman. He needs to marry a princess to break his enchantment. A Greek tale, good for older children.

"The Wonderful Tree" in Heady, Eleanor, *Jambo, Sungura!*

> East African trickster story of Sungura the hare, and the tortoise Kamba—and a tree whose magic name gave food when that name was pronounced. A variant of "The Bojabi Tree," witty and very tellable.

Mythological Animals

"The Fox, the Dog, and the Griffin" in Anderson, Poul, *The Fox, the Dog and the Griffin*

> A long short story which must be abridged and adapted for use in the story hour. The plot is strong and the action good. A fox and a dog compete for a lovely wife, with odd results.

"The Golden Phoenix" in Barbeau, Marius, *The Golden Phoenix*

> A fairly familiar, long fairy story of the golden bird who guarded the garden's treasure. Romantic, well-told Canadian version.

"The Beast with the Single Horn" in Jacobson, Helen, *The First Book of Mythical Beasts*

> Brief Chinese legend of the unicorn. Must be retold.

Monkey Island

"The Green Monkey" in Lang, Andrew, *The Yellow Fairy Book*

> The prince was turned into a small green monkey, and it seemed that nobody would recognize him and break his enchantment.

"Grandmother and the Apes" in Kalibala, Ernest Balintuma, and Davis, M. G., *Wakaima and Clay Man*

> A pourquoi story from Africa with animal protagonists, short, easy and amusing.

"Why Monkeys Live in Trees" in Kalibala, Ernest Balintuma, and Davis, M. G., *Wakaima and Clay Man*

> Lively and easy to tell—the reason monkeys take to the air!

Bears, Badgers, and Diggers

"Badger and the Green Giant" in Hill, Kay, *Glooscap and His Magic*

> A Glooscap legend from the Wabanaki Indians about famine and the mischiefmaker, Badger. Well-integrated plot, easy story line, well-paced.

"Kunikdjuaq" in Leach, Maria, *The Rainbow Book of American Folk Tales and Legends*

> Tender story of the old woman who adopted an orphan polar bear, only to lose him to jealous villagers. Excellent, and dramatic.

"Little Nichet's Baby Sister" in Arbuthnot, May Hill, *Time for Fairy Tales*

> Taken from the delightful French-Canadian stories in *Sashes Red and Blue* by Natalie Carlson, this is the story of an adventurous and curious little fellow who stirred up trouble when he set out to ask the Indians for a baby sister. Funny.

Rabbits, Rodents, and Sly Ones

"The Race between the Hare and the Hedgehog" in Wiggin, Kate D., and Smith, Nora, *Tales of Laughter*

> Variant of the fable "The Hare and the Tortoise," but this is set in England, and the turtle has become a hedgehog.

"The Mouse Princess" in Arbuthnot, May Hill, *Time for Fairy Tales*

> "Go find a wife," said the king to his sons, but the third son found only a wee mouse living in a ruined tower. A long fairy tale with a poignancy that appeals to children. Easy to tell.

"The King of the Leaves" in Greene, Lila, *Folk Tales of Spain and Latin America*

> An animal trickster tale full of nonsense and Latin American flavor, just the right length to tell.

Creepers and Crawlers

"Little Cricket" in Chamoud, Simone, *Picture Tales from France*

> So small he was called Little Cricket, but so clever a wizard, he won a fortune from the king! Play on words, witty and very clever.

"How Spider Got a Thin Waist" in Arkhurst, Joyce, *The Adventures of Spider*

> Greedy Anansi, pulled in two ways by two feasts, and nearly pulled in half, to boot! Obvious humor, delightful to tell.

"Juan Bobo and the Veiled Ladies" in Greene, Lila, *Folk Tales of Spain and Latin America*

> Juan Bobo, the Silly Jean of Latin America, finds himself in a fine stew with flies all around him, but in his noodleheaded way he solves the problem.

Tall Tale Critters

"The Squonk, the Goofus Bird, and the Whifflepoofle" in Stoutenberg, Adrien, *American Tall Tale Animals*

> Must be retold for effect, but the tall tale materials are amusing enough to warrant it. Onomatopoeic effect is good.

"The Fast Sooner Hound" in Bontemps, Arna, *The Fast Sooner Hound*

> Hilarious tall tale of the lop-eared hound who could outrun, outsmart, and outlast the mighty Cannonball train! Especially for older boys, but tell it straight-faced!

"Saved by a Turkey" in Credle, Ellis, *Tall Tales from the High Hills*

> A most remarkable bird "saved Jess from an awful end. . . ." Appalachian tall tale, dramatic and outrageous.

People Who Became Animals

"The Enchanted Mule" in Haviland, Virginia, *Favorite Fairy Tales Told in Spain*

> The mule somehow got mixed into the bishop's retinue, and all kinds of complications ensued. Difficult to tell but funny, with delightful Spanish folk flavor.

"The Gull" in Deutsch, Babette, *Tales of Faraway Folk*

> By the magic of singing, Ilmarinen the smith turned his reluctant bride into a gull. The language is rich and rhythmic, romantic for older girls, drawn from the Finnish Kalevala sources.

"Compair Taureau and Jean Malin" in Field, Rachel, *American Folk and Fairy Tales*

> A cajun tale of magic and enchantment from the Louisiana bayous, with a precocious lad named Jean Malin as hero. Difficult to tell, a little strange, but interesting. Needs some adapting for use in this story program.

Animals Who Turned into People

"The Hedgehog Who Became a Prince" in Baker, Augusta, *The Golden Lynx*

> "Though it were even a hedgehog, yet would I praise God for a child of my own!" So said the woman, and Jendza granted her request. Whimsical twist, good to tell.

"The Giant Okab" in Mehdevi, Ann S., *Persian Folk and Fairy Tales*

> "The giant Okab's wings were as wide as a river, and its feathers were all of copper . . ." —and everyone was terrified! A tale of love and magic for older children; longer and more complex.

"Peterkin and the Little Gray Hare" in Fenner, Phyllis, *Giants and Witches and a Dragon or Two*

> One of Pyle's wonderful retellings of the old folk story on the Boots and the Troll theme. This time it is a gay younger son who sets out with two pennies to win his fortune, and does so. Rhythmic, humorous, distinctive.

Closing Story Zoo Party
> Stuffed animal show
> Animal parade
> Live animal show
> Animal cookies.

STORY HOUR MAGIC

> Did you ever see a giant,
> Or a goblin, or a ghost?
> Did you ever watch the witches
> When they ride?
> Did you ever catch a leprechaun
> And find his pot of gold?
> Or see a tomte
> Seek his fireside?
> Ah, here are giants bold and big!
> Here elves dance merrily,
> And little folk come forth; and trolls;
> And mermaids from the sea!
> Within the pages of these books
> They'll come alive for you—
> And troop, in story magic,
> In and out, the whole year through!
> —de Wit

With these words this story program begins with the purpose of exploring various creatures of faery, seen and unseen, known and unknown to most children. But, since the world of the unconscious and the unknown impinges on children in the form of unidentified flying objects and witchcraft through television, and science fantasy and astrological projections through magazines, newspapers, and theaters, why should children not take an interest in magic? Research led to dictionaries and encyclopedias about mystical creatures, into notes and commentaries by distinguished authors—Tolkien and Hartland, for example—and far afield. When the program was finally arranged, illustrations of the various faery creatures to be presented in the separate story hours were used, including imps, goblins, gnomes, nisse, ellefolk, giants, brownies, leprechauns, and mermaids. Lest any not believe, in Scotland adults see full-grown kelpies and seal-men, and Andersen was not averse to investing even the lowly shirt collar with the magic of speech.

At each story hour, the magic person for that particular session was first introduced, using pictures and music where possible. Then the storyteller proceeded directly to the tales. Story hours for that year's program were still one half hour in length, ranging from the first week in October through April.

Magicians and Sorcerers: Since October is the witching month, it was appropriate to begin with magic and sorcery, and very natural to use the music of "The Sorcerer's Apprentice" by Dukas as a background for the first story, the medieval tale "The Sorcerer's Apprentice." The plot was familiar to the children, and well liked. This was followed by the magic of shape changing in "Black Magic," and concluded with a pungent, unusual Baltic story, "A Tale of Stolen Time."

Witches and More Witches: As the story program moved toward Halloween, the bony "Spearfinger, the Witch" came into focus, but she was offset by "Lazy Hans," who merrily tricked his witch. Last, to sweeten the witches' brew, was a fairy tale, "The Knights of the Fish"; this, however, is far from sugary, and ends with the dramatic collapse of the castle of Albatroz.

Imps and Goblins: A brief story, "The Imp Goblin of the Pitcher" strikes a strange note, followed by "Tom Tit Tot," the English variant of Rumplestiltskin; and finally, a delicious modern fantasy, "The Goblin Who Turned into a Doorknocker!"

Specters and Spooks: The following week opened with an atmospheric tale of misty appearances in the Dutch marshlands, "The Three Misty Women"; then, a cumulative spook story, "The Golden Arm," with an explosive ending. After that came a variant of the same theme, but this time a jolly one, "The Boy Who Was Never Afraid."

Ghosts and Ghoulies: The Halloween story hour's first tale was "The Giant Bones," with its Gaelic color; then the absurd "The Giant Ghost." An ornery Irish plow was featured in an unfamiliar story to finish off the session, "Jack O'Leary's Plow."

Devils and Demons: So much for the scary folk of October! In November, a Japanese folktale with hidden humor started off, "The Dumpling and the Demons," followed by a medieval French legend, "The Bridge of St. Cloud," wherein the devil himself was outwitted. Finally, a well-plotted, straightforward account of "The Smithy of Smee."

Gnomes and Pookas: Laurence Housman's creative fairy tale, "The Ratcatcher's Daughter" came first, beautifully styled and imaginative; then the short "Earth Gnome," with Wanda Gág's fresh, energetic version. To tie together the gnomes and the pookas, a modern Irish fantasy, "Philip and the Pooka," was used.

Wizards: The previous week's program laid a good foundation for the magic of the following week, Wizards, beginning with "The Luck Egg," a strange, short Baltic folktale. Howard Pyle came next, retelling the Spanish fairy tale "Black Magic" used in the first story hour, but now flavored with his distinctive style and entitled "The Clever Student and the Master of the Black Arts." To conclude, the broad humor of a Czech variant of the flying ship motif, "Long, Broad, and Sharpsight," was used. If the last of these tales had not been so well paced, the program would have been overlong.

The Small Ones: No special emphasis was given to Thanksgiving; the program at that season was called Small Ones and concerned the one-inch people; "Pyelkin," a brave Russian folklore character; "Issun Boshi, the Inchling," Japanese, brave, and very colorful; and "Little Cricket," always a funny play on words, familiar from the previous year. Incidentally, this is from one of the beloved picture tales—*Picture Tales from France*, rescued from obscurity by Eulalie Ross and included in her *The Buried Treasure*.

Godmothers and Genii and Jinn: This theme brought to mind probably the best-known of all fairy tales, "Cinderella," in a version by Lang. This was preceded by a brisk, short Grimm fairy tale, "The Blue Light" in which a godmother also appeared. These two were then offset by a different sort of magic-workers, the Middle-East Jinn, in *"The Half-pint Jinni,"* a delightful story that must be somewhat abridged in order to fit into an afterschool story hour.

Tomte and Nisse: For Christmas, "The Yule Tomte" pleasantly revealed those small folk from Sweden, the nisse, and the tomte from Norway. The other two Christmas stories were both by Ruth Sawyer, filled with fun and Christmas spirit—"The Christmas That Was Nearly Lost," and the priceless "The Voyage of the Wee Red Cap," where Irish Christmas elves abound.

Elves and Ellefolk: Before the New Year began, there was time to include a story hour with more Christmas emphases, introduced by a brief animal tale, the Irish "The Elf-ridden Pig," followed by a funny folk tale, "The Girl Who Didn't Know How to Spin," and her magic helpers. The story hour concluded with "The Little Green Elf's Christmas," for younger listeners, and the ever-popular "The Elves and the Shoemaker," seasonal and traditional, for everyone.

Dragons and Monsters: The New Year came in with a roar; "Mighty Mikko," the Finnish Puss in Boots, started out, followed by "Stan Bolovan," a Rumanian variant of Grimm's Gallant Tailor. Both of these stories are vigorous and adventurous. The third tale was "The Calabash Man," fast paced and beautifully written, with a scary monster from the South American jungles for atmosphere. Since the first two stories were jaunty, they balanced the heavier, more dramatic third number. Children usually join in the refrain of "Mighty Mikko," chanting it with delight every time it appears.

Dwarfs and Boggarts: Howard Pyle's "Farmer Grigg's Boggart" began this hour followed by an ancient Mexican legend, "The Dwarf Who Became King" with its keen humor. "Dwarf Long Nose" is long but brisk and satisfying.

Jesters, Jokers, and Noodleheads: This was a fun program, from its name to its last laugh, beginning with the delightful Polish tale, "The Jester Who Fooled a King"; then the droll, "Discreet Hans," amusingly improper; and finally the flavorful dialogue from the Appalachian hills, "Soap, Soap, Soap!"

Giants and Ogres: This program presented three different species of those towering figures, from the Irish "The Two Giants," often called "The Legend of Knockmany," broad and funny, to the horrid "The Hairy-armed Ogre of Kyoto," and the braggadocio of "How Big-mouth Wrestled the Giant," relaxed and undemanding.

Tricksters, Rascals, and Rogues: Very different in humor from the noodleheads and the jesters were the tricksters, who imbued their stories with a sly, subtle kind of humor, almost always with a wry twist, as though the trickster was making a commentary on human nature, as indeed was often the case. One such trickster figure was "Juan Cigarron," a variant of the Little Cricket motif, but typically Spanish. "Tricky Peik," a rogue who tricks the kingdom and the king in a Scandinavian droll, followed; shrewd "Kisander, the Cat" reflected Jamaican Anansi wit at the end.

Trolls: Here, an exaggerated bravado characterized "The Terrible Olli," the sharp-witted Finnish boy who completely foils the stupid but fierce troll. In contrast was the bright, cheerful "Hans Humdrum" from Denmark; and a variant on the same motif as "Olli," full of cumulative humor, called "Boots and the Troll." "Boots" however, was easier, and the two stories had enough difference in incident and background color to make them usable and interesting together.

Princes and Princesses: No story program would be adequate without a judicious sprinkling of princess stories, so February romantically first introduced "Esben Ashblower" who in short order proved that he could give a princess her comeuppance (one she nevertheless liked!). The second story featured a country girl who rescued a royal child from her tearless state with an onion in "The Princess Who Could Not Cry." The third princess story was romantic, longer, and very smooth—"The Grateful Prince."

Brownies and Fairies: Here there was much room for choice. First a sturdy Dutch folktale, "The Black-bearded Brownies of Bonenberg," balanced against a rhythmic Scotch story, "The Woman Who Flummoxed the Fairies," filled with whimsy. Finally, the fantasy "Fairy Cobbler" by Rose Fyleman. This program probably pleased the girls more than the boys, though all enjoyed the humor.

Pixies and Piskey Folk: Another kind of fairy appeared on the next week's program, the Cornish piskey. "The Spinning Plate" is unpredictable and short, "The Pixie's Scarf" modern and long. "The Tune of Iolo ap Hugh" is very short, very mysterious, very Welsh, and also suitable for a Halloween occasion, since the violinist met his fate on All-Hallows Eve.

Leprechauns and Little People: These stories are naturals for a St. Patrick's season. The mischievous hillman in "The Hillman and the Housewife," witty, with a hint of dialect, began the program; then time was telescoped as the little folk worked a strange magic in "The Widow and the Korrigans"; and finally Patrick O'Donnell rollicked through a fortune but came out laughing (as the children do!) at "Patrick O'Donnell and the Leprechauns."

Water Nixies, Sprites, and Nymphs: The last three programs in Story Magic involved water creatures, kings, and queens—very few of them remain today, at least in our hemisphere! The first program began with "The Water Nixy," a somewhat pathetic story found in Lang's version in *The Yellow Fairy Book*, drawn from Grimm sources; as an antidote, a gay Swedish story, just right for this spot, "The Boy and the Water-Sprite"; and at long last, an opportunity to use a myth, not always easy to incorporate into a story program, the picturesque "Echo and Narcissus."

Mermaids and Kelpies: These stories were of different character—two traditional fairy tales: "The Mermaid and the Boy" and "The Three Mermaids." The third, however, had a brisk, turn-of-the-tables ending, "Rake-up!" No "happily ever after" here!

Kings and Queens: The last program included the short, familiar "The Frog King"; a long and exciting fairy tale, "Queen Crane"; and the zestful Russian toast "To Your Good Health" that is not all that it seems! To conclude the season, we introduced riddles and guessing games, using shadow tableaux based on a dozen or more of the stories told over the year, and asked the children, "Can you name that one?" Most of the children found they could!

Themes and Stories

Magicians and Sorcerers

"The Sorcerer's Apprentice" in Rostron, Richard, *The Sorcerer's Apprentice*

> The apprentice knew how to get magic started but he didn't know how to turn it off. Lively, familiar to many.

"Black Magic" in Boggs, Ralph, and Davis, M. G., *Three Golden Oranges*

> From bird to fish to ring . . . the cunning went on and on until the master wizard met his finish at the hands of his clever helper.

"A Tale of Stolen Time" in Schvarts, Evgeny, *A Tale of Stolen Time*

> One morning he was a lazy boy—the next a wrinkled old man—what, oh, what had happened to him? Different sort of magic.

Witches and More Witches

"Spearfinger, the Witch" in Bell, Corydon, *John Rattling-gourd*

> Wonderfully scary story from the Cherokee about a dreadful witch with a long bony finger like a spear on one hand. See also Holiday Stories, page 116.

"Lazy Hans" in Manning-Sanders, Ruth, *A Book of Witches*

> Too lazy to work, but he found his come-uppance when the witch turned him first

into a pig to fatten him to eat, then into a gander . . . and then he escaped.

"The Knights of the Fish" in Lang, Andrew, *The Rose Fairy Book*

> A cobbler who cobbled in vain turned to fishing to feed his family but caught nothing until one morning he drew out a beautiful fish. "Take me back to your hut," said the fish. "Eat, give some to your wife, and bury part of me in the garden. . . ." An unusual witch story.

Imps and Goblins

"The Imp Goblin of the Pitcher" in Harper, Wilhelmina, *Ghosts and Goblins*

> The pitcher never failed to give water—but that was because Yan-Copek, the pitcher imp, began to work his magic. A most unusual tale of enchantment.

"Tom Tit Tot" in Jacobs, Joseph, *English Fairy Tales*

> Rumplestiltskin in a country English dress, with That twirling its tail and mystifying everyone who couldn't identify an imp. Lusty and merry.

"The Goblin Who Turned into a Doorknocker" in Fyleman, Rose, *Tea Time Tales*

> A small green goblin tricks a wizard, and sets a chain of events in motion that bewilders even the wisest. Delightful to tell, and to hear. See also Holiday Stories, page 117.

Specters and Spooks

"The Three Misty Women" in Spicer, Dorothy, *13 Witches*

> Three white, strange women lived in a deep hole in the misty fields of Holland, and made the passersby quake in their boots. Unusual, with a bit of humor to balance the shivers.

"The Golden Arm" in Fenner, Phyllis, *Ghosts, Ghosts, Ghosts*

> A variant of "The Boy Who Was Never Afraid" (Hatch—*More*), but just different enough to make it delightful. Scary ending may be hissed for effect.

"The Boy Who Was Never Afraid" in Hatch, Mary, *More Danish Tales*

> "Good for nothing!" said the parents of lazy, incorrigible Hans—but the Troll found Hans good for plenty of things!

Ghosts and Ghoulies

"The Giant Bones" in Nic Leodhas, Sorche, *Gaelic Ghosts*

> Horrible—the enormous bones everyone knew had been buried in the caves centuries before, but could not find! Scary, atmospheric, with a hint of Scotch dialect.

"The Giant Ghost" in Harper, Wilhelmina, *Ghosts and Goblins*

> A "critter" ghost—ungainly and funny makes for a short, unusual, ghost tale.

"Jack O'Leary's Plow" in Spicer, Dorothy, *13 Ghosts*

> A plow that was bewitched? Impossible! Yet this plow disappeared when angry words were hurled at the earth it turned over.

Devils and Demons

"The Dumpling and the Demons" in Stamm, Claus, *The Dumpling and the Demons*

> Rice dumplings do not talk—but this one did, and rolled its way into a cave of the Jizo of children, with the old man hustling along afterwards. What a magic! Fun to tell.

"The Bridge of St. Cloud" in Courlander, Harold, *Ride with the Sun*

> From the Middle Ages, the delightful contest between a wily devil and his victim—decided by a cat! Subtle humor.

"The Smithy of Smee" in Fisher, Agnes, *Once upon a Time*

> The Flemish city of Ghent is known as Ghent-the-Good because the goodly and godly smithy once bested the sulphurous devil at his own game.

Gnomes and Pookas

"The Ratcatcher's Daughter" in Davis, Mary Gould, *A Baker's Dozen*

> Housman's beautiful story of the girl whose greedy father turned her over to the gnomes. Very unusual—be sure Housman's language is followed.

"The Earth Gnome" in Gág, Wanda, *More Tales from Grimm*

> Rich though he was, the king prized his apple tree and his three daughters almost equally. But the apples were enchanted, he found to his sorrow. Only Dull Hansl could help, and then only after the daughters had foolishly confided their secret to the big kitchen stove.

"Philip and the Pooka" in Green, Kathleen, *Philip and the Pooka*

> Irish magic when the white pooka gets into Philip's pasture and bewitches not only the horses, but others as well. Humorous, and a bit fey! A modern accent.

Wizards

"The Luck Egg" in Olcott, Frances, *Wonder Tales from Baltic Wizards*

> One might have guessed something unusual would happen when the ninth child of the poor man had a beggar and a rich noble woman as godparents—and it did! Whimsical, short.

"Clever Student and the Master of the Black Arts" in Pyle, Howard, *The Wonder Clock*

> Witty retelling on Ralph Boggs's "Black Magic" motif from Spain but with Pyle's distinctive flavor. Excellent. See also Story Hour Canvas, page 108.

"Long, Broad, and Sharpsight" in Manning-Sanders, Ruth, *Book of Wizards*

> Czech variant of the men with the remarkable gifts who helped the luckless hero win a kingdom. Variant of the Russian "The Flying Ship" (Haviland—*Russia*).

The Small Ones

"Pyelkin" in Gottschalk, Fruma, *The Runaway Soldier*

> Thumb-size Pyelkin proved valiant in any situation. A Russian folk tale, especially good with younger children.

"Issun Boshi, the Inchling" in Ishii, Momoko, *Issun Boshi, the Inchling*

> Illustrated single edition of a familiar and beloved Japanese Tom Thumb folk tale.

"Little Cricket" in Ross, Eulalie S., *The Buried Treasure*

> Serendipity brought the unfortunate little fellow into the king's presence, and made it appear he was a wizard. An old plot with a delightful twist. See also Story Hour Zoo, page 77.

Godmothers and Genii and Jinn

"The Blue Light" in Grimm, Jakob, and Grimm, Wilhelm, *Grimm's Fairy Tales*, (ed. Hunt)

Traditional fairy tale of a hero who sought a bane, and found a boon, through a magic genii.

"Cinderella" in Lang, Andrew, *The Blue Fairy Book*

Perrault's well-loved traditional fairy tale, godmother and all, with the cinder-girl who became a princess.

"The Half-pint Jinni" in Dolbier, Maurice, *The Half-pint Jinni*

"In the years of enchantment . . . when Baghdad was the wonder of the world, there lived a boy . . . in a fishing village"—who, by chance, found a bottle with a half-grown jinni. When commanded, he, the Jinni, could work only half magic! Trouble!

Tomte and Nisse

"The Yule Tomte" in Luckhardt, Mildred, *Christmas Comes Again*

See Holiday Stories, page 118.

"The Christmas That Was Nearly Lost" in Sawyer, Ruth, *This Way to Christmas*

See Holiday Stories, page 118.

"The Voyage of the Wee Red Cap" in Sawyer, Ruth, *This Way to Christmas*

See Holiday Stories, page 118.

Elves and Ellefolk

"The Elf-ridden Pig" in Foyle, Kathleen, *The Little Good People*

Brief glimpse of elves who work their witchery on a pig in the full of the moon, with a bit of the Irish dialect for accent!

"The Girl Who Didn't Know How to Spin" in Belting, Natalia, *Elves and Ellefolk*

Lazy she was until the nisse who lived in the house showed her the magic in her own fingers. Short, very tellable.

"The Little Green Elf's Christmas" in Walters, Maude, A., *A Book of Christmas Stories*

See Holiday Stories, page 119.

"The Elves and the Shoemaker" in Grimm, Jakob, and Grimm, Wilhelm, *Grimm's Fairy Tales* (ed. Hunt)

See Holiday Stories, page 118. Listed as "The Elves" in the table of contents.

Dragons and Monsters

"Mighty Mikko" in Davis, Mary Gould, *A Baker's Dozen*

Finnish variant of Puss in Boots, with an unusual fox as protagonist, and a catchy refrain. Very rhythmical.

"Stan Bolovan" in Lang, Andrew, *The Violet Fairy Book*

Grimm's "The Gallant Tailor" (*Household*) in a most delightful variant, aided by Stan Bolovan's hundred children. Vigorous, hearty humor.

"The Calabash Man" in Finger, Charles, *Tales from Silver Lands*

A monster, scary and not to be tampered with! Very good South American atmosphere. Difficult to tell; long, dramatic.

Dwarfs and Boggarts

"Farmer Grigg's Boggart" in Pyle, Howard, *Pepper and Salt*

Wherever he moved, the irrepressible boggart moved also. Funny.

"The Dwarf Who Became King" in Purnell, Idella, *The Talking Bird*

The Dwarf of Uxmal struck a golden cymbal with silver sticks to fulfill the prophecy of becoming king through wit and witchery. Unusual, with an old Mexican myth as background.

"Dwarf Long Nose" in Lang, Andrew, *The Violet Fairy Book*

A dwarf he was indeed, but his skill at cooking was gigantic, and Danish soup and Hamburg dumplings merely commonplace in his hands. Very long, but a delightful fairy tale.

Jesters, Jokers, and Noodleheads

"The Jester Who Fooled a King" in Haviland, Virginia, *Favorite Fairy Tales Told in Poland*

It is one thing to be dead—quite another to seem to be dead, and the old jester reaped a just reward.

"Discreet Hans" in Wiggin, Kate D., and Smith, Nora, *Tales of Laughter*

"Behave well, Hans!" said his mother, and foolish Hans did, always at the wrong time, and in the wrong way. Hilarious.

"Soap, Soap, Soap!" in Chase, Richard, *Grandfather Tales*

A mountain riddle story, a play on words reminiscent of Little Cricket, but with a distinctive style. Requires skill to tell, very amusing.

Giants and Ogres

"The Two Giants" in Van Stockum, Hilda, *The Cottage at Bantry Bay*

"'Tis the Giant of Knockmany, forsooth, outwitted by a wee puny woman!" Rich in Irish feeling, fun to tell and to hear. Also known as "The Legend of Knockmany," one version of which is found in *Celtic Fairy Tales* by Joseph Jacobs.

"The Hairy-armed Ogre of Kyoto" in Spicer, Dorothy, *13 Giants*

"Once on a time a band of man-eating ogres plagued the fair land of Japan. . . ." So begins a satisfying monster story, not too hard to tell, especially good with older boys.

"How Big-mouth Wrestled the Giant" in Conger, Lesley, *Three Giant Stories*

A braggart giant, who in the long run is saved by his tricky tongue. Short and breezy.

Tricksters, Rascals, and Rogues

"Juan Cigarron" in Haviland, Virginia, *Favorite Fairy Tales Told in Spain*

Said Juan, "I am such a good rascal, I will make a better wizard. . . ." and he went on to serve apprentice to all the wizards in Spain. A merry variant of Grimm's "Dr. Know-All" (*Household*).

"Tricky Peik" in Hardendorff, Jeanne, *Tricky Peik*

A Scandinavian droll in which, for all his knavery, Peik manages to win both crown and queen.

"Kisander, the Cat" in Sherlock, Philip, *Anansi, the Spider Man*

Anansi was not afraid to skin up Kisander's dookanoo tree and throw down some delicious puddings . . . but there was a price to be paid! Jamaican, with a lilt to the words and bouncy humor.

Trolls

"The Terrible Olli" in Fillmore, Parker, *The Shepherd's Nosegay*

The youngest of the three brothers knew if a troll looked full at the rising sun, he would burst—but that took a bit of doing! A satisfying Finnish variant of "Esben and the Witch." (Manning-Sanders—*Witches*).

"Hans Humdrum" in Hatch, Mary, *13 Danish Tales*

The first to complain would forfeit the prize, but "foolish Hans" proved both witty and resourceful. Delightful.

"Boots and the Troll" in Haviland, Virginia, *Favorite Fairy Tales Told in Norway*

Cumulative nonsense in a familiar droll from Norway, a variant of Esben but just enough different to be interesting.

Princes and Princesses

"Esben Ashblower" in Hatch, Mary, *13 Danish Tales*

Not the witch-Esben tale, but another Esben who outwitted both his fine brothers, and the princess who chattered like a jay-bird. Easy pace, obvious humor, and well-liked.

"The Princess Who Could Not Cry" in Adams, Kathleen, and Atchinson, Frances, *A Book of Princess Stories*

Not that she couldn't cry, but that she laughed at the most unsuitable times! That was the problem. Now who could make this unfeeling bit of royalty behave?

"The Grateful Prince" in Lang, Andrew, *The Violet Fairy Book*

An exchange in babies, many mysterious happenings, smooth story line, and romance. Good fairy lore.

Brownies and Fairies

"The Black-bearded Brownies of Bonenberg" in Spicer, Dorothy, *13 Witches*

Since brownies come in all shapes and sizes, why not try this one with a witch and a Dutch flavor, for size?

"The Woman Who Flummoxed the Fairies" in Nic Leodhas, Sorche, *Heather and Broom*

Not by wit alone, but with a delicious cake also, did the clever housewife get the best of the mischievous fairies. Fun.

"The Fairy Cobbler" in Fyleman, Rose, *Tea Time Tales*

Modern whimsy. See Cobbler's Bench program, page 88.

Pixies and Piskey Folk

"The Spinning Plate" in Bleeker, Mary N., *Big Music*

West Cornwall, a clan of piskey men, and a plate with a mind of its own, befuddle a miner and his wife in this droll.

"The Pixie's Scarf" in Werner, Jane, *The Giant Golden Book of Elves and Fairies*

> A pocketful of pixie marbles in exchange for the scarf he found among the whortle-berries—but the marbles were worth a fortune!

"The Tune of Iolo ap Hugh" in Belting, Natalia, *Elves and Ellefolk*

> A violinist, a strange little tune, a haunted cave, and a bit of Welsh uncanniness. Short, interesting, with an All-Hallows Eve setting, so it might also be used at Halloween.

Leprechauns and Little People

"The Hillman and the Housewife" in Hutchinson, Veronica, *Candlelight Stories*

> The stingy housewife cheated the wee hill-man with a leaky pan, and the deed was returned in kind after all, plus! Short, funny, and flavorful.

"The Widow and the Korrigans" in Belting, Natalia, *Elves and Ellefolk*

> The gift of the tiny korrigans was more than the kindly widow had bargained for in this fascinating, short tale from Brittany.

"Patrick O'Donnell and the Leprechauns" in Haviland, Virginia, *Favorite Fairy Tales Told in Ireland*

> A stout spade to dig the treasure the leprechauns had pointed out, but whenever did a wee leprechaun keep his word? Easy to tell, bounces along with the "luck o' the Irish" for flavor.

Water Nixies, Sprites, and Nymphs

"The Water Nixy" in Lang, Andrew, *The Yellow Fairy Book*

> Poverty-stricken, the miller was desperate, so when the nixy asked for the youngest thing in his household, he promised it, to his sorrow. An unusual Grimm märchen.

"The Boy and the Water-Sprite" in Haviland, Virginia, *Favorite Fairy Tales Told in Sweden*

> What can you do when your inheritance is a piece of rope? A lot—if you have the wit and the will. Easy to tell.

"Echo and Narcissus" in White, Anne T., *The Golden Treasury of Myth and Legend*

> The lovely Greek myth of the nymph and the vain young man.

Mermaids and Kelpies

"The Mermaid and the Boy" in Lang, Andrew, *The Brown Fairy Book*

> The mermaid claimed the firstborn child, and to elude her, the boy ran away, but met with a series of enchantments. Not too long, and intriguing.

"The Three Mermaids" in Manning-Sanders, Ruth, *A Book of Mermaids* (Also in her collection *A Choice of Magic*.)

> The story is reminiscent of "Mother Holle" (Arbuthnot — *Time*) — goodness rewarded, rudeness punished. Well paced and full of action.

"Rake-up" in Manning-Sanders, Ruth, *A Choice of Magic*

> The mermaid who kept the sea cattle on the village meadow agreed to pay the debt with three jeweled girdles . . . which led to an interesting state of affairs for the greedy villagers! Little-known Danish tale.

Kings and Queens

"The Frog King" in Arbuthnot, May Hill, *Time for Fairy Tales*

> Spoiled princess, golden ball, and helpful ugly frog . . . and the king made his daughter keep her promise, willy nilly!

"Queen Crane" in Baker, Augusta, *The Golden Lynx*

> Romantic fairy story of enchantment and trials and rewards. Good, and not too difficult.

"To Your Good Health!" in Lang, Andrew, *The Crimson Fairy Book*

> Of course the young man would toast the king—but on his own terms.

THE COBBLER'S BENCH

There was a little cobbler,
I never heard his name.
I never saw his little shop,
I know him, just the same.

He bent above his cobbler's bench,
And sang a merry song;
Old shoes he patched, torn shoes he sewed
And made them whole and strong.

A bit of news he'd pass along;
Old stories he could tell.
Sometimes he'd pull an aching tooth,
Or tan a hide, as well.

The cobbler busy at his bench
Was loved by young and old,
Both for the shoes he made like new,
And for the tales he told.

O many little cobblers
Whose names we'll never know,
The self-same stories that you told
Are ours, from long ago!

—de Wit

In far-off days in Europe, the village cobbler was often the agent for passing on information, gossip, news, and tales heard from many sources to customers. When cobblers and shoemakers (there was a difference; originally the shoemaker made new footwear, while the cobbler only mended the old ones) joined the stream of people emigrating to the new hemisphere, they continued in their traditional position until the Industrial Revolution, with its technology, pushed them out of practice.

In America, as the frontier opened and people moved west, the cobbler often became itinerant, traveling to the remote settlements as shoemender, and often dentist as well; wherever a small shop was opened, it became the forum for public debate in the east and farther west, as patrons waited for their footgear, and lively points of view were exchanged. Old cobblers are fascinating, with the possibilities they might have had as raconteurs and as a channel for the oral tradition. How many treasures might have been chucked into those little drawers and cubbyholes in the old cobbler's bench! This seemed to be a picture that might intrigue American children, with their varied immigrant roots and inheritances of folklore and customs from many ethnic backgrounds. Perhaps a story hour built around this picturesque personality might encourage ethnic pride, as well as enjoyment in a community rapidly changing and Americanizing! Thus was the first priority established for A Cobbler's Bench story hour.

The second objective was to include in this program some audiovisual material and some poetry. The poetry is not included in this book, but was a part of the children's brochures. Films cannot take the place of storytelling, and they are everywhere around us, while storytelling is seldom experienced by modern children outside of the public library. Nevertheless, there are times when a film or a filmstrip can supplement a story hour and add vividness. And the love of poetry should be a factor cultivated more intensively by those who work with children.

Finally, many modern well-written fantasies can spice the storytelling program. In preparation for this particular program, the storyteller browsed widely in this genre of literature. In the storytelling brochure, many varieties of footgear were used as line sketches to set off the programs and the poetry.

Introducing the Shoemaker's Shop: To begin the season, the shop and the cobbler as an intriguing purveyor of oral tradition were introduced. First, a whimsical fantasy told in another program, "The Fairy Cobbler," then a lively film version of an Anansi spider story showing how the African tales took their name; finally, a variant of that same story in quite different illustrative form by Gail Haley, "A Story, a Story."

Shoemakers and Cobblers: From that program the stories journeyed to meet the shoemakers of Germany, England, and Denmark: "The Cobbler's Dilemma," an amusing picture story; a lyrical retelling of "The Elves and the Shoemaker" called "The Secret Shoemakers"; and finally, from Denmark, "The Obstinate Shoemaker" as found in an old Danish folk collection.

Shoemakers and Saints: The third program introduced the halo around the head of the old shoemaker in the legend of "St. Martin and the Honest Man," in Padraic Colum's version. St. Crispin is the shoemaker's saint, and a rhymed description of his celebration is found in Natalia Belting's A Winter's Eve. The storyteller used portions of the verse, "St. Crispin, the Shoemaker's Saint," then gave a brief retelling, illustrated with pictures from that book that engendered group participation. The concluding story, "The Cobbler's Luck," was taken from a very old Italian collection.

Halloween Shoemaking: The Halloween story hour was next, opening with "The Witches' Shoes," a story that reflected the superstitions of Appalachia, followed by "Queer Company," an eerie, cumulative tale from England, and completed with "The Tale of the Hairy Toe," a variant of "Chunk o' Meat'' and ''The Golden Arm'' with the same sort of scare ending.

Cobbler's Magic: This program included the film ''Shoemaker and the Elves,'' followed by an Arabic play-on-words tale called ''The Cobbler Astrologer and the Forty Thieves.''

Apprentice Helpers: The hour opened with a merry Polish folktale, ''Cobbler Kopytko and Drake Kwak,'' then a droll from the Grimm *Household Tales*, ''Lucky Hans,'' and finished with an easy-going variant of ''The Pedlar of Swaffham,'' ''The Fortunate Shoemaker.''

Leather and Cobbler's Aprons: The first story was a funny one repeated from the previous year, ''The Shoemaker's Apron,'' and that sly humor was offset by a Finnish droll about ''The Mouse Who Turned Tailor.'' The program concluded with a short, cheerful story entitled simply ''The Cobbler's Tale.'' After this series of programs introducing the cobbler as a teller of tales, the program switched emphasis to related areas involving footgear and such activities as dancing, racing, and walking, lest the listeners tire of hearing ''shoemaker,'' ad infinitum!

Thanksgiving: ''The Quick-running Squash'' opened up, followed by ''Slipfoot,'' from Carl Sandburg's *Rootabaga Stories*. To retain the distinctive word patterns, the storyteller read this, then concluded the story hour with an animal folktale from Russia, ''The Cobbler's Dog.''

Boots Magic: A. A. Milne's verse on ''waterproof boots and Macintoshes'' plunged the story group into December, and Boots Magic. Of course the most famous ones are the seven league boots of ''Hop o' My Thumb,'' somewhat familiar to many, as was ''Puss in Boots'' in Perrault's elegant fairy tale, told through a film with puppet protagonists. In complete contrast, the final story was a tall tale to elicit chuckles, ''The Moaning Boots.''

One Foot, Two Foot: This program began with an American droll, ''Brother Rabbit and His Famous Foot,'' followed by ''Nippit Fit and Clippit Fit,'' rhymed and tart; and a short, clever animal story from India, ''Little Toe Bone.''

Stockings and Socks: ''How the Flamingos Got Their Pink Stockings'' had a subtle Amazon flavor. Eleanor Farjeon's lovely retelling of the legend of ''Bertha Goldfoot'' was followed by a modern fantasy, ''A Hole in Your Stocking,'' quietly humorous.

Cobbler's Christmas: This story hour opened with Coppée's ''The Sabot of Little Wolff,'' then, to everyone's satisfaction, appeared the most delightful of all cobblers at Christmas, ''Schnitzle, Schnotzle, and Schnootzle.'' That could be used every year and not fail! ''Baby Bears' Christmas Stockings'' is very short, and especially for the younger children.

A New Year—A New Step: The Spanish teller says, ''Shoes mended, story ended! Come further, here's another!'' And another it was, on Twelfth Night or Three Kings' Day, January 6, which coincided with the first story hour of the new year. First, from Italy, was the quick short story of ''Piccola'' and her wooden shoe. De la Mare's Twelfth Night version of ''Cinderella'' followed, and then a modern story about the traditional Mummer's Parade held each New Year's Day in Philadelphia, ''Patrick and the Golden Slippers.'' This beautiful retelling of the Cinderella story is enhanced if Marcia Brown's lavishly illustrated edition is also shown, because she has pictured the palace setting so elegantly.

Legs and Other Such: This opened with ''Blue Legs,'' a strong Acoma Indian tale. It needed the scary fun of ''The Leg of Gold'' and the naiveté of the black folktale ''The Knee-hi Man'' to balance it.

Puddle-walking: ''The Galoshes of Fortune'' is appropriate, and can be used with this group if only the first section is told with very minor abridgements. Exactly opposite to Andersen's rather sophisticated plot was the down-to-earth wit of ''A Man and His Boots,'' an Uncle Remus tale giving insight into human nature. In contrast, the nitwit behavior of ''Where Were the Rubbers?'' and Mrs. Goose affords a change of pace.

A Stamp, a Kick, or a Jump: ''The Butterfly That Stamped'' is one of the more sophisticated *Just So Stories*; a good contrast is ''Jump, Jump, Jump the Highest,'' a funny why story from Groningen, Holland. The program closed with the short Navajo legend surrounding a huge rock, ''The-Giant-Who-Kicks-People-Down-Cliffs.''

Just Shoes: ''Squeaky Shoes'' was adapted from *Down, Down the Mountain*, a Blue Ridge story written in simple, unaffected style. Then came ''Nannie's Shoes,'' a somewhat imaginative and sentimental story, and ''Mr. Dog's New Shoes,'' Uncle Remus trickster-fun, with humor as broad as the shoes themselves!

Not Just Shoes: This program had a nice variety to it: a modern funny story, "The King Who Said Shoes Were Hats"; a noodlehead tale from Jewish sources, "All Because of a Pair of Shoes"; and finally, a variant of the Gullah Sea-Island tale, "Buh Fox's Numbah Nine Shoes." If the last is told gently, with very deliberate timing, it is very witty.

A Matter of Slippers: "Abu Kassim's Slippers" is an age-old Near East legend. It contrasts with the brief, sad story from China, "The Magic Silk Slippers," in every way. "The White Slipper" is a romantic fairy tale, neither too long nor demanding.

For Special Wear: Two modern fantasies were programmed, the first an illustrated story, "The Horse with the High-heeled Shoes," and second "The Shoes Fit for a King." Neither is a lasting tale, but both are whimsical, move quickly, and contrasted well with "The Magic Flying Shoes," a science fiction folktale from ancient China!

A Kind of a Sort of a Shoe: The opening story, "Singeli's Silver Slippers" is set in Sweden; "A Matter of Brogues," Ruth Sawyer's warm Irish story, is drawn from traditional sources; and "The Magic Moccasins" is an unusual Indian fairy tale.

Time for Dancing began with the Grimm variant "The Dancing Shoes," a traditional fairy story, more familiarly known as "The Twelve Dancing Princesses." "Nella's Dancing Shoes" is a gentle moral tale in Farjeon's beautiful style. Against these was balanced a trickster tale from Tyll Eulenspiegel, "The Tale of a Merry Dance," wherein, as usual, Tyll comes out on top!

Fairy Shoemakers for Saint Patrick: St. Patrick's Day calls for the leprechauns; therefore the program began with an Irish story, "Where Hidden Treasure Lies," a modern tale. Then a rare Irish fairy tale, "Murdoch's Rath," rich in fancy; and finally the lilt of Scotland in "The Laird's Lass and the Gobha's Son."

Frisky Feet: This program opened with an Indian trickster tale of foolish Manabozo, "The Goose Dance," then jumped to Japan and the merry folktale "The Dancing Kettle," and finished with a modern Highland-fling story, "The Patchwork Kilt." This particular program really frisked along!

Let's Go Walking: "The Cat That Walked by Himself," a *Just So* story, long, complex, and without equal for its genre, started the program; the two following stories needed to be very brief and informal—a humorous Welsh bit, "The Fairy Walk-ing Stick," and an excerpt from a long Irish narrative, "Boots on the Wrong Feet." However, in retrospect, a short animal fable might have provided a better balance.

Feet That Won't Behave: The same can be said of the first section of the following program; although "The Skipping Shoes" was an interesting sidelight into Louisa May Alcott, it proved not to be as good for oral presentation as for silent reading, sounding somewhat old-fashioned. "The King's Stilts," a Seuss fantasy with an outrageous plot and rollicking action, on the other hand, made for excellent telling and did not need the pictures to be enjoyed. "The Travelling Companions," a delightful variant on the "Bremen Town Musicians," provided a good contrast.

Footprints and Footsteps for Easter: "The Country Bunny and the Little Gold Shoes" was excellent, but was so long that time only allowed for the brief allegory, "Unda Marina's Footprints," retold from Topelius, and a bit of folklore from the Isle of Rogen, "The Little Glass Slipper."

Running Races: This program was interesting because it was comprised of all Indian stories—a Saynday trickster story from the Kiowa tribe, "How Saynday Ran a Race with Coyote"; and two variants on the fable of the hare and the tortoise race: "Coyote Helps Turtle Win a Race with Paisano, the Roadrunner," from the Southwest near Mexico; and a Big-Long-Man story from the Navajo, "How Badger Won a Race with Grey Rabbit." All of the stories were humorous, and since each had different characters and a different sort of local color, this was refreshing for a change.

Well-shod and Merry, Let's Go on a Journey: Three stories, well-known and well-liked were used to end the year's program: "How Six Traveled the World," the Grimm variant on the Flying Ship motif; "With a Wig, with a Wag," the rhythmic American variant of an old Irish droll; and "Travels of a Fox," a cumulative story especially liked by younger children.

Themes and Stories
Introducing the Shoemaker's Shop
"The Fairy Cobbler" in Fyleman, Rose, *Tea Time Tales*

> There was magic in the cobbler's leather, and it was good or bad depending on whose shoes the cobbler mended. A whimsical story

somewhat similar to "Murdoch's Rath" (Power—*Stories*), easy to tell and rather short.

Anansi, the Spider, 16mm film, color, 10 min. Distributed by Texture Films, 1600 Broadway, New York, N.Y. 10019

"A Story, a Story" in Haley, Gail, *A Story, a Story*

> A beautifully illustrated single edition of the African story explaining why Anansi stories are called spider stories. Excellent atmosphere. A Caldecott winner.

Shoemakers and Cobblers

"The Cobbler's Dilemma" in Werth, Kurt, *The Cobbler's Dilemma*

> An Italian variant of "The Lad Who Went to the North Wind" (Power—*Caravan*), but the villain in this droll is Cobbler Simon's own busy tongue. Fun to tell, rhythmic, of average length.

"The Secret Shoemakers" in Reeves, James, *Secret Shoemakers*

> James Reeves's simple and lovely version of the familiar Grimm tale, "The Elves and the Shoemaker," in short, flowing style.

"The Obstinate Shoemaker" in Bay, Jens C., *Danish Fairy and Folk Tales*

> Old Danish droll—the question: who would speak—not the last word, but the first! Short, epigrammatic.

Shoemakers and Saints

"St. Martin and the Honest Man" in Colum, Padraic, *The Stone of Victory*

> St. Martin, the good saint, disguises himself to see if he can find an honest man somewhere, and does, with surprising results.

"St. Crispin, the Shoemaker's Saint" in Belting, Natalia, *A Winter's Eve*

> A poetic version of the festival of the shoemakers on St. Crispin's Eve in medieval times. Must be well timed, but affords an interesting contrast.

"The Cobbler's Luck" in MacDonell, Anne, *The Italian Fairy Book*

> Good and easy to tell. Similar to "The Boy Who Was Never Afraid" (Hatch—*More Danish*). It is very long and in several parts; use only the first part, and add the end formula, "In a year and a day, the cobbler met the princess as she had promised and they married, for happy years to come!"

Halloween Shoemaking

"The Witches' Shoes" in Harper, Wilhelmina, *Ghosts and Goblins*

> Scary, and eerie enough for Halloween . . . See Holiday Stories, page 117.

"Queer Company" in Jacobs, Joseph, *English Fairy Tales*

> "And still she sat . . . and still . . . she rocked . . . and still she watched for company. . . ." Rhythmic, spell-binding, short. See also Holiday Stories, page 117.

"The Tale of the Hairy Toe" in Jagendorf, Moritz, *Ghostly Tales*

> Variant of old scare story. See Holiday Stories, page 117.

Cobbler's Magic

The Elves and the Shoemaker, 16mm film, color, 27 min. Distributed by International Film Bureau, 332 South Michigan Ave., Chicago, Ill. 60604.

"The Cobbler Astrologer and the Forty Thieves" in Hardendorff, Jeanne, *The Frog's Saddle Horse*

> Here is a subtle parallel to "Dr. Know-All" (Grimm—*Fairy* tr. Lucas) with the flavor of the Arabian Nights. Better for older children because of the play on words, and not difficult to tell, though somewhat long.

Apprentice Helpers

"Cobbler Kopytko and Drake Kwak" in Borski, Lucia, *The Jolly Tailor*

> The humor is very obvious and exaggerated in this Polish tale of a mischievous apprentice who learned compassion and won a princess for a wife. The story must be tightened, only a little of the introductory remarks given to sketch the unloved boy. Second and third grade children like it.

"Lucky Hans" in Wiggin, Kate D., and Smith, Nora, *Tales of Laughter*

> After working long for his money, Hans bargained it off, each time for something less valuable, till he ended with a stone. A Grimm (*Household*) variant of "What the Good Man Does Is Always Right" (Andersen—*Fairy* tr. Paull). Fun to tell, and very funny.

"The Fortunate Shoemaker" in Hardendorff, Jeanne, *Tricky Peik*

> Dutch Frisian variant of "The Pedlar of Swaffham" (Jacobs—*More English*) with a cobbler getting his rewards, justly or not. Witty and short.

Leather and Cobbler's Aprons

"The Shoemaker's Apron" in Fillmore, Parker, *The Shepherd's Nosegay*

> The terrible little shoemaker who outwitted the devil could not get into heaven either, till he threw his apron in first. Czech variant of an old devil legend, sly and humorous.

"The Mouse Who Turned Tailor" in Bowman, Cloyd, *Tales from a Finnish Tupa*

> Very short, witty, with the mouse outwitting the greedy puss, by giving him the short end of the leather! Also known as "Not Enough Leather."

"The Cobbler's Tale" in Association of Childhood Education, *Told under the Magic Umbrella*

> The king needed a soft—a very soft—shoe for his aching toes, and one day he found it, courtesy of the court cat! Whimsical and friendly.

Thanksgiving

"The Quick-running Squash" in Aspinwall, Alicia, *Short Tales for Short People*

> For Thanksgiving. See Holiday Stories, page 118.

"Slipfoot" in Sandburg, Carl, *Rootabaga Stories*

> One of the rhythmic, nonsense fantasies Sandburg created so well, which must be told in his language. Appeals especially to younger children.

"The Cobbler Dog" in Borski, Lucia, *The Gypsy and the Bear*

> A Russian pourquoi story of how the dog came to live with man.

Boots Magic

"Hop o' My Thumb" in Rackham, Arthur, *Arthur Rackham's Fairy Book*

> Hop o' My Thumb won the ogre's gold and saved his six brothers though he was no bigger than his father's thumb. Swashbuckling adventure with Rackham's vivid pictures.

"Puss in Boots" 16mm film, animated paper silhouettes, 10 min. Distributed by Madison Project, c/o Weston Woods Studio, Weston Woods, Conn. 06880

"The Moaning Boots" in Rounds, Glen, *Ol' Paul*

> One winter Ol' Paul got a hoodoo in his boots that moaned every time trouble was about to hit! A hilarious tall tale for older children, especially boys. Not easy to tell.

One Foot, Two Foot

"Brother Rabbit and His Famous Foot" in Harris, Joel Chandler, *Nights with Uncle Remus*

> A rabbit's foot is luck even for Br'er Rabbit until Br'er Wolf steals it! Short and funny. Modify the dialect, the children love the humor; or use Margaret Wise Brown's version, from *Br'er Rabbit*.

"Nippit Fit and Clippit Fit" in Grierson, Elizabeth, *The Scottish Fairy Book*

> A Scotch variant of Cinderella, with the emphasis on the glass slipper, a talking bird, and a huge cauldron. Nice for a change.

"Little Toe Bone" in Williston, Teresa, *Hindu Folk and Fairy Tales*

> A strange, eerie little story from India with a surprise ending that might be used to finish off a story hour. The situation is so ridiculous it would not frighten little children.

Stockings and Socks

"How the Flamingos Got Their Pink Stockings" in Quiroga, Horacio, *South American Jungle Tales*

> The flamingos dressed their skinny legs in coral snake skins, and the coral snakes recognized that! Different and funny, a pourquoi story from the Amazon Indians.

"Bertha Goldfoot" in Farjeon, Eleanor, *Old Nurse's Stocking Basket*

> To the baron's newborn daughter, the lorelei gave the gift of a gold foot—the imp, the gift of a perpetual hole in her stocking! One gift won a husband, the other lost a king. Short, with lilting style.

"A Hole in Your Stocking" in Reeves, James, *A Golden Land*

> Reeves's distinguished style in a bit of fantasy. Short and delightful.

Cobbler's Christmas

"The Sabot of Little Wolff" in Walters, Maude A., *A Book of Christmas Stories*

> See Holiday Stories, page 119.

"Schnitzle, Schnotzle, and Schnootzle" in Sawyer, Ruth, *The Long Christmas*

> See Holiday Stories, page 118.

"Baby Bears' Christmas Stockings" in Walters, Maude A., *A Book of Christmas Stories*

> See Holiday Stories, page 119.

A New Year—A New Step

"Piccola" in Walters, Maude A., *A Book of Christmas Stories*

> See Holiday Stories, page 119.

"Cinderella" in de la Mare, Walter, *Told Again*

> Beautiful prose, in a Twelfth Night version of this tale. See Holiday Stories, page 115.

"Patrick and the Golden Slippers" in Milhous, Katherine, *Patrick and the Golden Slippers*

> See New Year's Holiday Stories, page 115.

Legs and Other Such

"Blue Legs" in Rushmore, Helen, *The Dancing Horses of Acoma*

> A stark Acoma Indian tale of cruelty and punishment, told with dignity, and an atmospheric feeling for the hot desert place of this tribe. Long; for older children.

"The Leg of Gold" in Manning-Sanders, Ruth, *Book of Ghosts and Goblins*

> Scare story, this time with a fine French touch. Good, very short.

"The Knee-hi Man" in Carmer, Carl, *America Sings*

> Brief, pointed, and humorous. Carmer's style is more lilting than that of Julius Lester, who also tells this in his book of the same title. Story should end with the little knee-high man walking off into the swamp singing. Both tell very well.

Puddle-walking

"The Galoshes of Fortune" in Andersen, Hans Christian, *Fairy Tales* (tr. Lucas)

> An unusual story. The introduction and the councillor's tale make interesting fare for older children, with the 300-year flashback of past and present. Should be tightened a bit. This story can be used with junior high children also.

"A Man and His Boots" in Field, Rachel, *American Folk and Fairy Tales*

> Uncle Remus story, witty and full of wisdom concerning keeping what doesn't belong to one. Delete much of the dialect.

"Where Were the Rubbers?" in Potter, Miriam, *Mrs. Goose*

> An excerpt from the modern tale about absent-minded Mrs. Goose, who always does everything upside down. Fun for younger ones.

A Stamp, a Kick, or a Jump

"Butterfly That Stamped" in Kipling, Rudyard, *Just So Stories*

> This should be told in Kipling's words, but may be slightly abridged for the story hour. The story stars the wise Balkis who could make the sultan toe the line by her clever wiles.

"Jump, Jump, Jump the Highest!" in Olcott, Frances, *Wonder Tales from Windmill Lands*

> Abelstickdrawbridge in Groningen has its own version of how that remarkable name came about! Funny and short.

"The - Giant - Who - Kicks - People - Down - Cliffs" in Hogner, Dorothy, *Navajo Winter Nights*

> The Navajos have a legend about a terrible but stupid giant. They can even point to the place he occupied.

Just Shoes

"Squeaky Shoes" in Credle, Ellis, *Down, Down the Mountain*

> Blue Ridge tale of two children who raised turnips to buy the wonderful squeaky shoes they so coveted. Well-liked.

"Nannie's Shoes" in Colum, Padraic, *The Big Tree of Bunlahy*

> Somehow the people in the big house, and the new shoes, and the man who was drowned when Nannie was a baby were all mixed up, wound together around a ball of blue yarn. Written in Padraic Colum's fine style.

"Mr. Dog's New Shoes" in Harris, Joel Chandler, *Favorite Uncle Remus*

> If one tries on one shoe, he ought to try on the other, shouldn't he? So Br'er Rabbit thought, and proved! Can be told without strong dialect, and is just as funny.

Not Just Shoes

"The King Who Said Shoes Were Hats" in Alker, Dorothy, *Stories*

> King Dobble was always right, so when he decreed that shoes were hats, and hats were shoes—that's the way it was! A light, humorous story.

"All because of a Pair of Shoes!" in Simon, Solomon, *The Wise Men of Helm and Their Merry Pranks*

> Pinya, sometime philosopher for the noodle-

heads of Helm, was sent to Warsaw to solve the big problem—but how to get to Warsaw? He would set his shoes pointing there and on waking he would know the direction. So what happened?

"Buh Fox's Numbah Nine Shoes" in Courlander, Harold, *Terrapin's Pot of Sense*

One trickster outsmarts another in this amusing story from the Georgia Sea Islands. However, the Gullah dialect should be modified for better understanding.

A Matter of Slippers

"Abu Kassim's Slippers" in Green, Nancy, *Abu Kassim's Slippers*

A wise and funny legend from Arabia about the stingy rich man and the shoes that betrayed him over and over. Funny, many variants. Long.

"The Magic Silk Slipper" in Lim, Sian-Tek, *More Folk Tales from China*

When a silk slipper can produce a wonderful wife, what more could a Chinese scholar want? Short and wise, a transformation story.

"The White Slipper" in Lang, Andrew, *The Orange Fairy Book*

Only the young apprentice knew the secret alchemy which would cure the king's ailing foot—and he was willing to undertake the difficulties involved. Romantic and good, very satisfying.

For Special Wear

"The Horse with the High-heeled Shoes" in Slobodkin, Louis, *The Horse with the High-heeled Shoes*

A modern illustrated fantasy about a very special sort of horse, in a very special sort of place. Lots of fun to tell.

"The Shoes Fit for a King" in Bill, Helen, *Shoes Fit for a King*

Modern make-believe concerning a most remarkable pair of shoes that suited a king, when the shoes had almost given up all hope of being used.

"The Magic Flying Shoes" in Lim, Sian-Tek, *More Folk Tales from China*

A brief bit of magic, almost an epigram, of shoes that were not what they seemed, in this ancient Chinese tale.

A Kind of a Sort of a Shoe

"Singeli's Silver Slippers" in Werner, Jane, *The Giant Golden Book of Elves and Fairies*

A Swedish fairy story of the little one who sewed silver slippers and became a queen. Even today they say a falling star is the passing of her silver slippers across the sky. Charming.

"A Matter of Brogues" in Sawyer, Ruth, *The Way of the Storyteller*

With the lilt of the Irish, and the magic of love and fiddle music, the shoes have a way of their own. Delightful to tell.

"The Magic Moccasins" in Judd, Mary C., *Wigwam Tales*

A strange and thoughtful Indian story of moccasins that were bewitched, and the unusual journeys they took. For older children.

Time for Dancing

"The Dancing Shoes" in Grimm, Jakob, and Grimm, Wilhelm, *Household Stories*

Variant of the "Twelve Dancing Princesses" (Dalgleish), shorter and less beautiful, but brisker.

"Nella's Dancing Shoes" in Farjeon, Eleanor, *Italian Peep Show*

Red velvet dancing slippers made Nella the loveliest dancer in all of Florence—until the day they disappeared. Modern fantasy by a modern poet.

"The Tale of a Merry Dance" in Jagendorf, Moritz, *Tyll Eulenspiegel's Merry Pranks*

Naughty Tyll became a high-wire artist, using everyone's shoes—to the dismay of all the villagers who had come to the fair. Of course he won! Wry humor.

Fairy Shoemakers for Saint Patrick

"Where Hidden Treasure Lies" in Werner, Jane, *The Giant Golden Book of Elves and Fairies*

Leprechauns and hidden gold—but ah, the trickery of them all! Modern Irish fantasy but with a folklore feeling.

"Murdoch's Rath" in Power, Effie, *Stories to Shorten the Road*

Mystery and magic, and dancing shoes all on a fairy rath. An old, choice story.

"The Laird's Lass and the Gobha's Son" in Nic Leodhas, Sorche, *Thistle and Thyme*

The gobha's son was a blacksmith, too, and the lass was very willful . . . but so lovely! Not for the blacksmith, though, was she! Tight plot, good feeling for place.

Frisky Feet

"The Goose Dance" in Leekley, Thomas, *The World of Manabozo*

Manabozo, the trickster of the Central Woodland Indians, tricks the foolish geese into becoming a delightful dinner. Witty.

"The Dancing Kettle" in Uchida, Yoshiko, *The Dancing Kettle*

Brave little, curious little, merry little kettle that danced a fortune into the kind priest's empty pockets.

"The Patchwork Kilt" in Watts, Mabel, *The Patchwork Kilt*

Stunning black and white illustrations and a winsome lass who, for lack of a kiltie, made one, taking a bit of her uncle's shirt, and a bit of the auntie's scarf, and so on and on! She did her highland fling!

Let's Go Walking

"The Cat That Walked by Himself" in Kipling, Rudyard, *Just So Stories*

An irresistible story fantasized by a master of the art, presenting the cat who is never quite domesticated! Must use Kipling's words.

"The Fairy Walking Stick" in Thomas, William, *The Welsh Fairy Book*

So wee, and so forlorn was the tiny girl the Welsh farmer rescued—and he did not expect any reward—but it came. Short, and good.

"Boots on the Wrong Feet" in Lynch, Patricia, *The Turfcutter's Donkey*

A brief enticing excerpt from the long Irish story of two children who caught a leprechaun. An ending should be added, since this is an excerpt.

Feet That Won't Behave

"The Skipping Shoes" in Alcott, Louisa May, *Lulu's Library*

Midsummer Day, and the shoes had a mind of their own . . . and nothing Kitty could say would stop them from doing what they wanted to do, whether or not Kitty liked it. A little old-fashioned.

"The King's Stilts" in Seuss, Dr., *The King's Stilts*

Marvelous stilts of King Bitrim, his joy in life until the day they disappeared. Then the whole kingdom began to fall apart. Modern fantasy on a grand scale. Very rhythmic.

"The Travelling Companions" in Fisher, Agnes, *Once upon a Time*

Amusing variant of the "Bremen Town Musicians" (Grimm—*Bremen*), with two children as the protagonists, plus a pig, a needle, duck, fish, rooster, horse, and a merry goblin to boot.

Footprints and Footsteps for Easter

"The Country Bunny and The Little Gold Shoes" in Heyward, DuBose, *"The Country Bunny and the Little Gold Shoes*

Long, well-loved story of the first Easter bunny and her houseful of industrious children. Very nice.

"Unda Marina's Footprints" in Topelius, Zacharias, *Canute Whistlewinks*

Finnish allegory of the waves and the pattern they leave on the sand. Must be adapted.

"The Little Glass Slipper" in Olcott, Frances, *Wonder Tales from Goblin Hills*

Greedy farmer, mischievous brown dwarfs, and a tiny glass shoe. Unusual, a tale from the Baltic Sea island of Rogen.

Running Races

"How Saynday Ran a Race with Coyote" in Marriott, Alice, *Winter Telling Stories*

The wry, funny story of old Saynday, Kiowa trickster, who got his comeuppance from sly coyote as he deserved.

"Coyote Helps Turtle Win a Race with Paisano, the Roadrunner" in Peck, Leigh, *Don Coyote*

Southwest Spanish-Indian story of his highness, the rascal Don Coyote, this time in a variant of "Hare and Turtle."

"How Badger Won a Race With Grey Rabbit" in Hogner, Dorothy, *Navajo Winter Nights*

Another variant of the "Hare and Turtle" race, but colored with a bright Navajo design. Short and funny.

Well-shod and Merry, Let's Go on a Journey

"How Six Traveled the World" in Grimm, Jakob, and Grimm, Wilhelm, *Grimm's Fairy Tales*

A variant of the Flying Ship motif, but with a rough and tumble, earthy flavor from the

German countryside. Easy to tell and full of action.

"With a Wig, with a Wag" in Cothran, Jean, *With a Wig, with a Wag*

An old hag who tries to best three fortune-seeking brothers, finds herself outwitted by the youngest. A variant, country style, of the Irish story, "Old Hag's Long Leather Bag" (Wiggin-Smith—*Fairy*). Brisk and rhythmic.

"Travels of a Fox" in Arbuthnot, May Hill, *Time for Fairy Tales*

Rollicking along with a bag that never gets emptied until the last, fatal trade is made! Familiar, and lots of fun to tell.

STORY JOURNEYS

One of the objectives of this program was to weave good modern fantasies and modern short stories into the traditional folklore of the story hours wherever possible. Another objective was to use any well-illustrated editions of folk and fairy tales available; too many children today do nothing to help their artistic appreciations grow after leaving preschool and kindergarten picture story presentations, and so many of the illustrated editions far too difficult to use in the younger story periods are unknown to the children of school age. This is particularly true of such outstanding illustrators as Shulevitz, Brown, Daugherty, and Duvoisin. The story hour had been lengthened to forty-five minutes this year, allowing for more freedom of choice.

By Foot and Walking Stick: This imaginative Journeys story program began with an old American variant of "Gingerbread Boy," the merry "Journey Cake, Ho!" The second story was Howard Pyle's pungent tale, "Claus and His Wonderful Staff," both magic and commonsensical; then a droll, "The Kettle That Would Not Walk," and finally, for variety, a Juan Bobo nonsense tale from Costa Rica, "The Magic Stick."

In Boats, Canoes, and Kayaks: The program opened with a nitwit tale of foolish fishermen, very brief and funny—"The People of Mols." "Hidden Laiva and the Golden Ship," long and romantic, had as its counterfoil a brusque comical tale, "The

Canoe in the Rapids," with French-Canadian syntax in its style. The final story was a most unusual Arctic Indian legend of a young boy's bravery, "Blanket Boy and the Shaman."

With Faggots, Brooms, and Broomsticks: This began with the eerie "Fate and the Faggot-Gatherer," and continued with a modern fantasy by Rose Fyleman, "The Broom." A break in tempo then with the amusing illustrated fantasy by Carl Sandburg, "The Wedding Procession of the Rag Doll and the Broom Handle," followed by an enchanted touch of "The Sorcerer's Apprentice" in the Wanda Gág version.

Halloween Journeys: The Halloween program began with a short, scary tale, "The Ride on a Gravestone," retold from Russian sources. Then followed "The Witches' Ride," rhymed and witty with a Costa Rican rhyme to keynote the tale. "The Coffin That Moved Itself" is shivery; and a traditional hair-raising Russian witch story, "Baba Yaga and the Little Girl," finished the program with Baba Yaga racing through the air in her mortar and pestle!

Aloft on a Magic Carpet: "The Carpet of Solomon" opened here; it is very long and thought-provoking, but must be abridged and adapted for use in this story program. In contrast, "The Red Carpet" is rhymed, popular, a humorous picture story. The most beautiful and exciting in this group, however, was the Arabic romance, "The Flying Carpet," retold by Marcia Brown.

Horses! Horses! Horses!: This program spoke for itself through the genial folk character, Padre Porko, and "The General's Horse." These Spanish folktales, imbued with Celtic whimsy, are comfortable and gently paced; beside them, the Jugoslav tale of "The Sun Horse" was quite dramatic. Balance was maintained with the exaggerated humor of Baron Munchausen and "The Baron's Steed." To finish off, "The Little Horse of Seven Colors," brief and colorful Portuguese fairy story with the dry humor characteristic of that country, was used.

Perambulator, Pillow, Patchwork Quilt, and Litter: The next program featured exotic ways of journeying. "The Magic Perambulator" is a modern fantasy; "The Pillow of Content" is an epigram from ancient China; and "The Cock and the Cats Who Bore His Litter," is a fable that needed to be fleshed out somewhat in telling. "The Flying Patchwork Quilt" is make-believe that could happen anywhere at all, and just might. The program for this week did not have much humor per se, but the imaginative quality of the journeys made up for that.

Thanksgiving Journeys: The Thanksgiving program opened with the African trickster tale of "Kalulu's Pumpkins," clever and amusing; then "The Thanksgiving Dinner That Flew Away," a bit from colonial America; and finally the tall, tall tale from the Southern mountains, "The Perambulatin' Pumpkin," never to be taken seriously.

Riding a Bear, a Camel, a Tiger: This program was an adventure in planning. "Ali and the Camels" from Tripoli, and "Nine in a Line" from Arabia, are both variants on the miscounting motif, but since the backgrounds were different, and the style of narrative dissimilar, they balanced. (The second is also a picture version.) "The Man Who Rode a Bear" is the North Carolina variant of the Gallant Tailor told in colloquial mountain speech. "It All Began with a Drip" is a simplified Indic variant of the same tale in an illustrated format. The children recognized the relationships and found them amusing. However, such a program should be devised only once in a long while and then only for variety's sake.

Car, Carriage, Cart, or Pike?: A humorous modern story, "Gears and Gasoline," started off the next lap of journeys, followed by a short, beautifully written folktale, "At the Pike's Behest," with an alliterative refrain that invites participation. An illustrated edition of "The Deacon's One-Hoss Shay," a long Holmes poem, served as contrast to the Hindu tale, "The Cartman's Story." The rhythm of this particular story hour was erratic, but seemed acceptable, as a change of pace.

By Way of Water—Gondola, Lily Pad, or Peach: Timed for just before Christmas was a very traditional but beautiful story hour in which "Felice," the gondola cat of Italy, was set against Andersen's "Thumbelina." Both have unusual illustrations in the editions used. "Momotaro," the boy in the peach, pursues a merry course, slaying his ferocious enemies very cheerfully. The illustrations in "Thumbelina" should be shown afterwards, so as not to interrupt the line of the very long story.

Christmas Journeys: "The Voyage of the Wee Red Cap" opened the Christmas Journeys, and set the mood for "Torten's Christmas Secret," a magic journey on an amiable polar bear. Finally, the story "About a Noble Camel," about a camel immortalized by love, was used. "Torten" must be abridged for use in this program, but it is very suitable, and worth the effort.

On Sleigh, Snowshoes, and Skis: This program started with Baron Munchausen nonsense, "The Wolf and the Sled"; from there to Hawaii, with "The Strange Sled Race," a myth of the goddess Pele. "The Magic Snowshoes" returned the hour back to the Wabanaki Indians of Canada for a Glooscap tale; and then the listeners were hurled into a Swiss snowbank with Don Freeman's modern picture story of the St. Bernard "Ski-pup." That was a stretch of imagination for the children!

Journey into a New Year on a Flying Horse and Furry Feet: This program began with a fairy tale from Lithuania, "One Hundred Hares," a variant on "Jesper Who Herded the Hares." From that point the journey branched out to the Greek myth of "Pegasus, the Winged Horse," followed by a picture-format edition of a modern fantasy, "Two Hundred Rabbits"—ubiquitous setting, delightful humor! In "Gifts for the King," an Arabian Nights ebony horse rides to adventure and romance.

Trailer? Trendel? Or Top and Ball?: This program began with an eerie imaginative tale, "The Haunted Trailer," then introduced the Jewish Tom Thumb in "How K'tonton Took a Ride on a Runaway Trendel," a very merry ride indeed! The bittersweet irony of Andersen's "The Top and the Ball" added sharp contrast.

Swift as a Stag or a Deer: This story hour began with the fine Indian ghost tale "The Ghost of the Great White Stag," difficult to tell, long, and very appealing to older children. "The Banyan Deer" is a Jataka tale, moving and short. "Parrak, the White Reindeer" is a beautifully illustrated picture story from Lapland.

Aboard Engines, Arks, and Chariots: Journeys in innovative ways continued, this time with a fantasy based on the Biblical Ark, "The Giant Who Rode on the Ark"; then switched to an American tall tale, "The Fast Sooner Hound," followed by "The Chariot of Phaeton," a dramatic Greek myth. "The Wondrous Flying Chariot" conjured up an ancient space vehicle from China.

The Bigger the Better—Elephants and Whales: This program featured "The Little Elephant Who Wanted to Fly," wish fulfillment that went amiss.

Next to India, through the gay picture story of "The Elephants and the Mice" and Kipling's priceless "How the Whale Got His Throat," with its marvelous imagery and humor. An American popular tale from colonial New England, "Little Annie and the Whaler Captain," finished the story hour on a grand scale.

Things That Fly—Wax Wings, Airplanes, and Arrows: First offered were the wax wings of "Daedalus and Icarus," a contribution from Greek mythology. "Loopy," picture story of an obstreperous single-winged plane, followed, and contrasted with a Tlingit Indian legend, "The Angry Moon," with its startling graphics.

Donkeys and Goats and Little Gray Burros: Donkeys have always been an intriguing part of folklore, and "The Talking Donkey" proved to be no exception. Bechstein's retelling of this old German tale is smooth and finished. Then "Uncle Bouki Buys a Burro" in a Haitian folktale. The dramatic, illustrated Tsimshim legend "The Mountain Goats of Temlaham" fitted here; and adding a chuckle at the end was "Some Impatient Mule-drivers" with their ridiculous logic!

Cannonball, Clay Pot, Chopping Knife, and Drum: This program boasted real imagination in journeying, beginning with Baron Munchausen's "Ride on a Cannonball"; from that tall tale we went to Alexei Tolstoi's version of the folktale, "The Clay Manikin," a walking clay pot. Then a second and nearly fatal K'tonton adventure, "How K'tonton Took a Ride on a Chopping Knife," that contrasted with a witty picture version of the African folktale "When the Drum Sang."

Windy March Blows Kites, Bluebottles, and Baskets Aloft: In March, story kites were aloft, in China with "Fish in the Air"; while in France, Jonnikin took to the air in "Jonnikin and the Flying Basket," a long fairy tale. To finish, the pseudo-sad whimsey of the foolish "The Bluebottle Who Went Courting" and "The Picnic Basket" that took off by itself, a modern imaginative story.

Mules, Mares, Foals, and Fillies: Three fairy tales, each very distinctive, afforded sharp contrast to a Pennsylvania Dutch tall tale in this story program: "Fifine and the White Mare" (must be abridged); "The Prince and the Sky-Blue Filly," and the "Seven Foals," from Scandinavia, all versus "Soft-soap Satan," who literally foams at the mouth!

The Slow Way—Tugboat, Turtle, and Tortoise: This program found a Rip Van Winkle motif in the Japanese story of "Urashima Taro"; then an abrupt change in tone was provided in the picture story of redoubtable "Little Toot" the tugboat, and a rhythmic Anansi story from Jamaica, the tortoise "Bandalee."

Wind, Windwagon, and Wagon: A change of pace was indicated in "The Ride in the Night," a funny ghost story from New England; then, the cocky "Gillespie and the Guards," the picture story triumph of a little red wagon. "High Wind for Kansas," a prairie tall tale introducing Windwagon Smith, preceded the starkly beautiful "Ride the Cold Wind," a short story from Ecuador; the program was completed with "The Journey of the Breton Fishermen," a bit of French noodlehead folklore.

Easter Journeys: This program opened with the symbolic "Legend of St. Christopher" as retold by Eleanor Farjeon. A Kootenai Indian folktale, "Stealing the Springtime," introducing Skinkoots, the trickster, followed. In conclusion, the tender fantasy "The Song of the Little Donkey" made a good contrast.

Over the Deep in Schooner and Ship: To the roll of the ocean, the story program moved on, this time in three ghostly, very different, sea tales: "The Phantom Ship," from the Dutch canals; "The Skipper and the Witch," from the New England coasts; and "The Spectral Ship," a long engrossing narrative retold by Wilhelm Hauff from Moslem sources.

All of a Sudden—Umbrellas in the Air: With April came umbrellas, first with "The Umbrella-maker's Kozo," a brief bit from Japan; then a funny Haitian spook story, "Monsieur Jolicoeur's Umbrella." A recording by Sandburg of his Rootabaga tale, "How Six Umbrellas Took Off," was used, followed by an uncanny shred of Americana, "The Big Black Umbrella," and a picture story, "Professor Bull's Umbrella." This program may seem long, but it had much variety, and each selection was brief so the story hour as a whole was well-paced and delightful.

Bicycles, Birds, and Balloons: The items featured in this program were natural for trip-taking: "The Windbird and the Sun," an African pourquoi tale; "The Red Balloon," a photographic story based on a French adventure; "Jo-Ji and the

Dragon," following the excursion of a Japanese scarecrow in an exciting confrontation with a ghost; and finally, a bit of poetry about a weathervane, "The Pedaling Man."

Peacock Machines and Other Strange Things: And so the story season ended. From Ceylon, an ancient space ship, "The Wonderful Wooden Peacock Flying Machine" started this final journey; then a Caldecott picture fairy tale in marvelous color, "The Fool of the World and the Flying Ship." Next came a short Korean tale, "The Magic Snuff Box"; and, to bring the journeys to a conclusion, Andersen's delightful "The Flying Trunk." A closing party followed; the storyteller created a series of story riddles for the party that the children enjoyed and guessed surprisingly well.

Themes and Stories

Off and away on an arrow so bright!
To the moon on a wooden peacock flight!
Flying a ship with sails unfurled—
Story journeys all over the world—
In the really-real or the make-believe,
Wherever the story patterns weave
Caught on an umbrella—thrown to the wind—
Defying the sun with wings that bind,
Away on a journey, treasure to find!
Off and away in clay pot, and peach . . .
No limit where story journeys reach!

—de Wit

By Foot and Walking Stick

"Journey Cake, Ho!" in Sawyer, Ruth, *Journey Cake, Ho!*

> Mountain version of "The Gingerbread Boy," and delightfully illustrated with Robert McCloskey's art. American.

"Claus and His Wonderful Staff" in Pyle, Howard, *Pepper and Salt*

> A shape changing story, with Pyle's homely proverbs to heighten the delight and set off his unusual style. Possibly German.

"The Kettle That Would Not Walk" in Hutchinson, Veronica, *Fireside Stories*

> If one has two legs, he walks; if he has three, he carries another. So reasoned the merry men from Gotham. A familiar droll, short and brisk. English.

"The Magic Stick" in Osma, Lupe de, *The Witches' Ride*

> With his magic stick, Juan Bobo set off to marry the princess, all outfitted in his wide sombrero and red neckerchief, but she would not! Lots of adventure and laughter here, set in Costa Rican folklore.

In Boats, Canoes, and Kayaks

"The People of Mols" in Ross, Eulalie S., *The Buried Treasure*

> Like "The Wise Men of Helm" (Simon and "The Wise Men of Gotham" (Jacobs—*More English*), the people of Mols always came up with the wrong question for the right answer! Short, noodlehead humor. Scandinavian.

"Hidden Laiva and the Golden Ship" in Arbuthnot, May Hill, *Time for Fairy Tales*

> Finland's fairy tale variant of "The Flying Ship" (Ransome—*Old Peter's*), but yet unexpected. Similar to the "Nose Tree" (Jagendorf—*World*), only horns, not noses, grow.

"The Canoe in the Rapids" in Carlson, Natalie, *The Talking Cat*

> French-Canadian humor, with Sylvain Gagnon as the most skillful boatman of any— that is, until the bear came along!

"Blanket Boy and the Shaman" in Newell, Hope, *The Rescue of the Sun*

> The stark, arctic landscape is background for this story of a boy's courage in the face of strong magic. Not an easy story to tell, but a good one, especially for older boys.

With Faggots, Brooms, and Broomsticks

"Fate and the Faggot-Gatherer" in Jewett, Eleanor, *Which Was Witch?*

> When an unseen thief kept stealing his faggots, Kim Khodoury bound himself into the middle of one bundle to catch the man, but found himself pulled into the air and aloft on a magic flight who knew where? Intriguing Korean flavor.

"The Broom" in Fyleman, Rose, *Tea Time Tales*

> It certainly was strange to see the broom rise and streak for the moon! Could it have been lost by a witch? Short, humorous fantasy by a modern poet.

"The Wedding Procession of the Rag Doll and the Broom Handle" in Sandburg, Carl, *The Wedding Procession of the Rag Doll and the Broom Handle*

> From the Rootabaga stories, Sandburg's delicious nonsense in a single colorful edition, illustrated by Harriet Pincus.

"The Sorcerer's Apprentice" in Gág, Wanda, *More Tales from Grimm*

> A merry, but not very wise, apprentice tries to use his master's power—with dire results. German.

Halloween Journeys

"The Ride on a Gravestone" in Ralston, W. R. Sheddon, *Russian Fairy Tales*

> The bridegroom had only a few moments rest at his old friend's tomb . . . or had he? This story must be retold from the brief old sources Ralston gives, but it makes a good tale to tell. See page 53.

"The Witches' Ride" in Osma, Lupe de, *The Witches' Ride*

> No doubt of it, the broom was bewitched, but a riddle and a rhyme and a gift of laughter turned the trick nicely. The rhyme is the cue to this funny Costa Rican folk tale.

"The Coffin That Moved Itself" in Spicer, Dorothy, *13 Ghosts*

> A huge, slimy hole in North Gelderland, Holland, is spooky—and when the clouds are black across the full moon, then the ghost of the shepherd Klaas haunts the place. Good Halloween fare. See also Holiday Stories, page 117.

"Baba Yaga and the Little Girl" in Hoke, Helen, *Witches, Witches, Witches*

> Through the air in her mortar, steered by the pestle, flies Baba Yaga, looking for witchcraft . . . finding a little girl. . . . Russian.

Aloft on a Magic Carpet

"The Carpet of Solomon" in Ish-Kishor, Judith, *The Carpet of Solomon*

> An ancient legend of good and evil and mighty King Solomon. Beautifully written; must be abridged and adapted for story hour use, but well worth the effort. Good for older children.

"The Red Carpet" in Parkin, Rex, *The Red Carpet*

> A long rhymed extravaganza of the unpredictable carpet at the hotel. A favorite of many younger children.

"The Flying Carpet" in Brown, Marcia, *The Flying Carpet*

> A version, stunningly illustrated, of the old Arabian tale, with magic apple, spyglass, carpet and all.

Horses! Horses! Horses!

"The General's Horse" in Davis, Robert, *Padre Porko*

> The delightful Spanish gentleman-pig eases the general's horse of a painful nail in his hoof through cooperative dental work. Whimsical and likable.

"The Sun Horse" in Dobsinsky, Pavol, *The Enchanted Castle*

> A Slovakian fairy tale, somewhat long and romantic, on the same theme as "The Giant Who Had No Heart in His Body" (Dasent).

"The Baron's Steed" (or "The Divided Lithuanian") in Kästner, Erich, *Baron Munchausen*

> One of the Baron's exaggerated anecdotes, about the too-soon gate and the too-late horse, and the sad result! Very short and funny.

"The Little Horse of Seven Colors" in Lowe, Patricia, *The Little Horse of Seven Colors*

> Portuguese wry humor, and a magic horse waiting to work out a happy ending for the royal couple.

Perambulator, Pillow, Patchwork Quilt, and Litter

"The Magic Perambulator" in Brooks, Jeremy, *The Magic Perambulator*

> Modern fantasy of a sultan who had a lonely little daughter, much too young to ride on a magic carpet in her search for friends. But a magic perambulator—that might do the trick! Good illustrations, light fantasy.

"The Pillow of Content" in Lim, Sian-Tek, *More Folk Tales from China*

> The emptiness of riches, in a brief, telling epigram.

"The Cock and the Cats Who Bore His Litter" in Cooper, Frederick T., *An Argosy of Fables*

> A fable of the disdainful cock and the scheming cats. This has dramatic impact, but must be retold and amplified. Chinese. See page 52.

"The Flying Patchwork Quilt" in Brenner, Barbara, *The Flying Patchwork Quilt*

> Present-day fantasy of a quilt that was not content to stay in the bottom of the trunk, and thereby started a remarkable adventure. Fun to hear, easy to tell.

Thanksgiving Journeys

"Kalulu's Pumpkins" in Elliott, Geraldine, *Where the Long Grass Whispers*

> A very funny African tale about the trickster Kalulu and his remarkable pumpkins, with the elephant bearing the brunt of it all!

"Thanksgiving Dinner That Flew Away" in Harper, Wilhelmina, *The Harvest Feast*

> Fantasy of a different sort for Thanksgiving, short and easy to tell.

"The Perambulatin' Pumpkin" in Credle, Ellis, *Tall Tales from the High Hills*

> Wherever the pumpkin rolled, it left a trail of amazement and destruction. Long, tall tale humor, very funny.

Riding a Bear, a Camel, a Tiger

"Ali and the Camels" in Gilstrap, Robert, *The Sultan's Fool*

> Poor Ali could not count his fingers, his camels, or his beads! Tripolitan.

"The Man Who Rode a Bear" in Credle, Ellis, *Tall Tales from the High Hills*

> Told in Blue Ridge vernacular, the Gallant Tailor unrolls its serendipitious history. This is long, but very amusing.

"It All Began with a Drip" in Lexau, Joan, *It All Began with a Drip*

> A colorful variant of the Gallant Tailor in an attractive illustrated single edition. Indic.

"Nine in a Line" in Kirn, Ann, *Nine in a Line*

> A variant of the story of the man who could not count. Picture version. Arabian.

Car, Carriage, Cart, or Pike?

"Gears and Gasoline" in Fenner, Phyllis, *Adventures Rare and Magical*

> Modern fantasy in humorous vein about an obstreperous vehicle. A good change of pace from folktale materials.

"At the Pike's Behest" in Tolstoi, Alexei, *Russian Tales for Children*

> "At the pike's behest, at my own request . . ." —whatever Emelya wished would be done, even to having water walk uphill for him! Not too long, fun to tell.

"The Deacon's One-Hoss Shay" in Holmes, Oliver Wendell, *The Deacon's One-Hoss Shay*

> An amusing illustrated version of the famous long poem of a shay which went a hundred years to the day, and then utterly collapsed! Used with the illustrations, this makes an interesting poetic contrast.

"The Cartman's Story" in Spellman, John, *The Beautiful Blue Jay*

> When the cartman hired out his cart to earn a few rupees, the merchant gave him three pieces of advice, which earned him a fortune. Indic.

By Way of Water—Gondola, Lily Pad, or Peach

"Felice" in Brown, Marcia, *Felice*

> Striped little cat, hungry and lonely, who prowled among the gondolas of Venice and found a magic basket dropping food to him. Brilliant color, delightful plot.

"Thumbelina" in Andersen, Hans Christian, *Thumbelina*

> Journey on a lily pad by a wee, lovely traveller. If some of these illustrations by Adrienne Adams are shown after the story is told, the effect is enhanced. Danish.

"Momotaro" in Uchida, Yoshiko, *The Dancing Kettle*

> In the heart of a giant peach, a tiny lad sails into the life of a lonely couple and changes their fortunes through his bravery. Japanese.

Christmas Journeys

"The Voyage of the Wee Red Cap" in Sawyer, Ruth, *This Way to Christmas*

> Irish. See Holiday Stories, page 118.

"Torten's Christmas Secret" in Dolbier, Maurice, *Torten's Christmas Secret*

> Delightful story of an accommodating bear and a canny dwarf on Santa's big night. Must be abridged.

"About a Noble Camel" in Eaton, Anne, *The Animals' Christmas*

> Short and tender. From the Near East. See Holiday Stories, page 118.

On Sleigh, Snowshoes, and Skis

"The Wolf and the Sled" in Raspé, Rudolf Erich, *Baron Munchausen*

> Tale of a remarkable sled race, but a fun accent to the program. Very short. German.

"The Strange Sled Race" in Thompson, Vivian, *Hawaiian Myths of Earth and Sky*

> The mountainside was very steep, but the coconut frond sleds performed beautifully in this legend of Pele, goddess of volcanoes.

"The Magic Snowshoes" in Hill, Kay, *More Glooscap Stories*

> Folk tale of the Wabanaki Indians, and their genial culture hero, Glooscap, this time involving snowshoes which could take to the air.

"Ski-pup" in Freeman, Don, *Ski-pup*

> Bungling, good-natured Hugo, the St. Bernard pup at the ski lodge, earns his honors and becomes a hero in this illustrated story.

Journey into a New Year on a Flying Horse and Furry Feet

"One Hundred Hares" in Olcott, Frances, *Wonder Tales from Baltic Wizards*

> If the king would kiss the donkey, the boy would mind his hundred hares, and win the princess. A Baltic variant of "Jesper Who Herded the Hares" (Lang), with a delightful new twist. Lithuanian.

"Pegasus, the Winged Horse" in Elgin, Katherine, *The First Book of Mythology*

> Brief retelling of a familiar Greek myth that should be amplified by the storyteller.

"Two Hundred Rabbits' in Anderson, Alonzo, *Two Hundred Rabbits*

> Fantasy of two hundred rabbits who entertained the king and made him world-renowned, in delightful picture format.

"Gifts for the King" in White, Anne T., *Sinbad the Seaman—The Ebony Horse: Two Arabian Tales*

> Romance adapted from the "Arabian Nights" about a carved ebony horse with remarkable properties. Good plot, strong action. Must, however, be further adapted for story hour use. (See page 48.)

Trailer? Trendel? Or Top and Ball?

"The Haunted Trailer" in Ireson, Barbara, *Haunting Tales*

> Unusual modern story of a deposed ghost who would not desert his trailer home after it was sold, no matter where the trailer went. Must be abridged somewhat.

"How K'tonton Took a Ride on a Runaway Trendel" in Weilerstein, Sadie, *The Adventures of K'tonton*

> Pint-sized K'tonton gets a new trendel for Hannukah, but the trendel has a mind of its own, and off it goes! Different, fun. Jewish.

"The Top and the Ball" in Andersen, Hans Christian, *It's Perfectly True*

> Whimsical fantasy of the proud ball and haughty top who both came to a sad end. In Andersen's fine style, but not sad to tell! Danish.

Swift as a Stag or a Deer

"The Ghost of the Great White Stag" in Gruenberg, Sidonie, *More Favorite Stories*

> Seneca Indian ghost story, beautiful and difficult to tell, of a mighty stag cruelly killed, who thereafter haunted the New York mountains. May also be found in Parker, *Skunny-Wundy*.

"The Banyan Deer" in Babbitt, Ellen, *Jataka Tales*

> A moving allegory from the great Indian story treasure, of a beautiful deer who offered his life for his followers.

"Parrak, the White Reindeer" in Borg, Ingrid, *Parrak the White Reindeer*

> Beautifully illustrated glimpse of life among the Laplanders, centering on the appearance of a rare white reindeer.

Aboard Engines, Arks, and Chariots

"The Giant Who Rode on an Ark" in Stoutenberg, Adrien, *Fee-Fi-Fo-Fum*

> Freckle-faced giant Hurtali straddled Noah's Ark and paddled it to safety, then remained for the companionship. An irreverent bit of whimsy, fun to tell.

"The Fast Sooner Hound" in Bontemps, Arna, *The Fast Sooner Hound*

> Sooner run than eat, the hound that beat the Cannonball. An American tall tale somewhat difficult to tell, but very funny.

"The Chariot of Phaeton" in Benson, Sally, *Stories of Gods and Heroes*

> Dramatic myth of Apollo's son, who wanted to drive the fiery horses of the sun, to his own destruction. Good version for telling. Greek myth.

"The Wondrous Flying Chariot" in Lim, Sian-Tek, *Folk Tales from China*

> In the eighteenth century B.C. an artisan created a chariot that would fly, but the emperor feared it. Brief and interesting, but needs amplification.

The Bigger the Better—Elephants and Whales

"Little Elephant Who Wanted to Fly" in Lobagola, *Folk Tales of a Savage*

> The discontented elephant got his wish, but, oh, the consequences! Humorous animal story from Africa, succinct.

"The Elephants and the Mice" in Hirsh, Marilyn, *The Elephants and the Mice*

> Full of movement, color, and the Oriental splendor of a palace, a fable from India's *Panchatantra* literature.

"How the Whale Got His Throat" in Kipling, Rudyard, *Just So Stories*

> Irrepressible fun in this fantasy of the ingenious Hibernian and his remarkable suspenders. Use Kipling's language, however.

"Little Annie and the Whaler Captain" in Jagendorf, Mortiz, *The New England Bean Pot*

> Big baby whale Annie took the harpoon in her mouth and played ring-a-rosy with the old whaler captain. Tall tale from New England.

Things That Fly—Wax Wings,
Airplanes, and Arrows

"Daedalus and Icarus" in Untermeyer, Louis, *The World's Greatest Stories*

> Poetic retelling of the Greek myth of wax wings.

"Loopy" in Gramatky, Hardie, *Loopy*

> Show-off hedge-hopper plane who learned to skywrite with a flourish. Very gay picture story; appeals to boys.

"The Angry Moon" in Sleator, William, *The Angry Moon*

> Northwest Indian legend of the arrow-chain to the moon, magnificently illustrated in stunning color.

Donkeys and Goats and Little Gray Burros

"The Talking Donkey" in Bechstein, Ludwig, *The Fairy Tales of Ludwig Bechstein*

> A mischievous mountain spirit resembling Robin Hood tricks the stingy and rewards

the good by first fooling the glass seller, then turning into a talking donkey for the selfish innkeeper. A fine retelling of a German folk tale by a recognized artist.

"Uncle Bouki Buys a Burro" in Courlander, Harold, *Uncle Bouki of Haiti*

> Lovable, slow-witted Bouki is once again tricked by crafty Ti Malice over a contrary burro, but still can't figure out quite how! Understated humor from Haiti; must be well-timed.

"The Mountain Goats of Temlaham" in Toye, William, *The Mountain Goats of Temlaham*

> Single edition in brilliant color of a Tsimshim Indian legend about the totem of the goat and a cruel young prince. Stunning, but a better version, without illustrations, is that of Christie Harris in *Once Upon a Totem*. That, however, is much longer.

"Some Impatient Mule-drivers" in Brenner, Anita, *The Boy Who Could Do Anything*

> Some dim-witted mule-drivers with a cargo of sponges and chili peppers play a trick on their four-footed helpers that backfires. Also known as "The Donkeys and the Salt Bags" and "The Stubborn Muleteer." Mexican.

Cannonball, Clay Pot, Chopping Knife, and Drum

"The Ride on a Cannonball" in Kästner, Erich, *Baron Munchausen*

> One of the Baron's farfetched experiences on an extraordinary vehicle. Pungent, short. German.

"The Clay Manikin" in Tolstoi, Alexei, *Russian Tales for Children*

> The greedy clay-pot boy starts out to seek his fortune, but meets a sad end. Cynthia Jameson has a delightful pictured version of this same story.

"How K'tonton Took a Ride on a Chopping Knife," that contrasted with a witty picture version of the African folktale "When the Drum Sang."

> K'tonton jumped on his mother's big curved chopper as she made gefilte fish for the Sabbath—and lost his balance and nearly his life! Short and funny. Jewish.

"When the Drum Sang" in Rockwell, Ann, *When the Drum Sang*

> An African child is kidnapped and hidden in a drum by a wicked wandering beggar, where she is forced to sing for his supper.

The African Zmwi is caught in his own foils with his singing drum. Illustrated folk tale.

Windy March Blows Kites, Bluebottles, and Baskets Aloft

"Fish in the Air" in Wiese, Kurt, *Fish in the Air*

Picture story about the Lantern Festival in China and a huge fish-kite that carried its owner off into the blue. Nice atmosphere.

"Jonnikin and the Flying Basket" in Manning-Sanders, Ruth, *Jonnikin and the Flying Basket*

Scrubby Jonnikin knew a bit of magic, so when his sister was in danger, he invented a basket that could fly and loaded his sister into it. Colloquial style, French touch, humorous.

"The Bluebottle Who Went Courting" in Wiggin, Kate D., and Smith, Nora, *Tales of Laughter*

The fussy bluebottle was only a fly, of course, but how very important he felt himself to be! Droll, and easy to tell. English.

"The Picnic Basket" in Clark, Margery, *The Poppy Seed Cakes*

Wherein a picnic basket goes for a sail and Andrewshek nearly misses a wonderful lunch, until Auntie Katushka saves the day with her big umbrella. Mild humor, appropriate for young children. Russian.

Mules, Mares, Foals, and Fillies

"Fifine and the White Mare" in Fenner, Phyllis, *Magic Hoofs*

Fifine was the king's youngest daughter, and her fate would have been sad indeed without the help of the white mare. Romantic fairy tale. French.

"Soft-soap Satan" in DuMond, Frank, *Tall Tales from the Catskills*

Satan the mule ate everything in sight because he was so pesky—but when he ate the soft soap, he really was in a lather!

"The Prince and the Sky-Blue Filly" in Manning-Sanders, Ruth, *A Book of Princes and Princesses*

See Story Hour Canvas annotation for this Jugoslav fairy tale, page 107.

"Seven Foals" in Fenner, Phyllis, *Magic Hoofs*

"Watch my seven foals for one day, and I'll give you the princess to wife. . . ." That was what the king asked, but of all the suitors, only Boots had the spirit to outwit the frisky foals. Fairy tale adventure from Scandinavia.

The Slow-Way—Tugboat, Turtle, and Tortoise

"Urashima Taro" in Uchida, Yoshiko, *The Dancing Kettle*

A Japanese variant of the Rip Van Winkle theme, lively and well-told, with a fisherman and a giant turtle as protagonists. Use the illustrations from Taro Yashima's *Seashore Story* to create atmosphere, but the Uchida version is superior to tell.

"Little Toot" in Gramatky, Hardie, *Little Toot*

The plucky little tugboat rises above his mischief when help is needed in the harbor. Even older children enjoy the gay pictures.

"Bandalee" in Arbuthnot, May Hill, *Time for Old Magic*

Jaunty Anansi story with a gay rhythm that makes the story move fast. Fun to tell, and fun for children who like tortoises! Jamaican.

Wind, Windwagon, and Wagon

"Ride in the Night" in Jagendorf, Mortiz, *New England Bean Pot*

Old Pete was a melon-miser, until the night he found himself rolled downhill and into the mill pond by the Devil himself, everyone said, because of his stinginess! Eerie, and funny.

"Gillespie and the Guards" in Elkin, Benjamin, *Gillespie and the Guards*

Daugherty's robust illustrations give this congenial spoof on dignity a hearty humor. Well paced, popular.

"High Wind for Kansas" in Calhoun, Mary, *High Wind for Kansas*

Wind-power and a sail for the Conestoga wagons of the West—a good idea with unpredictable results. Must be abridged, but is unusual and very funny, told in straight-faced tall tale style.

"Ride the Cold Wind" in Surany, Anico, *Ride the Cold Wind*

Striking illustrations in a story of two children who rode the cold wind of an Ecuadorian lake in their father's borrowed fishing craft, and nearly drowned. Dramatic illustrations.

"Journey of the Breton Fishermen" in Chamoud, Simone, *Picture Tales from France*

Noodlehead story of fisherfolk who hoisted a

sail to help their donkey wagon make speed, but found themselves outsmarted by that same donkey. Very short and funny.

Easter Journeys

"The Legend of St. Christopher" in Farjeon, Eleanor, *Ten Saints*

The legend of the Christ Child who was borne across the stream on the brawny shoulders of the good saint, told in beautiful and simple prose.

"Stealing the Springtime" in Bleeker, Mary N., *Big Music*

Kootenai Indian folk tale retold by Frank B. Linderman explaining the change of seasons. The trickster Skinkoots lends a bit of humor to this strong and beautiful tale—wonderful to tell. (Also in Rachel Field's *American Folk and Fairy Tales*.)

"The Song of the Little Donkey" in Association for Childhood Education, *Told under the Magic Umbrella*

See Holiday Stories, Easter, page 116.

Over the Deep in Schooner and Ship

"The Phantom Ship" in Spicer, Dorothy, *13 Ghosts*

A ghostly ship that leaves the sea and anchors in the moors of Holland brings terror to all who see it. Longer and spookier than most ghost stories.

"The Skipper and the Witch" in Jagendorf, Moritz, *New England Bean Pot*

Witchcraft on the Maine coast, with a stingy skipper and a fiendish hag toting a magic bridle. Good for scary story hours.

"The Spectral Ship" in Smith, Elva S., *Mystery Tales for Boys and Girls*

One of Wilhelm Hauff's strong, unusual stories based on folklore from Moslem sources. An East Indian setting, a ghostly crew, and a ghastly spectacle. Must be carefully told to retain the distinguished style of Hauff, but is excellent for older boys.

All of a Sudden—Umbrellas in the Air

"The Umbrella-maker's Kozo" in Sugimoto, Chiyono, *Japanese Holiday Picture Tales*

The little apprentice took a magic flight on the big black cloud, but the umbrella did its work well. Short and different.

"Monsieur Jolicoeur's Umbrella" in Surany, Anico, *Monsieur Jolicoeur's Umbrella*

Gorgeous color in a spooky Haitian picture story, drawn by Leonard Everett Fisher. Fun to tell and to see.

"How Six Umbrellas Took Off" in Sandburg, Carl, *Rootabaga Stories*

Rhythmic nonsense from a master storyteller. A recording of Sandburg reading this can be used very effectively.

"The Big Black Umbrella" in Leach, Maria, *Rainbow Book of American Folk Tales and Legends*

A good finish for any ghost story hour, the short weird tale of the umbrella that was left by a black-coated man who never was!

"Professor Bull's Umbrella" in Lipkind, William, *Professor Bull's Umbrella*

Philip, he called him—that big black umbrella he so cherished. Fantasy amusingly illustrated, with a very delightful story line.

Bicycles, Birds, and Balloons

"The Windbird and the Sun" in Arbuthnot, May Hill, *Arbuthnot Anthology of Children's Literature*

African pourquoi story of how the rainbow came to be. Unusual.

"The Red Balloon" in Lamorisse, Albert, *The Red Balloon*

Fantasy of Pascal, a little French boy who followed his red balloon up the streets and on into the sky, out of sight. Photographic fantasy.

"Jo-Ji and the Dragon" in Lifton, Betty J., *Jo-Ji and the Dragon*

Modern imaginative story of the sorry old scarecrow who was dragged in disgrace from the rice field, to make way for a fierce dragon. But the crows that Jo-Ji would not scare away cunningly scared the imposter and rescued Jo-Ji. Gentle humor.

"The Pedaling Man" in Hoban, Russell, *The Pedaling Man*

Long poem about the weathervane, nicely rhymed.

Peacock Machines and Other Strange Things

"The Wonderful Wooden Peacock Flying Machine" in Tooze, Ruth, *The Wonderful Wooden Peacock Flying Machine*

Magic adventure in a rare flying machine designed to look like a peacock. An intriguing fairy tale from Ceylon, with interesting atmosphere and smooth style.

"The Fool of the World and the Flying Ship" in Ransome, Arthur, *The Fool of the World*

> Delightful prose and scintillating illustrations in this Russian tale of the tsar who demanded a flying ship that would go as well by land as by sea as by air! Caldecott winner, wonderful to tell.

"The Magic Snuff Box" in Carpenter, Frances, *Tales of a Korean Grandmother*

> Young Chiko found along the highway a mysterious box which flew open to his touch saying, "What do you wish for?" From then on, fortune smiled on him. Unusual details, easy to tell.

"The Flying Trunk" in Tudor, Tasha, comp., *Tasha Tudor's Book of Fairy Tales*

> Andersen's amusing fantasy of a discontented prince who took refuge in a trunk with unsuspected powers.

STORY HOUR CANVAS

Behind the creation of this particular story program were several clear objectives, the first of which was to see what could be done with the idea of color in the titles or the content of stories, just for the fun of it. A second was to select stories from the most famous series of folk and fairy tales ever published for English-speaking children, the *Color Fairy Books* of Andrew Lang. The riches of several other very good and old series that, in some instances, are now out of print, were also explored, series such as those by Carpenter, Wiggins, and Olcott (see the Series Bibliography for complete citations). Surely among such wealth the imagination could find enough color to create a story canvas.

An actual canvas was created on the story board, in fact. Each week the color of each story hour was added as a part of a collage landscape of mountains, clouds, trees, water, and flowers, and the children also brought in pictures or objects that they had made, which then became part of the picture board as well. The collage technique was used because it was expandable, with a particular part of the canvas pasted on week by week. The story board was incidental to the program, but creative, and it encouraged participation.

A third objective was to use the new series of books by Ruth Manning-Sanders, her books of ghosts, witches, giants, wizards, and so on, wherever they offered material, so as to introduce the children to these books for individual reading. The second series which seemed intriguing was Dorothy Spicer's "13" series; *13 Ghosts, 13 Giants, 13 Saints, 13 Goblins,* and so on. Each of these authors tells a story in contagious fashion, and makes use of material not always familiar to storytellers and listeners. They skimp on identifying their sources, some of which are undoubtedly firsthand. Children, of course, are not especially interested in identification, but it is important to storytellers. Since stories were selected for their capacity to become part of this story canvas, not all of the individual titles in the two series were used; plenty of material remains. The fourth objective was to continue the use of well-illustrated editions where these were appropriate, and to make use of modern imaginative stories, insofar as possible.

Painter, Palette, and Paint: The first colorful storytelling program opened with "Pitidoe the Color Maker," a rhymed fantasy, used with the pictures; second was a modern, imaginative story, "The Little Painter." This was followed by the ridiculous folktale from Estonia, "Painting the Moon," and ended with "The Magic Paintbrush", again a picture story.

The Background of Blue: This program opened with a Jugoslav story used the previous year, "The Prince and the Sky-blue Filly," a gay fairy tale; then, "The Blue Jackal," an illustrated edition of an Indic animal story, followed by the foolish tale of "The Bluebottle Who Went Courting" and the amusing calamity of "The Great Blueness," a fully illustrated fantasy. Thus the story canvas sky was painted.

Tales from *The Blue Fairy Book*: Andrew Lang's stories were next, beginning with "Rumpelstiltskin," from France; "Why the Sea Is Salt," an old legend; the story of "Prince Hyacinth and the Princess," from French sources; and the witty "Princess on the Glass Hill." In spite of the fact that this program included several fairy tales, the styles were so different, that they fitted together well into the forty-five minute period.

Black for Outlines: The next color was black, and again Howard Pyle's "The Clever Student and the Master of the Black Arts" was used—the rhythm was contagious as a starter. From there to the strange "The Black Giant of Luckless River" from Serbia; then, an illustrated edition of a Chinese magician tale, "The Black Heart of Indri." The final story was "Granny's Blackie," a Jataka elephant tale.

The Colors of Halloween: This program opened with a marvelous spooky story, "Twelve Great Black Cats," with its Scottish eeriness; a brief, pourquoi Indian story from the Algonquin tribe, "Pitcher the Witch, and the Black Cats," a rollicking story, "The Ghost Goblin's Gold" from Wales, and finally the "Leg of Gold" to startle everyone!

A Brushful of Yellow: "The Wizard with the Yellow Eyeballs and the Gold Ax" made interesting introductory material but should be amplified into a real story. It led into the Chinese story about the great Yellow River, "The Yellow Dragon." A delightful contrast was "The Yellow-haired Witch" from Serbia, followed by a picture story, "The Big Yellow Balloon."

Tales from *The Yellow Fairy Book*: This Lang book provided two tales by Andersen, "The Tinder Box" and blundering "Blockhead Hans"; then there was the somewhat wistful "The Hazelnut Child" from Grimm, and the familiar and popular riddle story, "The Dragon and His Grandmother." Yellow became autumn foliage on the story canvas.

Brown for the Earthtones: This program was suitable for the November weather, with an Irish variant of Cinderella, "Fair, Brown and Trembling," and the tricky "Black-bearded Brownies of Bonenberg" as a contrast. An illustrated story of the magical "Kappa's Tug-of-war with Big Brown Horse" from Japan was followed by a lilting story, "The Brownie o' Fern Den," a touch of Gaelic humor.

Tales from *The Brown Fairy Book*: Chosen for this program were Lang's "Habogi," a short fairy tale with a clever twist, followed by a Middle East story proving that fate loves the lazy man, "Fortune and the Woodcutter." Contrasting with this was "The Husband of the Rat's Daughter," from the French, with its almost fable quality; and finally, the German tale that partially parallels the theme of Andersen's *Emperor's New Clothes*, "Which Was the Foolishest?"

Red Skies for Sunrise: As December came up on the calendar, the color red came into focus,

making glorious red streaks around a rising sun on the collage story canvas. The program opened with the jaunty "Sashes Red and Blue," with its ironic French-Canadian humor; on to "The Red Etin," a weird Scotch creature; followed by the lovely why-story of "The Redbird," the Cherokee Indian version; and finally a merry variant of "Drakestail" from Switzerland, "Red Chicken."

Tales from *The Red Fairy Book*: This program provided the fun-loving "Golden Goose" folktale, "Rapunzel" of the long golden braids; "Six Sillies," a variant of the ridiculous story of the girl who courted trouble before it came, and finally the Grimm story of "Mother Holle."

The Colors of Christmas, Framed in Gold: The Christmas program began with the ever popular, ever adaptable "Voyage of the Wee Red Cap," then the legend of "The Golden Cobwebs," and its little brown spinner; finally came the very beautiful Spanish story, "The Gold of Bernardino"; and a brief poem, "The Stars Are Silver Reindeer."

A Splotch of Orange on the Palette: This topic allowed for the brief Mexican story of magic fruit, "The Oranges," and then that long fairy tale filled with enchantment, "Three Golden Oranges" from Spain. A picture story from India, the "Legend of the Orange Princess," was followed by Eleanor Farjeon's delicate fantasy, "Oranges and Lemons."

Tales from *The Orange Fairy Book*: This book provided only two stories that fitted into the story hour theme—"The White Slipper," a fairy tale of the chemist's boy who healed a king; and the strange, haunting French legend of "The Stones of Plouhinec." Interspersed between these two were placed a Japanese fairy tale, "The Golden Crane," and a sardonic Greek folktale of three remarkable coins, "The Three Gold Pieces." *The Orange Fairy Book* has many stories too sophisticated for use, or too long for an after-school hour.

Rose Shades for Flame and Flower: This subject produced a small fire on the story canvas. A natural for the story was "Briar Rose," the German variant of the Sleeping Beauty motif, and "Snow White and Rose Red," by Grimm. These provided a sharp contrast to the Paiute Indian myth of how coyote found fire, "The Firebringer." The closing story was one from China, "How Molo Stole the Lovely Rose-Red."

Tales from *The Rose Fairy Book*: Again only two stories fitted in, "Bobino," a lively Italian folktale, and a gentle story, "The Sprig of Rosemary." Therefore a picture why-story of the Iroquois, explaining the Pleiades, "The Dancing Stars," was used; the program finished with the brash Russian humor of "The Peasant's Pea Patch."

A Hint of Crystal Ice and Snow in Early Morn: By this time snow and ice encircled the library and hung on the windows, so the title of this program was appropriate, with its first story, "The Silver Saucer and the Crystal Apple," indicating that even in long-ago Russia there was clairvoyance. Next followed "The Crystal Coffin," in which sorcery and great magic run to meet a poor tailor. A very familiar moral folktale, "Toads and Diamonds" followed; the program ended with a strange, short tale from the Harz mountains, "Ilse's Crystal Palace."

A Pink Glow Reflected on Snow-topped Mountains: This title pointed to the next story session and "The Peach Boy," a variant of "Momotaro," the tiny boy born in a peach; after this came a merry little satire from Holland, "The Little Town Pink and Clean," and a variant of "Esben and the Witch," with its singing refrain: "Are you not a great knave, Pinkel?" and Pinkel's lighthearted taunting to the witch: "Yes, dear mother, I am!"— "Pinkel and the Witch." A modern fantasy, simple and intimate, by Rose Fyleman, "The Pink Rabbit," finished that story hour.

Tales from *The Pink Fairy Book*: From this book was selected the Andersen tale of "The Flying Trunk," told a previous year; the story of the very "Cunning Shoemaker"; and the Norwegian droll, "Peter Bull." A variant of the sad Japanese story "The Sparrow with the Slit Tongue" completed the program. Children do not object to pathos or sadness in a story hour if they are balanced with other emotions.

Gray for Shadows: This topic was interesting, and the stories used were all delightful—a Navajo trickster tale, "Grey Rabbit Plays a Trick"; the long, beautifully illustrated story of "The Tale of Prince Ivan, the Firebird, and the Grey Wolf"; "The Mule's Egg," a nitwit tale, this time a Swiss variant; and the strange tale of the changeling from Scotland, "Greyling."

Tales from *The Grey Fairy Book*: This book is less well known than some of the other collections but had several good stories, among them a Sicilian variant of Cinderella called "The Bear"; a rogue story of a greedy dwarf, "The Little Grey Manikin,"

from the German; the ever popular flying-ship story, but this time in a merry Czech variant, "Long, Broad, and Quickeye"; and finally a story from France very like the Pooka anecdotes from Ireland, also suitable for Halloween use, "The Goblin Pony."

Green for Field and Forest: The program added evergreen trees and bushes to the story board canvas. Green introduced the funny picture story, "The Green Noses"; the whimsical fairy tale of the enchanted prince, "Alphege or the Green Monkey"; a most strange and eerie picture tale from ancient Britain, in brilliant colors, "The Green Children"; and a sinister Swiss story of besting-the-devil, "The Man with the Green Feather."

Tales from *The Green Fairy Book*: This book is one of the more popular Lang color fairy book titles, as proved by the cheeky "The Half-chick"; "Jorinda and Joringel," with its leering witch; "Hok Lee and the Dwarfs"; and "The Fisherman and His Wife." The rhyme in this last tale draws a response from the children every time! Margot Zemach has illustrated an excellent single edition of this story.

The Colors of Easter: Four stories were used here: "Why the Ivy Is Always Green," a modern holiday story; "Tico and the Golden Wings," a lovely picture story of self-sacrifice; "The White Blackbird," a modern story written in Padraic Colum's gracious prose; and an unusual adaptation of several ancient legends woven around the "Thirty Gilt Pennies," retold for use in this program.

Highlights of White: This session was somewhat different, as it contained three picture book stories, but each so different from the other that they afforded variety and gave balance to the story telling. The first, however, was not a picture book, but a fairy tale from Brittany, "The White Lamb," a story of enchantment and changelings; following this came a strange and sad story of the creation of the horsehead fiddle of Mongolia, "Suho and the White Horse," strikingly pictured. Then a gay, short folktale from Japan, "The Little White Hen," and at last the beloved "Snow White and the Seven Dwarfs," with stunning illustrations by Burkert. Here the story was told first, and the illustrations shown afterwards.

Accent Colors in Flower and Field: For this program the children cut out many bright flowers and put them on the canvas; after this came "The

Little Horse of Seven Colors," a merry tale; "The Golden Frog," with dramatic designs from the San Blas Indians highlighting the story; "Cherry," one of the bewitching Cornish tales, and last of all, "The Gold Bread," a moral tale.

Tales from *The Lilac, Crimson, Violet,* and *Olive Fairy Books*: One story from each book made up the next program: "Schippeitaro," the scary story from Japan; a hilarious word-play from Russia, "To Your Good Health"; a liar's tale with a moral, "A Long Bow Story," from the East; and finally, a mystery in a soup tureen, the witty "A Lost Paradise."

A Silver Slant of Raindrops: In April, the story board collage was completed. The silver was provided in a gay Hungarian story, "The Silver Penny" and Andersen's story of "How to Tell a Real Princess" contrasted with an Italian fairy tale, "Three Silver Balls," and a Robin Hood story, "The Silver Arrow."

And Over All a Rainbow with a Pot of Gold at Its Foot: At the last story hour session, first came the illustrated version of "Noah and the Rainbow," retold by a distinguished German writer and marvelously illustrated by Aichinger; a clever Russian variant of the talkative wife, "Tusya and the Pot of Gold"; a brief episode from Fyleman's fantasy on "The Rainbow Cat," and at last "The Crock of Gold," based on Jacobs's retelling of the "Pedlar of Swaffham," illustrated in bright colors by William Stobbs. The program closed with a pourquoi tale from China, "The Rain King's Daughter."

The story board, at the program's conclusion, had a landscape of high mountains, snow covered with a sunrise glow; bright autumn foliage and flowers; a campfire, dew on the bushes; and a bit of rain shining through the sun to create a rainbow. Perhaps an artist would not have liked it, but the story hour children did. The stories were fun, and proved that the old anthologies still provided treasure for the telling.

Themes and Stories
Painter, Palette, and Paint
"Pitidoe the Color Maker" in Dines, Glen, *Pitidoe the Color Maker*

> The wizard Resk had a helper whose eagerness to mix colors landed everything and everybody in a colossal mess! A modern

imaginative story, rhythmic and colorfully illustrated.

"The Little Painter" in Marchant, Ralph, and Marchant, Jill, *The Little Painter*

> Illustrated story of the tiny housepainter whose enthusiasm for color-splashing knew no bounds. Fun to tell, down-to-earth humor.

"Painting the Moon" in Withers, Carl, *Painting the Moon*

> Old folk tale from Estonia of the heavenly blacksmith, Illmarinen, whose brilliant moon was too bright for the sulky Devil and his undercover deeds. Unusual and a bit satirical.

"The Magic Paintbrush" in Damjan, Misha, *The Magic Paintbrush*

> Modern fantasy of an old pony who gave his kind little friend the gift of a magic paintbrush with wonderful powers of its own. Delightfully illustrated by Janosh.

The Background of Blue
"The Prince and the Sky-blue Filly" in Manning-Sanders, Ruth, *A Book of Princes and Princesses*

> Because the stepmother was jealous, the small prince went into the world to seek his fortune, and the first thing he discovered was a flute that made everything, and everyone, dance—including a sky-blue filly, a magic sword, and a giant. Romantic, with a brisk tempo, from Jugoslavia.

"The Blue Jackal" in Gobhai, Mehlli, *The Blue Jackal*

> Illustrated folk tale from India about a jackal of most strange hue, and the consequences of that! Had it been published at the time, I should have much preferred Marcia Brown's illustrated edition of this same folktale.

"The Bluebottle Who Went Courting" in Wiggin, Kate D., and Smith, Nora, *Tales of Laughter*

> Nobody wanted the foolish bluebottle fly but a kind lady-fly who agreed to nurse his wounds—and at last marry him out of charity!

Blueness
"The Great Blueness" in Lobel, Arnold, *The Great*

> What would you do if the world were all blue—or all red? A modern humorous story with gay illustrations.

Tales from The Blue Fairy Book

"Rumpelstiltskin" in Lang, Andrew, *The Blue Fairy Book*

Familiar German fairy story of the imp-helper whose name the young queen must guess if she would keep her child.

"Why the Sea Is Salt" in Lang, Andrew, *The Blue Fairy Book*

Rich brother, poor brother, and a quern which ground pottage and herrings, or anything else desired. It is still grinding out salt, at the bottom of the sea, so they say.

"Prince Hyacinth and the Princess" in Lang, Andrew, *The Blue Fairy Book*

She was a lovely princess, but only he who could step on her great cat's tail could marry her, for she was under a spell. A fairy tale with an unusual angle.

"The Princess on the Glass Hill" in Lang, Andrew, *The Blue Fairy Book*

Cinderlad, and the great horse—and the witchery of St. John's Eve, all combined to win the hand of the princess atop the glass hill. Wonderful to tell, and satisfying to hear.

Black for Outlines

"The Clever Student and the Master of the Black Arts" in Pyle, Howard, *Wonder Clock*

Alas, the student had not learned how to chop wood or bind faggots, nor anything useful—but indeed, he could change himself into a dapple gray nag, that he could! Flavorful, distinctive style.

"The Black Giant of Luckless River" in Spicer, Dorothy, *13 Giants*

Strange and engrossing story from Serbia.

"The Black Heart of Indri" in Hoge, Dorothy, *The Black Heart of Indri*

A peculiar and dangerous wizard named Indri, from old China, performs his magic in this illustrated single edition.

"Granny's Blackie" in Babbitt, Ellen C., *Jataka Tales*

From the Indian Jataka stories, the tale of the love between an old woman and her pet elephant. Very short and heartwarming.

The Colors of Halloween

"Twelve Great Black Cats" in Nic Leodhas, Sorche, *Twelve Great Black Cats*

Suspenseful and weird, this mysterious story from Scotland. Excellent for Halloween, with twelve huge black cats, and one red one!

"Pitcher the Witch, and the Black Cats" in Olcott, Frances, *The Red Indian Fairy Book*

An uncanny pourquoi story from the Algonquin Indians, explaining why we have mosquitoes. Somewhat strange, not easy to tell.

"The Ghost Goblin's Gold" in Spicer, Dorothy, *13 Ghosts*

Ghosts are one thing—goblins another; but when they are both involved with a treasure, you have a real spook story.

"Leg of Gold" in Manning-Sanders, Ruth, *A Book of Ghosts and Goblins*

A noble French woman, with a leg of gold . . . story with an eerie ending!

A Brushful of Yellow

"The Wizard with the Yellow Eyeballs and the Gold Ax" in Olcott, Frances, *Wonder Tales from Baltic Wizards*

Very brief bit of atmosphere from a strange part of the world, more anecdote than story but useful here.

"The Yellow Dragon" in Manning-Sanders, Ruth, *A Book of Dragons*

They say in China that the great Yellow River is a mighty dragon at times, or so it seems. . . .

"The Yellow-haired Witch" in Spicer, Dorothy, *13 Witches*

A most unusual witch, with a strange sort of power . . . good for Halloween.

"The Big Yellow Balloon" in Fenton, Edward, *The Big Yellow Balloon*

Modern picture story, fresh and funny, about a yellow balloon which attracted a motley procession in its wake.

Tales from The Yellow Fairy Book

"The Tinder Box" in Lang, Andrew, *The Yellow Fairy Book*

Behind the first magic door sat a huge dog, with eyes as big as saucers . . . behind the second door, a dog with eyes as big as millwheels . . . behind the third door a dog with eyes as big as a round tower. Andersen's delectable tale of the magic box and the demanding witch.

"Blockhead Hans" in Lang, Andrew, *The Yellow Fairy Book*

> The youngest son rode on a goat, and presented the princess with a dead crow—but he won her anyhow! Funny and fast-moving, from Andersen.

"The Hazelnut Child" in Lang, Andrew, *The Yellow Fairy Book*

> No bigger than a hazelnut, yet big enough to find a fortune, was this hero!

"The Dragon and His Grandmother" in Lang, Andrew, *The Yellow Fairy Book*

> The wily soldier, the stupid dragon, and the riddles the grandmother unwittingly answered, appeal to children every time.

Brown for the Earthtones

"Fair, Brown and Trembling" in Jacobs, Joseph, *Celtic Fairy Tales*

> Irish variant of Cinderella, with a henwife instead of a godmother.

"The Black-bearded Brownies of Bonenberg" in Spicer, Dorothy, *13 Ghosts*

> Deep inside the heather heath of North Gelderland rises a strange mount occupied by brownies who give treasure only to those who think of others more than of themselves . . . and so it proved to be!

"Kappa's Tug-of-war with Big Brown Horse" in Baruch, Dorothy, *Kappa's Tug-of-war with Big Brown Horse*

> Tastefully illustrated with Japanese watercolors, this is a merry tale of the tiny Kappa who stole the farmer's cucumbers, but met his match in the big brown horse.

"The Brownie o' Fern Den" in Haviland, Virginia, *Favorite Fairy Tales Told in Scotland*

> Since none of the men were brave enough to dare the moors at night when the good mistress was taken ill, the brownie did it himself. Appealing, and somewhat different. Good Scottish atmosphere.

Tales from The Brown Fairy Book

"Habogi" in Lang, Andrew, *The Brown Fairy Book*

> The youngest daughter would marry a man who bore the name of Habogi, and no one else . . . though why she said *that* name, she couldn't tell. Short, and good, somewhat ironic.

"Fortune and the Woodcutter" in Lang, Andrew, *The Brown Fairy Book*

> From Asia Minor, the short humorous story of the woodcutter who took to his bed, only to discover a fortune!

"The Husband of the Rat's Daughter" in Lang, Andrew, *The Brown Fairy Book*

> Neither the sun, the cloud, the mountain, the wall was good enough to be the rat-daughter's husband. A fable, well told, variant of the Stonecutter motif.

"Which Was the Foolishest?" in Lang, Andrew, *The Brown Fairy Book*

> A contest between two idiotic wives to see which could outsmart the other, and the dire and amusing results.

Red Skies for Sunrise

"Sashes Red and Blue" in Carlson, Natalie, *Sashes Red and Blue*

> Between the Quebec LeBlancs and the Montreal LeBlancs was an endless rivalry—and it made for great fun!

"The Red Etin" in Baker, Augusta, *The Golden Lynx*

> The Red Etin of Scotland was a dreadful creature with three heads that spared neither man nor beast; but the youngest son was a brave one, and so the adventure has a happy ending. Scotch, and full-flavored.

"The Redbird" in Cunningham, Caroline, *The Talking Stone*

> Short pourquoi story of the bright feathers of the redbird, from the Cherokee.

"Red Chicken" in Duvoisin, Roger, *The Three Sneezes*

> Swiss variant of "Drakestail" (Hutchinson—*Fireside*), with zesty humor, merry pace, brevity.

Tales from The Red Fairy Book

"The Golden Goose" in Lang, Andrew, *The Red Fairy Book*

> Dullhead won the princess, but first he won a golden goose that ensnared every greedy person who tried to touch it! A variant of "The Flying Ship" (Ransome—*Old Peter's*). Always good, very obvious humor.

"Rapunzel" in Lang, Andrew, *The Red Fairy Book*

> Beautiful girl with long, long golden braids, a nasty witch, and a prince who fell in love

with the voice in the tower—what more could a fairy tale have? Familiar and well-loved.

"The Six Sillies" in Lang, Andrew, *The Red Fairy Book*

The silly would-be-wed sat in the cellar and let the beer run out of the keg while she tried to think of a name for the child she might never have! A variant of "Jack and the Three Sillies" (Chase), and just as funny.

"Mother Holle" in Lang, Andrew, *The Red Fairy Book*

When it snows in Germany they say Mother Holle is shaking her feather bed, and Grimm tells why, in this brief märchen.

The Colors of Christmas, Framed in Gold

"The Voyage of the Wee Red Cap" in Sawyer, Ruth, *This Way to Christmas*

See Holiday Stories, page 118.

"The Golden Cobwebs" in Bryant, Sara Cone, *Best Stories to Tell to Children*

See Holiday Stories, page 118 (in Dickenson anthology).

"The Gold of Bernardino" in Sawyer, Ruth, *The Long Christmas*

Father Bernardino hoarded his gold for a great gift for the Holy Mother. But each time a needy person came to him, the treasure was tapped until he had given away all that he had. Yet he was blest!

"The Stars Are Silver Reindeer" in Belting, Natalia, *The Stars Are Silver Reindeer*

Brief and lovely poetry, from many primitive peoples.

A Splotch of Orange on the Palette

"The Oranges" in Henius, Frank, *Stories from the Americas*

A short, unusual tale of magic about a tree that grew and grew and provided wonderful oranges for the starving children. Unusual, Mexican background.

"Three Golden Oranges" in Boggs, Ralph, and Davis, M. G., *Three Golden Oranges*

Long, romantic fairy tale of a widow's only son who found three beautiful princesses, each in an orange, one of whom became his wife.

"The Legend of the Orange Princess" in Gobhai, Mehlli, *The Legend of The Orange Princess*

Lushly illustrated fairy tale from India of a princess kept in a beautiful palace in a secret place, but not in the form imagined.

"Oranges and Lemons" in Farjeon, Eleanor, *Italian Peep Show*

Brief, and fanciful, and should be told in the author's flowing style. From Italy, a colorful fantasy.

Tales from The Orange Fairy Book

"The White Slipper" in Lang, Andrew, *The Orange Fairy Book*

A wound that would not heal, a beautiful princess, and a brave chemist's helper interweave in a story of magic and bravery.

"The Golden Crane" in Yamaguchi, Tohr, *The Golden Crane*

Single edition, beautifully illustrated, of an enchanted Japanese crane. Not for the youngest children, however. Symbolic, and somewhat involved.

"The Stones of Plouhinec" in Lang, Andrew, *The Orange Fairy Book*

Uncanny and mysterious, the huge meniers of Brittany in this old, old legend of greed repaid. May be used with good effect with older children also.

"The Three Gold Pieces" in Aliki (Brandenburg), *The Three Gold Pieces*

Clever illustrations, very colorful, in this humorous Greek folk tale of the way in which three gold pieces influenced human events.

Rose Shades for Flame and Flower

"Briar Rose" in Wiggin, Kate D., and Smith, Nora, *The Fairy Ring*

Well known and loved story of the princess who fell asleep for a hundred years, but wakened to a prince's kiss.

"Snow White and Rose Red" in Grimm Brothers, *Snow White and Rose Red*

Illustrated version by Adrienne Adams, with beautiful color. An old tale of two loving sisters and the great bear who protected them.

"The Firebringer" in Hodges, Margaret, *The Firebringer*

Striking illustrations for the Paiute legend

of Coyote who stole fire and brought it to man. A stunning book, and a well-told tale.

"How Molo Stole the Lovely Rose-Red" in Baker, Augusta, *The Talking Tree*

A mighty sword-hero of ancient China rescues a lovely princess. Unusual, and the emphasis on courage appeals to the children.

Tales from The Rose Fairy Book

"Bobino" in Lang, Andrew, *The Rose Fairy Book*

To his father's dismay and great anger, his only son had learned only how to understand the animals' talk and nothing else! But that knowledge, though it threw the boy into the world to fend for himself, was the making of his fortune. Unusual, not too long, and absorbing.

"The Sprig of Rosemary" in Lang, Andrew, *The Rose Fairy Book*

A Spanish tale, not too long, but very romantic, about an evil spell that took a young bridegroom away from his plucky wife. With the aid of a sprig of rosemary and three walnuts, she rescued him.

"The Dancing Stars" in Rockwell, Anne, *The Dancing Stars*

Iroquois legend of the formation of the Pleiades, simple, colorful.

"The Peasant's Pea Patch" in Daniels, Guy, *The Peasant's Pea Patch*

A well-meaning peasant goes from one hilarious disaster to another, but in the end, comes out none the worse for his troubles. Funny, with very gay illustrations by Quackenbush.

A Hint of Crystal Ice and Snow in Early Morn

"The Silver Saucer and the Crystal Apple" in Ransome, Arthur, *Old Peter's Russian Tales*

Long and romantic, but well liked—the magic apple that enabled anyone to see what was happening anywhere in the world, a treasure indeed!

"The Crystal Coffin" in Lang, Andrew, *The Green Fairy Book*

Enchantment, sorcery, and a poor tailor's courage. Not as well known as many others, fairly short. A Grimm märchen.

"Toads and Diamonds" in Lang, Andrew, *The Blue Fairy Book*

For the kind sister, diamonds dropped from her lips; with the other sister, it was another matter. Well known story with an obvious point.

"Ilse's Crystal Palace" in Olcott, Frances, *Wonder Tales from Goblin Hills*

An enchanted princess beckoned from the distant crystal palace, but did she call for good, or for evil? Fantasy from the Harz Mountains.

A Pink Glow Reflected on Snow-topped Mountains

"Peach Boy" in Sugimoto, Chiyono, *Picture Tales from Japan*

Variation of the story, "Momotaro," told by Uchida. Tiny boy found in a peach becomes brave enough to overcome the demons and make the country safe for his parents. Always good.

"The Little Town Pink and Clean" in Olcott, Frances, *Wonder Tales from Windmill Lands*

The women of Broek, Holland, were so clean is was wicked! Very short, pourquoi story.

"Pinkel and the Witch" in Lang, Andrew, *The Orange Fairy Book*

A variant of "Esben and the Witch" (Manning-Sanders—*Witches*), with a lantern, a goat, and a golden cloak—but with the same rakish humor and lilting taunt.

"The Pink Rabbit" in Fyleman, Rose, *Tea Time Tales*

Wherein a little boy's pet toy rabbit comes alive, but all does not come true in rabbit's dream. Especially for younger ones, a charming fantasy.

Tales from The Pink Fairy Book

"The Flying Trunk" in Lang, Andrew, *The Pink Fairy Book*

Since the spendthrift had nothing to pack in the gift trunk but himself, he did just that—and found that the trunk was magic. A bittersweet, short story which could well be used with older boys and girls, from Hans Christian Andersen.

"The Cunning Shoemaker" in Lang, Andrew, *The Pink Fairy Book*

Similar to "Hudden and Dudden" (Jacobs—*Celtic*), but with slightly different aspects. Funny.

"Peter Bull" in Lang, Andrew, *The Pink Fairy Book*

> A rich, childless farmer and his wife decide to adopt the pretty little bull calf born to their stock, but the school clerk must teach that calf to read so that he may be a worthy heir. How the mistake was compounded and twisted out of shape makes for a good time.

"The Sparrow with the Slit Tongue" in Lang, Andrew, *The Pink Fairy Book*

> A somewhat starker version of "The Tongue Cut Sparrow" (Uchida—*Dancing*). Tenderness rewarded and greed brought to task, in a familiar Japanese folk tale.

Gray for Shadows

"Grey Rabbit Plays a Trick" in Hogner, Dorothy, *Navajo Winter Nights*

> Grey Rabbit, the trickster figure of the Navajo, is up to mischief again, in this amusing folk tale.

"The Tale of Prince Ivan, the Firebird, and the Grey Wolf" in Whitney, Thomas, *The Tale of Prince Ivan, the Firebird, and the Grey Wolf*

> Illustrated by Nanny Hogrogian in lovely color, this long traditional Russian fairy tale, romantic and full of adventure.

"The Mule's Egg" in Carpenter, Frances, *Tales from a Swiss Grandmother*

> Nitwit story of the fellows who believed they would hatch a colt from a melon or squash, here with a Swiss touch.

"Greyling" in Yolen, Jane, *Greyling*

> Somber and beautiful legend from the Shetland Islands of Scotland of the changeling found by a childless couple and raised with love.

Tales from The Grey Fairy Book

"The Bear" in Lang, Andrew, *The Grey Fairy Book*

> Sicilian variant of Cinderella with some strange and interesting differences. Short, fun to tell.

"The Little Grey Manikin" in Olcott, Frances, *Wonder Tales from Goblin Hills*

> The fisherman would be the knight in the ancient castle that shone above the rocks across the river, and this he asked of the manikin who appeared to him. But when the wishes were granted, he was not satisfied.

> A St. John's Day legend from northern Germany.

"Long, Broad, and Quickeye" in Lang, Andrew, *The Grey Fairy Book*

> Czech variant of three remarkable helpers who saved the princess with their magic abilities. Always a good story.

"The Goblin Pony" in Lang, Andrew, *The Grey Fairy Book*

> Somewhat sad and eerie story from France of the goblin pony who rides on Halloween and makes mischief. Very short and atmospheric.

Green for Field and Forest

"The Green Noses" in Weisner, William, *Green Noses*

> Mischievous old droll in a new dress. The unlikeliest succeeds, the rest win green noses. Picture story that is fun to tell.

"Alphege or the Green Monkey" in Wiggin, Kate D., and Smith, Nora, *Magic Casements*

> Rather complex fairy story of the prince turned into a charming green monkey because of his stepmother's jealousy. Found in Lang's *The Yellow Fairy Book* as well. Satisfactory ending pleases the children.

"The Green Children" in Crossley-Holland, Kevin, *The Green Children*

> Strange tale in a picture book format. An ancient British legend about the tiny green children found deep in the coffer pits. Colorful, and an interesting contrast to usual fare.

"The Man with the Green Feather" in Spicer, Dorothy, *13 Goblins*

> Sinister fellow with a sly offer, and sulphurous disposition, is outwitted by a villager. Brisk and funny.

Tales from The Green Fairy Book

"The Half-chick" in Lang, Andrew, *The Green Fairy Book*

> Medio Pollito had a roving spirit and a saucy tongue, and, though only half a chick, he got along very well! Short, cheerful.

"Jorinda and Joringel" in Lang, Andrew, *The Green Fairy Book*

> An old Grimm favorite about the wicked witch and her thousands of birds; a new illustrated edition is available which adds a further dimension to it.

"Hok Lee and the Dwarfs" in Lang, Andrew, *The Green Fairy Book*

> By day respectable, but by night a rascal! It is not at all surprising that the rich Hok Lee was found out by the merry little dwarfs. Fun!

"The Fisherman and His Wife" in Lang, Andrew, *The Green Fairy Book*

> Greedy wife, obliging fish, spineless husband, and a potent rhyme to invoke the magic. Margot Zemach has an illustrated version in stunning color, but Lang's text is more authentic.

The Colors of Easter

"Why the Ivy Is Always Green" in Sechrist, Elizabeth, *It's Time for Easter*

> Short and lovely story of the ivy that covers the ugly bare oak with a living spring garment. Symbolic.

"Tico and the Golden Wings" in Lionni, Leo, *Tico and the Golden Wings*

> Exquisite illustrated edition of the allegory of a golden bird who gives unselfishly to help others, but sacrifices himself. Serious, yet effective.

"The White Blackbird" in Sechrist, Elizabeth, *It's Time for Easter*

> An old story, little known and beautifully told by Padraic Colum, of the lonely boy who found an Easter awakening and a lost treasure. Also in Corrigan, *Holiday Ring*.

"Thirty Gilt Pennies" in Kelsey, Alice, *Thirty Gilt Pennies*

> Several meaningful and most interesting legends devolving around the pennies given to Joseph for the food from Egypt, the gift money of the Wise Men, and the betrayal money of Judas. Must be retold for use in this story hour, and has proved excellent for older children, also. A remarkable tale.

Highlights of White

"The White Lamb" in Manning-Sanders, Ruth, *A Book of Charms and Changelings*

> The sea captain had married a beauty, a jealous shrew who hated his daughter Rosalie. After he went to sea, the stepmother evicted the girl and consulted a witch, but Rosalie came back—as a lamb. . . .

"Suho and the White Horse" in Otsuka, Yuzo, *Suho and the White Horse*

> A haunting tale from Mongolia, illustrated in glowing colors and giving the background of the strange horsehead fiddle found among the nomadic peoples there.

"The Little White Hen" in Kijima, Hajime, *The Little White Hen*

> Gay Japanese variant of an old fox-and-the-hen story, with a lilt, and very attractive illustrations.

"Snow White and the Seven Dwarfs" in Grimm, Jakob, and Grimm, Wilhelm, *Snow White and the Seven Dwarfs*

> A recent edition of the Grimm story, illustrated by Nancy Burkert, brings many facets of the fairy tale into focus. Interesting version, exquisite illustrations.

Accent Colors in Flower and Field

"The Little Horse of Seven Colors" in Lowe, Patricia, *The Little Horse of Seven Colors*

> "If you will teach me something I know nothing about, I will marry you," said the three lovely princesses to the captive prince. But they did not want to learn what he would teach—except the youngest, who offered him a horse of seven colors to take her and flee. Wry humor.

"The Golden Frog" in Surany, Anico, *The Golden Frog*

> Brilliant illustrations based on the San Blas mola designs help tell the story of a boy who found, in an old tomb, one of the precious gold burial-totems, and thus helped his whole village. Unusual, and distinctive.

"Cherry" in Manning-Sanders, Ruth, *Peter and the Piskies*

> The pretty daughter was curious, and her curiosity nearly made an end of her, but just in time she learned her lesson. Somewhat unusual, and whimsical.

"The Gold Bread" in Wiggin, Kate D., and Smith, Nora, *Magic Casements*

> Strange, touching story of the proud maid who would have naught but a gold prince with all his gold trappings for her husband, but who, on receiving her wish, starved; the bread, too, was of gold!

Tales from The Lilac, Crimson, Violet, *and* Olive Fairy Books

"Schippeitaro" in Lang, Andrew, *The Violet Fairy Book*

A ruined temple, a stormy night, and a troop of monstrous cats. . . . Weird and hair-raising, for Halloween or any other time.

"To Your Good Health" in Lang, Andrew, *The Crimson Fairy Book*

Whenever the king sneezed, everyone in the country had to shout, "To your good health, Sire!" But the shepherd with the bright blue eyes would not . . . and a battle of wits began. Humorous, for older children.

"A Long Bow Story" in Lang, Andrew, *The Olive Fairy Book*

If the bunniah was a rich banker, the farmer was a poor sharp-wits. And he believed—never doubting—*everything* the bunniah said—for a price! Clever, rather subtle folk tale from the Far East.

"A Lost Paradise" in Lang, Andrew, *The Lilac Fairy Book*

The charcoal burner and his wife might, from thenceforward, have anything they wished of the king's bounty—only they must not lift the cover of the tureen which stood on the table at every meal. Not long, but intriguing, a reflection on human nature.

A Silver Slant of Raindrops

"The Silver Penny" in Manning-Sanders, Ruth, *A Book of Wizards*

Only a penny for an inheritance—but with the wizard's help, it did very well! Fairy tale fun from Hungary.

"How to Tell a Real Princess" in Lang, Andrew, *The Yellow Fairy Book*

Andersen's short delightful story of the pea and the sensitive girl.

"Three Silver Balls" in Manning-Sanders, Ruth, *A Book of Ghosts and Goblins*

The goblin's closet was dirty and smelly—and it moaned! Scary, fun.

"The Silver Arrow" in Power, Effie, *Bag o' Tales*

Crafty, lovable Robin Hood again outwits the wily Sheriff of Nottingham, and wins a silver arrow. Always good to tell.

And Over All a Rainbow with a Pot of Gold at Its Foot

"Noah and the Rainbow" in Bollinger, Max, *Noah and the Rainbow*

Beautiful, illustrated version of the Old Testament story in dignified and quiet prose.

"Tusya and the Pot of Gold" in Yaroslava, *Tusya and the Pot of Gold*

A Russian variant of the Polish story, "The Fish in the Forest" (Walters—*Clever*), in which the old woman who cannot hold her tongue is made ridiculous. Very funny, but not for the very young, in spite of the delightful pictures.

"The Rainbow Cat" in Fyleman, Rose, *The Rainbow Cat*

Just the first brief part of this modern fantasy will make a short delightful animal story for young children.

"The Crock of Gold" in Jacobs, Joseph, *The Crock of Gold*

Bright and cheerful, the single edition of "The Pedlar of Swaffham (Jacobs—*More*) brought vividly to life by Stobbs's illustrations, and told with British succinctness.

"Rain King's Daughter" in Chrisman, Arthur, *Shen of the Sea*

How the rainbow came to be, from this author's Chinese folktale treasury.

10
Annotations
for Holiday Stories

These stories are grouped in chronological order as the holidays appear during the story year. Many stories in this particular list are taken from the afternoon story hour programs included in this work, and represent stories chosen to fit into the time limits and the program sequence, as discussed in an earlier chapter. Since most of the story hour children are in the first through the fourth grades, the stories represent children of younger age; also, stories used in programs such as these are chosen to fit together and reflect the overall story theme.

This is not necessarily true of other holiday stories used in other storytelling programs—in the schools, or for special occasions. Yet it is worthwhile mentioning these other holiday stories; good stories are not easy to find, and when one is considering the total storytelling program of a community, these suggestions are valid. They have been used with success in an overall program. Even when a very brief annotation has been given for lack of space, the very mention of the story as a usable title with a source will be helpful to new storytellers.

The following stories, for the most part, are taken from six years of after-school storytelling, and their annotations may appear in the story programs as well, if the annotations help illustrate the various themes more fully.

NEW YEAR'S DAY AND THREE KINGS DAY (January 6, also known as "Old Christmas")

"The Three Young Kings" by George S. Albee in Wernecke, H. H., *Christmas Stories from Many Lands*

> Three young high school boys play Three Kings for the poor children of Cardenas, Cuba, by giving away the gifts intended for the rich children. Unusual and good.

"Cinderella" in De la Mare, Walter, *Told Again: Old Tales Told Again*

> "On Twelfth Night there was to be a great ball at the Palace, with dancing and feasting and revelry as had never been known in that country before. Bonfires were to be lit on the hills. . . ." Cinderella in a dramatic, beautiful Twelfth Night variant.

"Patrick and the Golden Slippers" in Milhous, Katherine, *Patrick and the Golden Slippers*

> Patrick gilded the Mummers' shoes to earn his mascot's costume for the traditional New Year's Mummers' Parade in Philadelphia, but at the last moment he saw he'd forgotten to gild his own! Good plot and colorful

background about a tradition still being observed. May be abridged for story programs.

"New Year's Hats for the Statues" in Uchida, Yoshiko, *The Sea of Gold*

Not even a bit of rice to celebrate the New Year! Still, one shares what one has—including a straw hat. Fine version of an old Japanese tale.

LENTENTIDE AND EASTER STORIES

"The Song of the Little Donkey" in Association for Childhood Education, *Told under the Magic Umbrella*

Columbus, the small gray donkey, drew the little cart that held the chairs of the cabinet-maker. One day he turned into a strange lane, and a strange encounter.

"Stealing the Springtime" in Bleeker, Mary N., *Big Music*

Skinkoots, trickster of the Kootenai Indians, dared to steal the moose-skin bag that kept spring captive in a distant lodge. Frank Linderman's fine version of an old, ever satisfying story.

"The Legend of Saint Christopher" in Farjeon, Eleanor, *Ten Saints*

The great giant looked for a beloved master whom he might serve forever and he found him in a little child at the ferry landing.

"The Country Bunny and The Little Gold Shoes" in Heyward, DuBose, *The Country Bunny and the Little Gold Shoes*

Mother Cottontail has 21 children and a pair of tiny gold shoes, and this is how she earned them. Modern fantasy, that must be abridged for young children.

"The Sugar Egg" in Lord, Priscilla, and Foley, Daniel, *An Easter Garland*

How sugar eggs, with their windows offering magic peeks, came to be.

"Where One Is Fed, a Hundred May Dine" in Sawyer, Ruth, *The Way of the Storyteller*

The unknown guest, friendless and hungry, brings a new meaning into the host's dwelling. Poignant and Symbolic.

"The White Blackbird" in Sechrist, Elizabeth, *It's Time for Easter*

Padraic Colum has written a lovely story of a lonely boy and the strange captive bird, freed by a little wren. (Also in *Holiday Ring* by Corrigan.)

HALLOWEEN

"Spearfinger, the Witch" in Bell, Corydon, *John Rattling-gourd*

Always hungry, always hunting for human livers—and she feared neither arrows nor fire. Indian, atmospheric.

"Schippeitaro and the Monster Cat" in Belting, Natalia, *Cat Tales*

Many had tried, all had failed—the monster lurked and waited to pounce! Suspenseful, dramatic. Also in Andrew Lang's *The Violet Fairy Book*

"Chunk o' Meat" in Chase, Richard, *Grandfather Tales*

The little boy found a strange Thing in the bean patch and reaped dire consequences when he appropriated it! Scary.

"Sop Doll" in Chase, Richard, *The Jack Tales*

"The sorriest bunch of witches the world has known"—but not to Jack. Good, and scary. (Also in Helen Hoke's *Spooks, Spooks, Spooks*.)

"Horace, the Happy Ghost" in Child Study Assoc., *The Holiday Story Book*

Horace was too naive and cheerful to be a good chain-clanker, so he failed the ghost test—but he was so lovable!

"Elizabeth the Cow Ghost" in DuBois, William, *Elizabeth the Cow Ghost*

An ungainly ghost, extraordinary happenings! Unusual.

"The Hobyahs" in Fenner, Phyllis, *Giants and Witches and a Dragon or Two*

The impossible critters who finished off little dog Turpie create scare nonsense. (Also in Joseph Jacobs's *More English Fairy Tales*.)

"The Hungry Old Witch" in Finger, Charles, *Tales from Silver Lands*

Bravery, gentleness, and greed combined in a chiller! Excellent.

"Travelling Companions" in Fisher, Agnes, *Once upon a Time*

How did a goblin get into "The Bremen Town Musicians?" But there he is, big as life, and lots of fun. May also be used for general storytelling.

"The Goblin Who Turned into a Doorknocker" in Fyleman, Rose, *Tea Time Tales*

Delicious fantasy—the mischievous wizard and the small green goblin who escaped by hiding on a door.

"Boy Who Drew Cats" in Gruenberg, Sidonie, *Favorite Stories Old and New*

The boy who drew cats, so natural they looked alive! And one night, one cat had blood on its mouth—from whence, why? Dramatic Japanese folktale.

"The Conjure Wives" in Harper, Wilhelmina, *Ghosts and Goblins*

Spooky, repetitive, spell-binding—short recipe for a good shiver if told in the original words.

"The Witches' Shoes" in Harper, Wilhelmina, *Ghosts and Goblins*

Iron can break a witch's spell, as the blacksmith's apprentice knew, luckily.

"The Buried Moon" in Jacobs, Joseph, *More English Fairy Tales*

Bogs, black water, and the very moon mired deep in the marsh grasses. Full of bogles, shivers, and atmosphere.

"The Hedley Kow" in Jacobs, Joseph, *More English Fairy Tales*

Big black pot turned itself into this, then that, and finally put out lanky legs and disappeared into the dusk with a mocking laugh—and the old woman felt herself blest!

"Mr. Miacca" in Ness, Evaline, *Mr. Miacca*

Tommy Grimes was sometimes good, sometimes bad: one day Mr. Miacca caught him and stuffed him into his dinner bag! (Also in Joseph Jacobs' *English Fairy Tales*.)

"Queer Company" in Jacobs, Joseph, *English Fairy Tales*

"In came a pair of small, small legs and sat down on the broad, broad soles. . . ." Rhythmic, scary, delightful!

"The Tale of the Hairy Toe" in Jagendorf, Moritz, *Ghostly Tales*

"The door opened with a crash, and in came the strangest creature ever seen in North Carolina. . . ." Short, eerie mountain folktale with a scare ending.

"The Big Black Umbrella" in Leach, Maria, *The Rainbow Book of American Fairy Tales*

An enigma—where did it come from—from whom? Was Death its owner? Brief, enigmatic.

"The Leg of Gold" in Manning-Sanders, Ruth, *A Book of Ghosts and Goblins*

Off went the lady's leg, on went its solid gold replacement—and then the trouble began!

"The Giant Bones" in Nic Leodhas, Sorche, *Gaelic Ghosts*

In Caledonia, on a lonely Scottish causeway, there dwelt once a race of men whose giant bones still moulder in some near unknown cave. Excellent, hard to tell.

"Black Cat of the Witch Dance" in Olcott, Frances, *Wonder Tales from Goblin Hills*

Magic herbs, moonlight, a black witch-cat. Short, good. (Also in Wilhelmina Harper's *Ghosts and Goblins*.)

"Baba Yaga and the Little Girl" in Ransome, Arthur, *Old Peter's Russian Tales*

A Russian witch riding mortar and pestle, a house on chicken legs, standing all scary in the woods, greedy eyes looking for a girl. . . .

"The Coffin That Moved Itself" in Spicer, Dorothy, *13 Ghosts*

Among the hills of Drie, Holland, a lonely shepherd ghost wanders still because, they say, he caused a coffin to jump! Good fare for shivers.

"Ghost Goblins' Gold" in Spicer, Dorothy, *13 Ghosts*

A foolish tongue runs away with the secret, and so a treasure is lost forever!

"The Three Misty Women" in Spicer, Dorothy, *13 Witches*

A honey cake, and a brave heart, can oust the wierdest witch!

THANKSGIVING

"The Ballad of the Pilgrim Cat" in Wibberley, Leonard, *The Ballad of the Pilgrim Cat*

In verse, obviously, but may be told in prose with some introductory verse. The plot is good; this is worth experimenting with.

"The Quick-running Squash" in Aspinwall, Alicia, *Short Stories for Short People*

The little boy planted a garden, but the garden squash ran away with the little boy—a fine howdy-do! (Also in Wilhelmina Harper's *The Harvest Feast*.)

"The First Thanksgiving" in Barksdale, Lena, *The First Thanksgiving*

Simplified background material which may be adapted to story form very easily.

"How the Turkey Got His White Tail Feathers" in Belting, Natalia, *The Long-Tailed Bear*

Tewa pourquoi story of the turkeys who scuttled to safety (almost!) during the Flood.

"The Perambulatin' Pumpkin" in Credle, Ellis, *Tall Tales from High Hills*

The pumpkin knew he was special, so he rolled down the hills, into the fairgrounds, carrying his mistress with him, right to the prize table. Sounds tall, and is!

"The Kingdom of the Greedy" in Harper, Wilhelmina, *The Harvest Feast*

The king saw that his subjects wanted only pastry, so he devised a clever ruse—they should have their cake and eat it too, every last crumb! Modern, and easy.

"The Pumpkin Child" in Mehdevi, Ann S., *Persian Folk and Fairy Tales*

A Persian parallel on the Cinderella motif, surprising and whimsical.

"The Pumpkin Giant" in Ross, Eulalie S., *The Lost Half Hour*

Aeneas saw his father overcome the Giant Shakes and slay the monster with a giant potato . . . upon which the pumpkin giant became the main ingredient in pumpkin pie, to everyone's delight! Also published as a retelling by Ellin Greene, "The Pumpkin Giant."

CHRISTMAS

"The Golden Cobwebs" in Dickenson, Alice, *Children's Book of Christmas Stories*

An old German folktale of the small brown spiders who covered the Christmas tree, leaving webs everywhere; an angel transformed them into gold.

"About a Noble Camel" in Eaton, Anne, *The Animals' Christmas*

A camel of the Wisemen offered to act as a toy for the camel driver's small son, except for a brief time every Three King's Day. Unusual, fetching, and appropriate for Epiphany, also.

"The Christmas Spider" in Eaton, Anne, *The Animals' Christmas*

Short Polish folktale of the silken-spun coverlet the spider wove to wrap the Child.

"The Lamb and the Child" in Frye, Dean, *The Lamb and the Child*

Medieval legend of the tricky shepherds whose knavery boomerangs and leads them to the Child. Illustrated by Duvoisin.

"The Shoemaker and the Elves" in Grimm, Jakob, and Grimm, Wilhelm, *The Shoemaker and the Elves*

Essence of Christmas, with the generous elves and the grateful shoemaker. Illustrated by Adams.

"Why the Evergreen Trees Keep Their Leaves" in Holbrooke, Florence, *A Book of Nature Myths*

The little evergreen that gave shelter, and showed kindness, was rewarded with evergreen foliage, to this day.

"The Yule Tomte" in Luckhardt, Mildred, *Christmas Comes Again*

Swedish Christmas, and the little tomte finds a way to bring joy to a hard-pressed family.

"The Christmas Apple" in Sawyer, Ruth, *This Way to Christmas*

The little clockmaker gives all he has, an apple saved for Christmas, at the great altar of the Cathedral—and Mary smiles. Well-liked.

"The Christmas That Was Nearly Lost" in Sawyer, Ruth, *This Way to Christmas*

When Santa Claus tried to take a vacation, it led to very upsetting events. Gay and heartwarming.

"Schnitzle, Schnotzle, Schnootzle" in Sawyer, Ruth, *The Long Christmas*

In the Tyrolean Alps, the Goblin King Laurin visits one family each Christmas Eve—and this was the year for the poor cobbler and his three small sons. Rollicking humor, perfect for telling.

"The Voyage of the Wee Red Cap" in Sawyer, Ruth, *This Way to Christmas.*

Tender, jaunty, never worn-out—the tale of the red caps of the fairy-folk who open Teig's eyes to Christmas!

"The Christmas Bear" in Sperry, Margaret, *Scandinavian Stories*

Freya, the polar bear, and her master Lars, started on a Christmas journey to the King of Denmark, but lodged en route with a woodsman whose house the trolls took over each Christmas Eve. Often called "The Cat on the Doverfell (Asbjornsen—*East*).

"The Baby Bears' Christmas Stockings" in Walters, Maude A., *A Book of Christmas Stories*

Small bears' search for a stocking-vine leads to a honey tree and a tumble-down shack. Obvious humor, especially for the very young.

"The Christmas Cuckoo" in Walters, Maude A., *A Book of Christmas Stories*

The gift of a merry heart or wealth. Which is better?

"The Little Green Elf's Christmas" in Walters, Maude A., *A Book of Christmas Stories*

C. S. Bailey's whimsical story of frost fairies and fireflies and stars to adorn a tree.

"Piccola" in Walters, Maude A., *A Book of Christmas Stories*

In Italy, Piccola put out her little wooden shoe, and found a most surprising present.

"The Sabot of Little Wolf" in Walters, Maude A., *A Book of Christmas Stories*

Miracle story by Francois Coppée of the Christ Child's visit to the great cathedral. Tell carefully to avoid saccharinity.

Additional Stories Used for School Visits and Other Occasions

The following stories have been repeatedly used in school programs where only one story at a time was needed, or in groups that were homogeneous in age and in interest. In general, they were tied into the particular yearly program theme of the public library after-school story hours. However, since school visiting programs allocate more time for each individual class story, these stories tend to be geared to a particular grade; they may be introduced with background material; and they may vary from twelve to twenty minutes in telling, or sometimes more. They have been carefully chosen, and are often presented in a more formal situation than in a story hour. As a resource for new storytellers, they suggest a wide selection of appropriate holiday materials.

NEW YEAR'S DAY AND TWELFTH NIGHT

"Babouscka" in Smith, Dorothy H., *Tall Book of Christmas*

For young children, first grade or kindergarten age, the short account of Babouscka and her continual search for the Child.

"The Three Magi" in Belpré, Pura, *The Tiger and the Rabbit*

The night the kings left there was general confusion, but even greater confusion existed when Father Time fell asleep and mixed up the schedule. Humorous turn to an old Puerto Rican tale, suitable for fourth and fifth grades.

"Frankincense and Myrrh" in Becker, May L., *The Home Book of Christmas*

Heywood Broun's touching short vignette of the three kings, suitable for sixth grade.

"The Legend of Befana" in Chafetz, Henry, *The Legend of Befana*

A long, beautifully written legend on the Befana theme, suitable for third and fourth grades, with lovely illustrations by the author.

"Old Christmas Eve: The Mummers Play" in Chase, Richard, *Grandfather Tales*

Authentic reenactment of the traditional Twelfth Night Play, still given in remote parts of the North Carolina mountains. May be used with a reading of the traditional Mummers Play; of interest to fourth and fifth grades.

"Torten's Christmas Secret" in Dolbier, Maurice, *Torten's Christmas Secret*

A sleigh, an astonished bear, and a worried boy help Santa.

"The Three Kings of Saba" in Evers, Alf, *The Three Kings of Saba*

A legend of the three kings and the visit they made to see the Christ Child; each saw himself reflected as he viewed the Child. Based on legendary material found in the ancient travel journals of Marco Polo. Grades five and six.

"The Twelfth Night Santons" in Garthwaite, Marion, *The Twelfth Night Santons*

A wonderful story of the old santon-maker in France, and the boy who yearned to work with him. Vivid French customs and smooth style, but the story must be abridged. Excellent for fourth or fifth grade.

"The Golden Legend" in Harper, Wilhelmina, and Hazeltine, Alice, *Merry Christmas to You*

Based on legendary material surrounding the journey and the entombment of the Eastern Magi. For fifth and sixth grades.

"The Months of the Year" in Herda, Helmutt, *Fairy Tales from Many Lands*

A traditional Czech tale of the proud and the pretty, girls who separately seek fruit and flowers in off-seasons, at the stepmother's behest. The twelve months are on hand to help. For third and fourth grades. (Also in Virginia Haviland's *Favorite Fairy Tales Told in Czechoslovakia*.)

"Baboushka and the Three Kings" in Robbins, Ruth, *Baboushka and the Three Kings*

Caldecott winner, in a single edition retelling of the Russian gift-giver and her penchant for sweeping that made her miss finding the Babe. For young children.

"The Legend of Befana" in Sechrist, Elizabeth, *Its Time for Christmas*

In warm Italy, busy little Befana missed the Manger because she had not yet finished her housework, so still she seeks the Baby with a basket of toys on her arm each anniversary of the Magi's visit. For very young children, a variant of the other Baboushka stories.

"Caspar's Story" in Sechrist, Elizabeth, *It's Time for Christmas*

John Oxenham has written a fantasy on the third wiseman, beautiful, long, and of interest to older children, perhaps sixth graders.

LENTENTIDE AND EASTER

"The Baker's Top-hat Bunny" in Child Study Assoc., *The Holiday Story Book*

An elegant fellow, the rabbit, in his black

topper! But he was sold for ten cents to the perfect buyer. For first and second graders.

"Ys and Her Bells" in Cothran, Jean, *Magic Bells*

"The ghost of poor King Gralon has been wandering over the small paths of Brittany through the golden mist, for over fifteen hundred years. . . ." So begins the legend of the old city of Ys, whose bells lie under the sea. For fourth and fifth grades.

"A Dust Rag for Easter Eggs" in Cuneo, Mary L., *Silver Stories, Golden Verse*

In the aftermath of World War II, the Gang-of-the-cat-who-goes-fishing finds a benefactor and wonderful eggs for Easter. Realism for third and fourth grades.

"The Giant and the Mite" in Farjeon, Eleanore, *The Little Bookroom*

Symbolic, and beautifully written. For fourth and fifth grades.

"The Girl Who Kissed the Peach Tree" in Farjeon, Eleanore, *The Little Bookroom*

Imaginative tale based on the Sicilian custom of peasants who cherish the fruit trees growing under the shadow of an active volcano. For third and fourth grades.

"The Pedlar of Ballaghadereen" in Fenner, Phyllis, *Feasts and Frolics*

Ruth Sawyer's charming retelling of the "Pedlar of Swaffham" makes it a choice for the Lenten season. For third and fourth grades.

"The Shepherd's Nosegay" in Fillmore, Parker, *The Shepherd's Nosegay*

A merry princess and a gay shepherd who made her say "please", and like it! For third and fourth grades.

"The Gypsy Woman and the Good Lord," in Jagendorf, Moritz, and Tillhagen, C., *The Gypsies' Fiddle*

Taikon's version of the legend of Christ who sought, in disguise, the hospitality of a villager. For fourth and fifth grades.

"An Egg Is for Wishing" in Kay, Helen, *An Egg Is for Wishing*

Charming illustrations, in a gay single edition tale of a small boy who found not only the right eggs for pysanky—Ukranian eggs—but his own pint-sized courage as well. For second and third grades.

"Who Makes the Heart to Sing" in Lillie, Amy, *The Book of Three Festivals*

From the Middle Ages and Cluny Abbey, a crusader tale with a serious and significant theme, for fifth and sixth grades.

"The Egg Tree" in Milhous, Katherine, *The Egg Tree*

Caldecott winner about the Pennsylvania Dutch custom of decorating egg-trees during Lent to celebrate the Easter season. Abridge somewhat, and use the author's illustrations afterwards. About third grade.

"The Princess and the Vagabone" in Sawyer, Ruth, *The Way of the Storyteller*

Beautiful princess, hateful temper, and love strong enough to tame it—a fine story for fourth and fifth grades. (Also in Sally Patrick Johnson's *The Princesses*.)

"The Boy Who Discovered the Spring" in Sechrist, Elizabeth, *It's Time for Easter*

A lonely hermit and an elf discover the secret of ongoing life. Somewhat sentimental, but a good presentation makes it significant. For second and third grades.

"Candles at Midnight" in Sechrist, Elizabeth, *It's Time for Easter*

Kelsey's story of post-World War II Greece, and the boy who longed for a tall white candle and a rocket to celebrate the holy season. For fourth and fifth grades.

"The Quest for the Holy Grail" in Sechrist, Elizabeth, *It's Time for Easter*

The old legend of Sir Galahad and his search for the Holy Grail, suitable for fourth and fifth grades. Should be tightened for best results.

"The Magic Mountain" in Spicer, Dorothy, *13 Witches*

In Bohemia, in the old days, they say strange things happen on Good Friday, and so Annie's greed led her to discover. For third and fourth grades.

"The Witch in the Hill" in Spicer, Dorothy, *13 Witches*

Shrove Tuesday, pancake day in England. But Witch Hitty fries her pancakes deep under Conger Hill, for a special reason. Unusual, for third and fourth grades.

HALLOWEEN

"The Three Pumpkins" in Barnet, George, *Stories for Fun*

A huge pumpkin, and a small grain of honest sense! The storyteller must improve the style, but the plot is right for first and second grades.

"The Tinker and the Ghost" in Boggs, Ralph, and Davis, M. G., *Three Golden Oranges*

Practical, rib-tickling variant of the scare story, "The Boy Who Was Never Afraid" (Hatch—*More Danish*), for second and third grades.

"The Fierce Yellow Pumpkin" in Gruenberg, Sidonie, *Favorite Stories Old and New*

Little pumpkin laughed a ziggety-zaggety chortle with his fierce small face, and scared away the mice! Jack-o-lantern fun for kindergarten and first grade.

"Tomson's Halloween" in Harper, Wilhelmina, *Ghosts and Goblins*

Tomson, the witch's big black cat; a talking broom; and one shy little cat—thus cat dreams come true! Fun for first and second grades.

"King o' the Cats" in Jacobs, Joseph, *More English Fairy Tales*

A sexton's wife listens to the husband's ghostly cat-story while Old Tom raises his hairs and yowls—word play on scary themes. For second and third grades.

"Teeny-Tiny" in Jacobs, Joseph, *English Fairy Tales*

For tiny people, a tiny scare, with a tiny screech to end it!

"The Eternal Wanderer of the Pampas" in Jagendorf, Moritz, *The King of the Mountain*

Neither home nor family was enough for the greedy weaver—so he lost all!

"Sandy MacNeil and His Dog" in Nic Leodhas, Sorche, *Gaelic Ghosts*

The ghost of the faithful canine still haunts his beloved master's steps. An unusual tale that even sixth graders enjoy.

"When Witches Rode Broomsticks" in Miller, Alice B., *Heroes, Outlaws, and Funny Fellows*

A New England legend of what happens when witches take political sides and outshriek their opponents. For fifth and sixth grades.

THANKSGIVING

"The Horn of Plenty" in Olcott, Frances, *Good Stories for Great Holidays*

An unfamiliar myth told by Ovid, suitable for fourth and fifth grades.

"Old Man Rabbit's Dinner Party" in Bailey, Carolyn S., *Old Man Rabbit's Dinner Party*

A dinner shared with others is a dinner doubled. For kindergarten and first grade, a cheerful picture story.

"Little Boy Pie" in Gruenberg, Sidonie, *Favorite Stories Old and New*

Turn the tables, and instead of "eating crow," the rook-crows are eating Little Boy Pie in a field of bread and butter. Delightful fantasy, for first and second grades.

"Black Sheep's Coat" in Harper, Wilhelmina, *The Harvest Feast*

Laid in the days of Squantum and the first settlement, a story both thoughtful and engrossing of the interaction between the English settlers and the Red Men. Should be tightened in telling to fifth and sixth grades, however. Written by an author who has carefully researched the background, Cornelia Meigs.

"Indian Summer" in Harper, Wilhelmina, *The Harvest Feast*

Rough Massachusetts terrain, a tiny settlement, and a raging fire that threatens everyone; in battling these mutual dangers, the Indian and white children lay a basis for future friendship. For fifth and sixth grades.

"The Spirit of the Corn" in Jagendorf, Moritz, *Kwi-Na the Eagle*

The origin of corn, according to the Indians of the New York forests. Grades three and four.

ST. NICHOLAS DAY, DECEMBER 6

"The Gift of St. Nicholas" in Association for Childhood Education, *Told under the Christmas Tree*

A wonderful pipe that got Klaas a chest of gold and the burgomeester a paddling. Delightful to tell, and funny. For third and fourth grades.

"The Gifts of the Bell-Schneckel" in Bailey, Carolyn S., *Tops and Whistles*

Among the Pennsylvania Dutch, the Holland "Sint Nicolaas" was transformed into "Sch-Neckel," and this is the story of the celebration of that good saint in the new land, based on actual events. Must be abridged for use with fourth and fifth grades, but is out-of-the-ordinary holiday fare.

"Mikulás, Bearer of Gifts" in Seredy, Kate, *The Good Master*

Hungary, in days past, called the birthday of St. Nicholas the day of Mikulás, and that day found all little boots set out on the windowsills overflowing with goodies.

HANUKKAH

"The Cruse of Oil" in Association for Childhood Education, *Told under the Christmas Tree*

The oil which lighted the great Menorah lasted miraculously, and in memory of that great day, Hanukkah candles are still burned. For third and fourth grades.

"How K'tonton Took a Ride on a Runaway Trendel" in Weilerstein, Sadie, *The Adventures of K'tonton*

Delightful story of the thumb-sized rascal whose big trendel took him on a merry adventure that was nearly fatal! (Also found in Association for Childhood Education's *Told Under the Christmas Tree*.) For second and third grades.

"The Festival of Lights" in Association for Childhood Education, *Told under the Christmas Tree*

The story of the great Temple, won back from the Greeks by Judas Maccabeus, and the miracle that took place at that time. For third and fourth grades.

CHRISTMAS

"Why the Chimes Rang" in Alden, Raymond, *Why the Chimes Rang*

Little Brother's piece of silver, not the king's golden crown, rang the wonderful carillon. For third and fourth grades; popular.

"The Fir Tree" in Andersen, Hans Christian, *Complete Andersen*

Bittersweet story of the little tree whose one desire was to be a Christmas tree, and whose wish was granted. For fourth and fifth grades.

"Pedro, the Angel of Olvera Street" in Angelo, Valenti, *Pedro, the Angel of Olvera Street*

Black-eyed and lively, but Pedro sang like an angel, and the red wings suited him perfectly when he led the Posada. For second and third grades; Mexican flavor.

"The Story of the First Christmas Tree" in Smith, Dorothy H., *Tall Book of Christmas*

When a storm covered the path, fairy lights showed the woodcutter safely home. Brief, good for kindergarten and first grade.

"O Children of the Wind and Pines" in Baker, Laura, *O Children of the Wind and Pines*

In the deep woodlands, the Huron Indians of Canada heard their first Christmas carol, Jesus Ahatonhia, from a French priest.

"Lullabye" in Bernhard, Josephine, *Lullabye*

The song the small gray pussy sang to the Babe. A Polish folktale, short, sweet, for the very young. (Also in Association of Childhood Education's *Told under the Christmas Tree*.)

"Pinto's Journey" in Bronson, Wilfred, *Pinto's Journey*

Big Earrings, the Pueblo silversmith whose turquoise jewelry supported the family, needed the stones hidden in the Saddle Range mountains but he could not get them. His grandson went forth secretly to bring him the turquoise for Christmas, facing much danger. Unusual, and strong, but must be somewhat abridged for telling. For fourth and fifth grades.

"The Little Pagan Faun" in Colwell, Eileen, *A Storyteller's Choice*

The merry little tune of the wee faun brought laughter to the Child on his first birthday, and a piece of cake for the piper. Unusual, whimsical, for third and fourth grades.

"The Little Juggler" in Cooney, Barbara, *The Little Juggler*

Beautifully illustrated and simply retold, another version of the Cluny Abbey miracle,

more restrained and rhythmic. For third and fourth grades.

"The Christmas Tree of Good St. Florentin" in Dalgleish, Alice, *Christmas*

A legend of the hermit saint, Florentin, and his tiny tree in the chapel. From Alsace-Lorraine, for third and fourth grades.

"The Bird Began to Sing" in Field, Rachel, *The Bird Began to Sing*

Old and not well remembered, but still good—the story of the bird in the carved box that sang again on Christmas Eve. For third and fourth grades.

"Christmas through a Knothole" in Gibson, Katherine, *The Tell-It-Again Book*

A sparkling little tale, bouyant and cheerful, of toys and the Christmas dinner that were shoved through the knothole of the jail. For second and third grades.

"One Luminaria for Antonio" in Hood, Flora, *One Luminaria for Antonio*

In New Mexico, the villagers create luminarias made from brown bags with a candle burning in sand inside to greet the Christmas Child. Antonio found only a broken bit of candle. Unusual and good, for second and third grades.

"The Christmas Nightingale" in Kelly, Eric, *The Christmas Nightingale*

A long, romantic Christmas story of the heir who at last found his heritage, with a rich background of old Polish customs. Must be abridged, but can be very absorbing for fourth and fifth grades.

"In Clean Hay" in Kelly, Eric, *In Clean Hay*

For 700 years the szopka puppet play of the Nativity had been performed on the streets of Krakow on Christmas Eve, but this year a miracle took place. Must be abridged, but is worth it.

"A Gift Should Be Given" in Luckhardt, Mildred, *Christmas Comes Again*

Gifts were prepared for the prince in the small mountain village on the Black Sea; but it was a stranded traveler, not the prince, who needed the gifts most. Meaningful, for fourth and fifth grades.

"How the Good Gifts Were Used by Two" in Pyle, Howard, *The Wonder Clock*

Told with zest, good humor, and Pyle's special ingredients of style. The Christmas spirit for third and fourth graders, in a pleasing guise.

"Juan's Burro" in Roehrenbeck, William, *Christmastide*

A goatboy finds his voice in time to sing a Christmas paean of praise in this Mexican miracle story of Juan-the-tongue-tied. Strong plot, but some adapting is necessary. For fourth and fifth grades.

"The Juggler of Notre Dame" in Sawyer, Ruth, *The Way of the Storyteller*

Beautiful retelling of the legend of the little juggler who dedicated his acrobatic talents to Our Lady of Cluny Abbey, especially liked by third and fourth graders.

"The Precious Herbs of Christmas" in Sawyer, Ruth, *Joy to the World*

A legend of Goodlad who set out to find the herbs of healing to brew for his mother. But the herbs must have the first snow on them, and by faith they must be gathered. Unusual and symbolic, for fourth and fifth grades.

"This Is the Christmas" in Sawyer, Ruth, *Joy to the World*

A strong, dramatic story hundreds of years old from Serbia, about the blind singer who found a radiant light. For sixth graders and up.

"San Froilan of the Wilderness" in Sawyer, Ruth, *Joy to the World*

Spanish legend says that in the years following the Goths, a Brother came to these pagan forests and, because of the small creches he erected at the crosspaths, became accepted by the people. A mixture of tragedy and joy, with a haunting quality. For fifth and sixth grades.

"Gifts for the First Birthday" in Sechrist, Elizabeth, *It's Time for Christmas*

An ancient gypsy legend, beautifully retold by Ruth Sawyer, explaining the origin of the robin's red breast. Grades two and three.

"The Tree That Didn't Get Trimmed" in Sechrist, Elizabeth, *It's Time for Christmas*

Cryptic and flavorful, an out-of-the-ordinary story by master storyteller Christopher Morley, especially good for upper grades.

"The Worker in Sandalwood" in Sechrist, Elizabeth, *It's Time for Christmas*

A desperately weary, awkward youth finds his cabinetwork on the Christmas Creche taken over by a Master Craftsman on Christmas Eve. Can be used with sixth graders and older.

"The Third Lamb" in Hazeltine, Alice, and Smith, E. S., *A Christmas Book of Legends*

From the Dolomite valley, the story of Dritte the Woodcarver, who dared to depart from carving saints for cathedrals to carving lambs for children. For fourth and fifth grades; beautiful to hear and to tell.

"Jared's Gift" in Vance, Marguerite, *Jared's Gift*

The Magi sought a jar to replace his own cracked jar, and his choice fell on Jared's vase. "A vessel fitting for a King's gift of myrrh. . . ." Story is excellent, but must be abridged. For fifth and sixth grades.

"Fulfilled" in Wiggin, Kate D., and Smith, Nora, *Magic Casements*

Two brothers each extend Christmas hospitality, each reap a reward reflecting the individual nature of each brother; but one is richly endowed, and the other punished for greed. For third and fourth grades.

Part 3

PROGRAM ENRICHMENT

11

Some Suggestions

Ask a child what programming is, and you will usually receive a blank stare and a shrug of indifference, yet that child may actually engage in a kind of programming, selecting programs from the variety offered on television. Perhaps the chosen programs feature adventure, travel, or contact with people or events from the past. The actual act of selection indicates an interest in a particular direction. Motivation for the selection may be a latent interest in the wide seas, in forests centuries old, in the white polar regions, or the beckoning challenge of outer space. Through today's pictorial media a child becomes a part of all these areas vicariously, through television, filmstrips, slides, wide screen productions, and occasionally stories or commentaries.

In direct line with the current technological explosion of information, however, the child has often become merely an onlooker, rather than a participant, in creative experience. As a spectator, the child may formulate many questions, such as "What makes a moon explorer?" or "How do you make a ship fly?" Within the periphery of a school community, some children indeed begin to discover principles, concepts, and forces they can use to reckon rationally. These are the children who will push the doors of science and knowledge ever wider

as they mature, the children who will eventually, become active, performing agents on the frontiers of unfolding knowledge and scientific development.

But what about the other boys and girls, those who wonder about many things, but possess no inner urge or compulsion to find their own answers? They also possess curiosity and imagination that should find fulfillment in daily living. And, to a limited degree, spectator sports and activities will satisfy this urge; participating as an audience in live theater, festivals, and concerts will help also to bridge the gap on a limited scale. But the most meaningful experiences for children as a whole come when they themselves begin to create word-patterns, scenes, characters, figures, pictures, and sounds in an informal recreational environment, as opposed to the more regimented formal setup of a curriculum-oriented time and place.

And today's informed children, with their wide exposure to the world, need just those experiences that build their inner spirits, stimulate their creative talents, challenge their imagination, and finally, satisfy their social instincts in meaningful work-play relationships. Because this is true, some additional suggestions to open up creative story programming are suggested below. Though these experiences have been developed in public library groups, they are valid for camps, neighborhood centers, vacation and play schools, recreation programs, church-oriented activities, and so on, as well. Today there are too few—if any—opportunities for children to hear good storytelling and to participate through informal dramatics in related story activities.

Librarians are in a unique position to help children find some of these opportunities. Why? Perhaps because they are not caught in a web of interpersonal relationships as tightly as a school librarian or a teacher. Teachers, administrators, and other personnel feel the constraint of curricula demands, standards of education, requirements of boards, the press of schedules, and the necessity to achieve specific goals within a defined time schedule. A librarian, of course, works with other staff personnel and with patrons, and yet has a certain independence in planning; and the librarian in a public children's department has more opportunities to discover and explore new techniques and to develop progressive activities for those children who choose to become a part of the program. "Choose" is a key term, at once indicative of both the strength and the weakness of library work with children. In a public library no child is forced, or even expected, to appear on schedule, and many do not choose to come. Yet those who do come, do so because they want to, and in most cases will remain as long as they feel satisfaction and refreshment.

Many years ago the librarian served as the person who "told the stories," and indeed this remains one of the librarian's most satisfying and exciting roles, providing stories for all ages, in endless variety. But the librarian can now supplement experiences with music, cassettes, tapes, filmstrips, puppets, and slides. Children can now be guided to write their own verse, create their own dramatic skits and plays, act out and record for themselves with cassettes and tapes, in puppet theaters, or through choral speech groups. The librarian has only to show the children and help them create displays, exhibits, paper-folding, origami, paper cutting, or papier-mâché projects. They themselves are capable of bringing songs, skits, stories, folktales, old ballads, poems, and historical figures to life through shadow plays, masques, pantomime, dialogue, marionette and puppet creations, or monologues. All of this is included in the concept of creative programming. The materials and direc-

tions are all around in a good library collection, and even in the most limited circumstances all kinds of creative experiences may be worked out by boys and girls.

From the storyteller's vantage point, it is eye-opening how many dramatists, artists, musicians, ballet choreographers, puppeteers, and marionettists have turned to the field of folklore for inspiration. In Germany alone there are more than 150 dramatizations of the Grimm stories. Perrault's *All the French Fairy Tales* has provided "Cinderella," "Beauty and the Beast," and "Red Riding Hood." Since 1830 more than 40 operas have been composed based on such Grimm favorites as "Hansel and Gretel," and "Briar Rose," both in the complete edition of *Grimm's Fairy Tales*. Countless choral and instrumental compositions have been written around such figures as Tyll Eulenspiegel, the Sorcerer's Apprentice, Peter and the Wolf—all of them rooted in folklore. The use of recordings from such literature can enrich the children's appreciation of the material. In one program, paper silhouettes illustrating a number of these music stories were cut and presented as shadowgraphs along with excerpts from the records. Shadowgraphs (scenes cut in silhouette, and shown against a shadow-screen) were used at another story hour session to illustrate scenes from the stories told during the year, asking the children to identify the tales. The story of the all-too-real princess, as told by Andersen ("The Real Princess"), was cut in silhouette scenes, and reflected as the story was read, to celebrate Andersen's birthday. For other programs, shadow-puppets have acted out stories, with taped dialogue.

In a spring puppet workshop, paper bag, finger, stick, and mitten puppets were created to form tableaux from many different stories, with a running narrative based on one of the story programs for the year. Again, tall tale figures were created and a separate cast read the dramatic adaptation from the story, as the puppets pantomimed the action.

Puppet plays dramatized from folktales, using many kinds of marionettes and puppets, have presented programs for special groups in the community; spur-of-the-moment puppetry has evolved by combining a recording of a storytelling record with sock-puppets and tabletop stages. Such recordings as those made by Anne Pellowski, Christine Price, Ruth Sawyer, and Ed Begley can be used. Such impromptu creativity can supplement story programs very well. With longer practise and more complex workshops, marionettes made of newspapers or styrofoam can be created. Material found in the well-known Arabian Nights tales may be written as scripts, or as a narrative text, using a marionette storyteller synchronized with a tape. Many African tales lend themselves to this sort of production very well. Masks, as well, are easy to make from papier-mâché, bags, paper plates, aluminum foil; these can be used with scripts, or in pantomime with a narrator.

A summer audiovisual workshop adapted several folk plays, dramatized them, and put them onto cassettes. The students used an overhead projector, placing on the projector frame a miscellany of seeds, plants, weeds, buttons, cellophane, colored paper, and cutouts. The reflected image was then photographed with a 35mm. slide camera, and music was synchronized with the slide narration.

Use of an opaque projector is interesting with, for instance, a Keats version of "John Henry," combined with a record of the old John Henry ballad (there are a number of such recordings by various artists—take your choice, or let the children sing the ballad and record it). Other tall tales may also be projected successfully.

A skillful librarian can adapt stories for creative dramatics, skits, or choral speech. Some long ballads and narrative poems make excellent choral speech presentations; chalk talk illustrations, flannel board figures, or stand-up characters can be coordinated with lively tales such as *I Know an Old Lady* (Bonne) or *The Sooner Hound* (Weiss).

One summer, a story-craft project proved successful. Carefully selected stories were matched to a craft suggested by the story. One popular session mated peanut puppets to easy folktales. Another combined a story and papier-mâché *animules* (newspaper-rolls).

A combination of some of the Richard Chase stories with play-party games or folk dances is fun, if good leadership is available. Play reading of dramatized folk plays can be taped and used at a later time; if some qualified person can add a session or two on stage makeup as a demonstration it adds to the fun. We used help from the local little theater group.

Contests can encourage creativity: creative writing of short stories, or poetry; posters, exhibits of art work, or displays of hobbies; illustrations for stories told, painted, drawn, or modeled from papier-mâché or clay are interesting. One year a number of children made bottle figurines and puppets of many different North and South American Indian tribes for use in the library story program; these were used at each session, but were also taken to workshops, school visits, and professional meetings, and later used with Cub Scouts, Indian Guides, and nursery schools in storytelling.

Professional filmstrips, movies, and tapes can be coordinated into storytelling programs. The secret is to know when and how to use them for contrast and effect, so they do not overshadow the oral presentation.

Finally, a few suggestions that might lend sparkle to specific story programs. Try, with a young group, a walk-on dramatization of *I Know an Old Lady* (Bonne) using large paperbag masks for April Fool's Day; perhaps use "The Horse Egg" (Jagendorf—*Noodlehead*), "Pumpkin Trees and Walnut Vines" (Kelsey—*Hodja*), and "A Short Horse" (Credle—*Hills*) or "The Man Who Rode a Bear" (Credle—*Hills*) for an April Fool's story hour for older children.

A spring seasonal program might include background material on *Purim* (Cone), with the beautiful story of Esther as told in *The Book of God* (Armstrong) or *The Bible Story for Boys and Girls* (Bowie). Another story program could be built around *An Egg Is for Wishing* (Kay), followed with a demonstration of the making of Ukrainian pysanky (decorated eggs in traditional style) and an exhibit of decorated eggs.

During the period preceding Easter and Purim there are stories on a thoughtful vein, as well as films, that can be coordinated into a spring or Lent-entide story program: for example, "The Apple Tree" and "The Boy Who Discovered the Spring," both from *It's Time for Easter* (Sechrist). Decorating an egg tree and then telling *The Egg Tree* (Milhous) is interesting.

A summer story program might be built around one particular collection of stories, such as *The Wonder Clock* (Pyle) or *The Jack Tales* (Chase). Or a combination of reader-plus-puppet-pantomime might be used for a story like *Tikki-Tikki-Tembo* (Mosel). A story hour could use an old favorite—"Puss in Boots" (Perrault—*French*), followed by a new variant, "Kuzma-Get-Rich-Quick"

(Duddington—*Russian*), to make an interesting change of pace.

The use of *Where the Wild Things Are* (Sendak) for Halloween with a younger audience in the sound-filmstrip form is good; an interesting contrast is provided by following this with the filmstrip again, as the storyteller tells it in person. Another special Halloween story hour might include excerpts from "A Night on Bald Mountain" (Moussorgsky) in any of several excellent recordings to introduce *Baba Yaga* (Lent), a shadowgraph presentation with a storyteller. Further, we have used the Leonard Everett Fisher edition of *The Legend of Sleepy Hollow* (Irving), showing the illustrations synchronized with a good recording—that of Boris Karloff, for instance.

One Three Kings Day story hour included the picture story *Baboushka and the Three Kings* (Robbins), a Russian tale; *The Legend of Befana* (Chafetz), a long Italian variant; and the brief Arabian parallel, "The Camel of Bethlehem" (Walters—*Christmas*). This program was an experiment in variants, and its success dependent on the mood the teller was able to create.

I have always felt that the story hour for afterschool children during the winter months, however, should contain mainly stories, well-told, well-arranged, and perceptively chosen, with a limited use of realia or special items to enhance them. Occasionally a film or filmstrip, if it is brief and suitable, is good. For summer activities, story programs are often more elastic, more informal, with larger groups, and often have informal physical circumstances. But there is no substitute for a fine, well-programmed story hour, and a storyteller who loves to tell stories.

12

In Summary

"Snip, snap, snout . . . this tale's run out!"

In the preceding chapters the storyteller has been examined as both a carrier of past oral traditions and experience and a present repository of the best of that past, as well as a channel for keeping alive the oral heritage. The oral heritage itself has been considered by exploring sources for stories, suggesting criteria for choice, and formulating some ideas for welding different types of materials into coherent, creative story periods for boys and girls, complete with demonstrations of programs that have been used with boys and girls over a six-year period.

Annotations and listings have been drawn up to enable storytellers with limited resources to reach out and identify story materials more quickly and easily, and several different sources for the same story are given deliberately to encourage comparison. The discussion of how to mold written matter into a form usable with children between first and sixth grades has been undertaken in light of the fact that storytelling programs are for recreation, are on a volunteer basis, and come after school in most library story programs, factors that limit the kind of stories, their length, and their subject matter.

Additional enrichment suggestions are included for those varieties of programming that librarians and other group recreational leaders may use in summer schedules, on special occasions, and for additional opportunities. In analyzing the process of building programs, many of the basic principles of balance, variety, appropriateness, rhythm, group rapport, and mood discussed may also be sound and useful for building programs other than storytelling.

Storytelling is by no means dead, but it is in danger of being pushed into the background because of the quantity of books available to boys, girls, and leaders—and because it is easier to read stories than to become a storyteller. The prevalence of the electronic media also discourages personalized story programs. But nothing actually quite takes the place of storytelling in the lives of children. In *Children and Books* (page 249) May Hill Arbuthnot states:

> On the whole, . . . if the magic makes wishes come true and paints the way to happiness, it does so only with struggles and hardship on the part of the hero or heroine . . . the magic of these tales is the magic of the "Terrible Meek," who does the best he can with the tools he finds at hand. And it is good magic for children to grow up with, because presently it will be absorbed into their spirits and become a part of their adult strength.

Material for storytelling abounds, as well as counsel on how to develop good technique and a wealth of information on the background of this ancient art. But not much is available on what, where, and how to put this all together in story-telling programs. This is important; storytelling as an art is important. This book, then, can serve those starting out on the storytelling journey as both an introductory guide and a source book. Ruth Sawyer, in *My Spain*, said, "In our story hours, through the stories told, the poetry shared, we can reveal the expectancy, wonder, compassion, understanding, laughter, and courage that are components of the image in which mankind was created."

But this is only an introduction! Each one of us must build through our own individual efforts, and to each of us, as we give, does the return come.

> A spark—a picture flashed upon the mind,
> A turn of phrase—a door just lightly pushed
>   aside
> To open up a glimpse of wider worlds,
> Horizons stretching limitless and far—
> A path that leads to who knows where?
> Thus unsuspectingly, the imprint
> Of some tale from immemorial time
> May stamp itself upon a questing mind!
> So would I leave a tale etched in the lives
> And hearts of children's faces, looking up!
>   —de Wit

Bibliography

SOURCES CITED IN THE TEXT

Adams, Kathleen, and Atchinson, Frances. *A Book of Princess Stories.* New York: Dodd, 1927.

Aesop. *The Fables of Aesop.* Selected by Joseph Jacobs. New York: Macmillan, 1950.

Af'anasev, Aleksandr N. *Russian Fairy Tales.* Translated by N. Guterman. New York: Pantheon, 1945.

Albee, George Sumner. "The Three Young Kings" in Herbert Wernecke, *Christmas Stories from Many Lands.* Philadelphia: Westminster, 1961.

Alcott, Louisa May. *Lulu's Library.* Boston: Little, Brown, 1930.

Alden, Raymond. *Why the Chimes Rang.* Boston: Bobbs-Merrill, 1908.

Aliki (Brandenburg). *The Three Gold Pieces.* New York: Pantheon, 1967.

Alker, Dorothy. *Stories.* Austin, Texas: Jenkins, 1956.

Andersen, Hans Christian. *Complete Andersen.* Edited and translated by Jean Hersholt. New York: Heritage, 1949.

——. *Emperor's New Clothes.* Illustrated by Virginia Burton. Boston: Houghton, 1949.

——. *Fairy Tales.* Translated by Mrs. E. M. Lucas. New York: Dutton, n.d.

——. *Fairy Tales.* Translated by Mrs. H. B. Paul. New York: Warne, n.d.

——. *It's Perfectly True.* Translated by Paul Leyssac. New York: Harcourt, 1938.

——. *The Swineherd.* Illustrated by Eric Blegvad. New York: Harcourt, 1958.

——. *Three Tales from Andersen.* Translated by R. P. Keigwin. New York: Macmillan, 1958.

——. *Thumbelina.* Illustrated by Adrienne Adams. New York: Scribners, 1961.

Anderson, Alonzo. *Two Hundred Rabbits.* New York: Viking, 1968.

Anderson, Poul. *The Fox, the Dog and the Griffin.* Garden City, N.Y.: Doubleday, 1966.

Angelo, Valenti. *Pedro, the Angel of Olvera Street.* New York: Scribners, 1946.

Arbuthnot, May Hill. *The Arbuthnot Anthology of Children's Literature.* 3rd ed. Glenview, Ill.: Scott, Foresman, 1971.

——. *Children and Books.* 3rd ed. Chicago: Scott, Foresman, 1964.

——. *Time for Fairy Tales.* Chicago: Scott, Foresman, 1961.

——, and Taylor, Mark. *Time for Old Magic.* Chicago: Scott, Foresman, 1970.

Arkhurst, Joyce. *The Adventures of Spider.* Boston: Little, Brown, 1964.

Armstrong, April. *The Book of God.* New York: Garden City Books, 1951.

Asbjornsen, Peter, and Moe, Jorgen. *East of the Sun and West of the Moon.* Translated by Sir George Dasent, edited by Ingri and Edgar d'Aulaire. New York: Macmillan, 1963.

————. *Norwegian Folk Tales*. New York: Viking, 1960.

————. *Popular Tales from the Norse*. Translated by Sir George Dasent. Edinburgh: D. Douglas, 1903.

————. *Three Billy Goats Gruff*. Retold by Marcia Brown. New York: Harcourt, Brace, 1957.

Aspinwall, Alicia. *Short Stories for Short People*. New York: Dutton, 1896.

Association for Childhood Education. *Told under the Christmas Tree*. New York: Macmillan, 1948.

————. *Told under the Magic Umbrella*. New York: Macmillan, 1962.

Babbitt, Ellen C., ret. *Jataka Tales*. New York: Appleton, 1912.

Bailey, Carolyn S. *Favorite Stories for Children*. New York: Platt and Munk, 1965.

————. *Old Man Rabbit's Dinner Party*. New York: Platt and Munk, 1949.

————. *The Story-Telling Hour*. New York: Dodd, 1934.

————. *Tops and Whistles*. New York: Viking, 1937.

Baker, Augusta. *The Golden Lynx*. Philadelphia: Lippincott, 1960.

————. *The Talking Tree*. Philadelphia: Lippincott, 1955.

Baker, Laura. *O Children of the Wind and Pines*. Philadelphia: Lippincott, 1967.

Baldwin, James. *The Story of Roland*. New York: Scribners, 1930.

————. *The Story of Siegfried*. New York: Scribners, 1882.

Barbeau, Marius. *The Golden Phoenix*. New York: Walck, 1958.

Barksdale, Lena. *The First Thanksgiving*. New York: Knopf, 1942.

Barlow, Genevieve. *Latin American Tales*. Chicago: Rand McNally, 1966.

Barnet, George. *Stories for Fun*. New York: Macmillan, 1959.

Baruch, Dorothy. *Kappa's Tug-of-war with Big Brown Horse*. Rutland, Vt.: Tuttle, 1962.

Bay, Jens C. *Danish Fairy and Folk Tales*. New York: Harper, 1899.

Bechstein, Ludwig. *The Fairy Tales of Ludwig Bechstein*. New York: Abelard-Schuman, 1967.

Becker, May L. *The Home Book of Christmas*. New York: Dodd-Mead, 1941.

Beckley, René. *Folklore of the World: Australia*. Leeds, England: C. Arnold, 1965.

Bell, Corydon. *John Rattling-gourd*. New York: Macmillan, 1955.

Belpré, Pura. *The Tiger and the Rabbit*. Boston: Houghton, 1944.

Belting, Natalia. *Cat Tales*. New York: Holt, 1959.

————. *Elves and Ellefolk*. New York: Holt, 1961.

————. *The Long-tailed Bear*. Indianapolis, Ind.: Bobbs-Merrill, 1961.

———— *The Stars Are Silver Reindeer*. New York: Holt, 1966.

————. *A Winter's Eve*. New York: Holt, 1969.

Benson, Sally. *Stories of Gods and Heroes*. New York: Dial, 1940.

Bernhard, Josephine. *Lullabye*. New York: Roy Publishers, 1944.

Bill, Helen. *The Shoes Fit for a King*. New York: Watts, 1956.

Blair, Walter. *Tall Tale America*. New York: Coward-McCann, 1944.

Bleeker, Mary N. *Big Music*. New York: Viking, 1946.

Boggs, Ralph, and Davis, M. G. *Three Golden Oranges*. New York: Longmans, 1936.

Bollinger, Max. *Noah and the Rainbow*. New York: Crowell, 1972.

Bonne, Rose. *I Know an Old Lady*. Chicago: Rand McNally, 1961.

Bontemps, Arna. *The Fast Sooner Hound*. Boston: Houghton, 1942.

Borg, Ingrid. *Parrak the White Reindeer*. London: Warne, 1959.

Borski, Lucia. *The Gypsy and the Bear*. New York: Longmans, 1933.

————. *The Jolly Tailor*. New York: Longmans, 1928.

Boucher, Alan. *Mead Moondaughter and Other Icelandic Folk Tales*. New York: Chilton, 1960.

Bowie, Walter. *The Bible Story for Boys and Girls—Old Testament*. Nashville, Tenn: Abingdon, 1952.

Bowman, Cloyd. *Winnebojo*. Chicago: Whitman, 1941.

————, and Bianco, M. *Tales from a Finnish Tupa*. Chicago: Whitman, 1936.

Brenner, Anita. *The Boy Who Could Do Anything*. New York: Scott, 1942.

Brenner, Barbara. *The Flying Patchwork Quilt*. New York: Young-Scott, 1965.

Bro, Marguerite H. *How the Mouse Deer Became King*. Garden City, N.Y.: Doubleday, 1966.

Bronson, Wilfred. *Pinto's Journey*. New York: Messner, 1948.

Brooks, Jeremy. *The Magic Perambulator*. New York: John Day, 1965.

Brown, Marcia. *The Blue Jackal*. New York: Scribners, 1977.

————. *The Bun*. New York: Harcourt, 1972.

————. *Cinderella*. New York: Scribners, 1954.

————. *Dick Whittington and His Cat*. New York: Scribners, 1950.

————. *Felice*. New York: Scribners, 1958.

————. *The Flying Carpet*. New York: Harcourt, 1956.

————. *The Neighbors*. New York: Scribners, 1967.

————. *Once a Mouse.* New York: Scribners, 1961.

————. *Puss in Boots.* New York: Scribners, 1952.

————. *Stone Soup.* New York: Scribners, 1947.

Bryant, Sara Cone. *Best Stories to Tell to Children.* Boston: Houghton, 1912.

————. *How to Tell Stories to Children.* Boston: Houghton, 1905.

Bryson, Bernarda. *Gilgamesh.* New York: Holt, 1966.

Burton, W. F. P. *The Magic Drum.* New York: Criterion, 1961.

Calhoun, Mary. *High Wind for Kansas.* New York: Morrow, 1965.

Campbell, Alfred S. *The Wizard and His Magic Powder.* New York: Knopf, 1954.

Carlson, Natalie. *Sashes Red and Blue.* New York: Harper, 1956.

————. *The Talking Cat.* New York: Harper, 1952.

Carmer, Carl. *America Sings.* New York: Knopf, 1942.

Carpenter, Frances. *The Elephant's Bathtub.* Garden City, N.Y.: Doubleday, 1962.

————. *Tales of a Basque Grandmother.* Garden City, N.Y.: Doubleday, 1930.

————. *Tales of a Chinese Grandmother.* Garden City, N.Y.: Doubleday, 1937.

————. *Tales of a Korean Grandmother.* Garden City, N.Y.: Doubleday, 1947.

————. *Tales of a Russian Grandmother.* Garden City, N.Y.: Doubleday, 1933.

————. *Tales of a Swiss Grandmother.* Garden City, N.Y.: Doubleday, 1940.

————. *Wonder Tales of Dogs and Cats.* Garden City, N.Y.: Doubleday, 1955.

————. *Wonder Tales of Horses and Heroes.* Garden City, N.Y.: Doubleday, 1952.

————. *Wonder Tales of Ships and Seas.* Garden City, N.Y.: Doubleday, 1959.

Carrick, Valery. *Tales of Wise and Foolish Animals.* New York: Stokes, 1928.

Carroll, Lewis. *Alice in Wonderland.* New York: Heritage, 1944.

Chafetz, Henry. *The Legend of Befana.* Boston: Houghton, 1958.

————. *Thunderbird.* New York: Pantheon, 1964.

Chamoud, Simone. *Picture Tales from France.* New York: Stokes, 1933.

Chase, Richard. *Grandfather Tales.* Boston: Houghton, 1948.

————. *Jack and the Three Sillies.* Illustrated by Joshua Tolford. Boston: Houghton, 1950.

————. *The Jack Tales.* Boston, Houghton: 1943.

Child Study Association. *Castles and Dragons.* New York: Crowell, 1958.

————. *The Holiday Story Book.* New York: Crowell, 1952.

Chrisman, Arthur B. *Shen of the Sea.* New York: Dutton, 1925.

Christopher, John. *City of Gold and Lead.* New York: Macmillan, 1967.

————. *Pool of Fire.* New York: Macmillan, 1968.

————. *White Mountains.* New York: Macmillan, 1967.

Church, Alfred J. *The Aeneid for Boys and Girls.* New York: Macmillan, 1942.

————. *The Iliad for Boys and Girls.* New York: Macmillan, 1964.

Clark, Margery. *The Poppy Seed Cakes.* Garden City, N.Y.: Doubleday, 1924.

Collodi, Lorenzo. *Pinocchio.* New York: Macmillan, 1951.

Colum, Padraic. *The Arabian Nights.* New York: Macmillan, 1923.

————. *The Big Tree of Bunlahy.* New York: Macmillan, 1933.

————. *The Stone of Victory.* New York: McGraw, 1966.

Colwell, Eileen, compiler. *A Second Storyteller's Choice.* New York: Walck, 1965.

————. *A Storyteller's Choice.* New York: Walck, 1964.

Cone, Molly. *Purim.* New York: Crowell, 1967.

Conger, Lesley. *Three Giant Stories.* New York: Four Winds, 1968.

Cooney, Barbara. *The Little Juggler.* New York: Hastings, 1961.

Cooper, Frederick T. *An Argosy of Fables.* New York: Stokes, 1921.

Corrigan, Adeline. *Holiday Ring.* Chicago: Whitman, 1975.

Cothran, Jean. *Magic Bells.* New York: Aladdin, 1955.

————. *The Magic Calabash.* New York: McKay, 1956.

————. *With a Wig, with a Wag.* New York: McKay, 1954.

Courlander, Harold. *The Fourth World of the Hopi.* New York: Harcourt, 1970.

————. *The Hat-shaking Dance.* New York: Harcourt, 1957.

————. *Kantchil's Lime Pit.* New York: Harcourt, 1950.

————. *The King's Drum.* New York: Harcourt, 1962.

————. *The People of the Short Blue Corn.* New York: Harcourt, 1970.

————. *The Piece of Fire.* New York: Harcourt, 1964.

————. *Ride with the Sun.* New York: McGraw, 1955.

————. *Terrapin's Pot of Sense.* New York: Holt, 1957.

————. *The Tiger's Whisker.* New York: Holt, 1959.

————. *Uncle Bouki of Haiti.* New York: Morrow, 1942.

————, and Herzog, G. *The Cowtail Switch.* New York: Holt, 1947.

————, and Wolf, Lesley. *The Fire on the Mountain.* New York: Holt, 1950.

Credle, Ellis. *Down, Down the Mountain.* New York: Nelson, 1934.

——. *Tall Tales from the High Hills.* New York: Nelson, 1957.

Crossley-Holland, Kevin. *The Green Children.* New York: Seabury, 1968.

Cuneo, Mary L. *Silver Stories, Golden Verse.* New York: Dodd-Mead, 1965.

Cunningham, Caroline. *The Talking Stone.* New York: Knopf, 1939.

Dalgleish, Alice. *Christmas.* New York: Scribners, 1950.

——. *The Enchanted Book.* New York: Scribners, 1947.

——. *St. George and the Dragon.* New York: Scribners, 1941.

Damjan, Misha. *The Magic Paintbrush.* New York: Walck, 1967.

Daniels, Guy. *The Peasant's Pea Patch.* New York: Delacorte, 1971.

Dasent, Sir George. *East of the Sun.* See Asbjornsen listing.

Davies, Anthea. *A White Horse with Wings.* New York: Macmillan, 1968.

Davis, Mary Gould. *A Baker's Dozen.* New York: Harcourt, 1930.

Davis, Robert. *Padre Porko.* New York: Holiday House, 1948.

Dayrell, Elphinstone. *Why Sun and Moon Live in the Sky.* Boston: Houghton, 1968.

De la Mare, Walter. *Animal Stories.* New York: Scribners, 1940.

——. *Told Again: Old Tales Told Again.* New York: Knopf, 1927.

——. *Stories from the Bible.* New York: Knopf, 1961.

De Leeuw, Adele. *Legends and Folk Tales of Holland.* New York: Nelson, 1963.

Deutsch, Babette. *Heroes of the Kalevala.* New York: Messner, 1940.

——. *Tales of Faraway Folk.* New York: Harper, 1952.

Dickenson, Alice. *Children's Book of Christmas Stories.* Garden City, N.Y.: Doubleday, 1913.

Dines, Glen. *Pitidoe the Color Maker.* New York: Macmillan, 1959.

Dobsinsky, Pavol. *The Enchanted Castle.* London: Hamlyn, 1967.

Dolbier, Maurice. *The Half-pint Jinni.* New York: Random, 1948.

——. *Torten's Christmas Secret.* Boston: Little, Brown, 1951.

Downing, Charles. *Russian Tales and Legends.* London: Oxford Univ. Pr., 1956.

DuBois, William. *Elizabeth the Cow Ghost.* New York: Viking, 1964.

——. *Lion.* New York: Viking, 1956.

Duddington, Natalie, trans. *Russian Folk Tales.* New York: Funk and Wagnalls, 1967.

DuMond, Frank. *Tall Tales from the Catskills.* New York: Atheneum, 1968.

Duvoisin, Roger. *The Three Sneezes.* New York: Knopf, 1941.

Eaton, Anne. *The Animals' Christmas.* New York: Viking, 1944.

Edmonds, I. G. *Trickster Tales.* Philadelphia: Lippincott, 1966.

Elgin, Katherine. *The First Book of Mythology.* New York: Watts, 1956.

Elkin, Benjamin. *Gillespie and the Guards.* New York: Viking, 1956.

Elliot, Geraldine. *Where the Long Grass Whispers.* London: Routledge and Kegan, 1949.

Emrich, Marion. *A Child's Book of Folk Lore.* New York: Dial, 1947.

Evers, Alf. *The Three Kings of Saba.* Philadelphia: Lippincott, 1955.

Farjeon, Eleanor. *Italian Peep Show.* New York: Walck, 1926.

——. *The Little Bookroom.* New York: Walck, 1956.

——. *Old Nurse's Stocking Basket.* New York: Walck, 1965.

——. *Ten Saints.* New York: Oxford Univ. Pr., 1936.

Fenner, Phyllis. *Adventures Rare and Magical.* New York: Knopf, 1945.

——. *Feasts and Frolics.* New York: Knopf, 1949.

——. *Ghosts, Ghosts, Ghosts.* New York: Watts, 1952.

——. *Giants and Witches and a Dragon or Two.* New York: Knopf, 1943.

——. *Magic Hoofs.* New York: Knopf, 1957.

Fenton, Edward. *Big Yellow Balloon.* Garden City, N.Y.: Doubleday, 1967.

Field, Rachel. *American Folk and Fairy Tales.* New York: Scribners, 1929.

——. *The Bird Began to Sing.* Eau Claire, Wis.: Hale, 1932.

Fillmore, Parker. *Mighty Mikko.* New York: Harcourt, 1922.

——. *The Shepherd's Nosegay.* New York: Harcourt, 1958.

Finger, Charles. *Tales from Silver Lands.* Garden City, N.Y.: Doubleday, 1924.

Fisher, Agnes. *Once upon a Time.* New York: Nelson, 1942.

Fournier, Catherine. *The Coconut Thieves.* New York: Scribners, 1964.

Foyle, Kathleen. *The Little Good People.* London: Warne, 1949.

Freeman, Don. *Ski-pup.* New York: Viking, 1963.

French, Allen. *Heroes of Iceland.* Boston: Little, Brown, 1905.

Frost, Frances. *Legends of the United Nations.* New York: McGraw, 1943.

Frye, Dean. *The Lamb and the Child.* New York: McGraw, 1963.

Fyleman, Rose. *The Rainbow Cat.* Garden City, N.Y.: Doubleday, 1923.

———. *Tea Time Tales.* Garden City, N.Y.: Doubleday, 1930.

Gág, Wanda. *Millions of Cats.* New York: Coward-McCann, 1928.

———. *More Tales from Grimm.* New York: Coward-McCann, 1947.

———. *Tales from Grimm.* New York: Coward-McCann, 1936.

———. *Three Gay Tales from Grimm.* New York: Coward-McCann, 1943.

Garthwaite, Marion. *The Twelfth Night Santons.* Garden City, N.Y.: Doubleday, 1965.

Gibson, Katherine. *The Tell-It-Again Book.* Boston: Little, Brown, 1942.

Gillham, Charles. *Beyond the Clapping Mountains.* New York: Macmillan, 1945.

Gilstrap, Robert. *The Sultan's Fool.* New York: Holt, 1958.

Gobhai, Mehlli. *The Blue Jackal.* Englewood Cliffs, N.J.: Prentice, 1968.

———. *The Legend of the Orange Princess.* New York: Holiday, 1971.

Gottschalk, Fruma. *The Runaway Soldier.* New York: Knopf, 1946.

Grahame, Kenneth. *The Wind in the Willows.* New York: Scribners, 1960.

Gramatky, Hardie. *Little Toot.* New York: Putnam, 1941.

———. *Loopy.* New York: Putnam, 1939.

Green, Kathleen. *Philip and the Pooka.* Philadelphia: Lippincott, 1966.

Green, Margaret. *The Big Book of Animal Fables.* New York: Watts, 1965.

Green, Nancy. *Abu Kassim's Slippers.* Chicago: Follett, 1963.

Green, Roger L. *Tales of Ancient Egypt.* New York: Walck, 1967.

Greene, Ellin, ret. *The Pumpkin Giant.* New York: Lothrop, 1970.

Greene, Lila. *Folk Tales of Spain and Latin America.* Morristown, N.J.: Silver Burdett, 1967.

Grey, Nicholas. *Mainly in Moonlight.* New York: Meredith, 1967.

Grierson, Elizabeth. *The Scottish Fairy Book.* Philadelphia: Lippincott, 1910.

Grimm, Jakob L., and Grimm, Wilhelm. *The Bremen Town Musicians.* Illustrated by Paul Galdone. New York: McGraw, 1968.

———. *Briar Rose.* Illustrated by Margery Gill. New York: Walck, 1972.

———. *Complete Grimm's Fairy Tales.* Translated by Margaret Hunt. New York: Pantheon, 1944.

———. *Grimm's Fairy Tales.* Translated by Mrs. E. M. Lucas. New York: Grosset & Dunlap, 1945.

———. *Household Stories.* Illustrated by Margery Gill. New York: Walck, 1972.

———. *Household Stories.* Translated by Lucy Crane. New York: Macmillan, 1926.

———. *The Shoemaker and the Elves.* Illustrated by Adrienne Adams. New York: Scribners, 1960.

———. *Of Wisemen and Simpletons.* Translated by Elizabeth Shub. New York: Macmillan, 1971.

———. *The Sleeping Beauty.* Illustrated by Felix Hoffmann. New York: Harcourt, 1959.

———. *Snow White and Rose Red.* Illustrated by Adrienne Adams. New York: Scribners, 1944.

———. *Snow White and the Seven Dwarfs.* Illustrated by Nancy Burkert, translated by Randall Jarrell. New York: Farrar, 1972.

———. *The Traveling Musicians.* Illustrated by Fischer. New York: Harcourt, 1944.

———. *The Twelve Dancing Princesses.* Translated by Elizabeth Shub, illustrated by Uri Shulevitz. New York: Scribners, 1966.

Grishna, Givago. *Peter Pea.* Philadelphia: Lippincott, 1926.

Gruenberg, Sidonie. *Favorite Stories Old and New.* Garden City, N.Y.: Doubleday, 1955.

———. *More Favorite Stories.* Garden City, N.Y.: Doubleday, 1960.

Haley, Gail. *A Story, a Story.* New York: Atheneum, 1970.

Hardendorff, Jeanne B. *The Frog's Saddle Horse.* Philadelphia: Lippincott, 1968.

———. *Tricky Peik.* Philadelphia: Lippincott, 1967.

Harper, Wilhelmina. *Easter Chimes.* New York: Dutton, 1942.

———. *Ghosts and Goblins.* New York: Dutton, 1965.

———. *The Harvest Feast.* New York: Dutton, 1938.

———, and Hazeltine, Alice. *Merry Christmas to You.* New York: Dutton, 1935.

Harris, Christie. *Once upon a Totem.* New York: Atheneum, 1963.

Harris, Joel Chandler. *Br'er Rabbit.* Retold by M. W. Brown. New York: Harper, 1941.

———. *Favorite Uncle Remus.* Boston: Houghton, 1948.

———. *Nights with Uncle Remus.* Boston: Houghton, 1883.

———. *Uncle Remus and His Friends.* Boston: Houghton, 1883.

———. *Uncle Remus: His Songs and Sayings.* Boston: Houghton, 1880.

Hart, Johan. *Picture Tales from Holland.* Philadelphia: Lippincott, 1935.

Hatch, Mary C. *More Danish Tales.* New York: Harcourt, 1949.

———. *13 Danish Tales.* New York: Harcourt, 1947.

Hauff, Wilhelm. *The Caravan.* Translated by Alma Overholt. New York: Crowell, 1964.

Haviland, Virginia. *Favorite Fairy Tales Told in Czechoslovakia.* Boston: Little, Brown, 1966.

———. *Favorite Fairy Tales Told in Denmark.* Boston: Little, Brown, 1971.

———. *Favorite Fairy Tales Told in England.* Boston: Little, Brown, 1959.

———. *Favorite Fairy Tales Told in France.* Boston: Little, Brown, 1959.

———. *Favorite Fairy Tales Told in Germany.* Boston: Little, Brown, 1959.

———. *Favorite Fairy Tales Told in Greece.* Boston: Little, Brown, 1970.

———. *Favorite Fairy Tales Told in India.* Boston: Little, Brown, 1973.

———. *Favorite Fairy Tales Told in Ireland.* Boston: Little, Brown, 1961.

———. *Favorite Fairy Tales Told in Italy.* Boston: Little, Brown, 1965.

———. *Favorite Fairy Tales Told in Japan.* Boston: Little, Brown, 1967.

———. *Favorite Fairy Tales Told in Norway.* Boston: Little, Brown, 1961.

———. *Favorite Fairy Tales Told in Poland.* Boston: Little, Brown, 1963.

———. *Favorite Fairy Tales Told in Russia.* Boston: Little, Brown, 1961.

———. *Favorite Fairy Tales Told in Scotland.* Boston: Little, Brown, 1963.

———. *Favorite Fairy Tales Told in Spain.* Boston: Little, Brown, 1962.

———. *Favorite Fairy Tales Told in Sweden.* Boston: Little, Brown, 1966.

Hawthorne, Nathaniel. *Tanglewood Tales.* Boston: Houghton, 1853.

Hazeltine, Alice, and Smith, E. S. *A Christmas Book of Legends and Stories.* New York: Lothrop-Lee, 1944.

———. *Hero Tales from Many Lands.* Nashville, Tenn.: Abingdon, 1961.

Heady, Eleanor. *Jambo, Sungura!* New York: Norton, 1965.

Hearn, Lafcadio. *The Boy Who Drew Cats.* New York: Macmillan, 1963.

Henderson, Gertrude. *The Ring of the Nibelungen.* New York: Knopf, 1932.

Henius, Frank. *Stories from the Americas.* New York: Scribners, 1944.

Herda, Helmutt. *Fairy Tales from Many Lands.* New York: Watts, 1956.

Heyward, DuBose. *The Country Bunny and the Little Gold Shoes.* Boston: Houghton, 1939.

Hill, Kay. *Glooscap and His Magic.* New York: Dodd-Mead, 1963.

———. *More Glooscap Stories.* New York: Dodd-Mead, 1970.

Hirsh, Marilyn. *The Elephants and the Mice.* Cleveland: World, 1967.

Hoban, Russell. *The Pedaling Man.* New York: Norton, 1968.

Hodges, Margaret. *The Firebringer.* Illustrated by Peter Parnall. Boston: Little, Brown, 1972.

Hoge, Dorothy. *The Black Heart of Indri.* New York: Scribners, 1966.

Hogner, Dorothy C. *Navajo Winter Nights.* New York: Oxford Univ. Pr., 1935.

Hogrogian, Nonny. *One Fine Day.* New York: Macmillan, 1971.

Hoke, Helen. *Spooks, Spooks, Spooks.* New York: Watts, 1966.

———. *Witches, Witches, Witches.* New York: Watts, 1966.

Holbrooke, Florence. *A Book of Nature Myths.* Boston: Houghton, 1930.

Holding, James. *The Sky-eater and Other Tales.* New York: Abelard, 1965.

Hollowell, Lillian. *A Book of Children's Literature.* New York: Holt, 1966.

Holmes, Oliver Wendell. *The Deacon's One-Hoss Shay.* Illustrated by Paul Galdone. New York: Macmillan, 1965.

Hood, Flora. *One Luminaria for Antonio.* New York: Putnam, 1966.

Hosford, Dorothy. *Sons of the Volsungs.* New York: Holt, 1949.

Housman, Laurence. *The Ratcatcher's Daughter: A Collection of Stories.* Selected by Ellin Greene. New York: Atheneum, 1974.

Houston, James. *Tikta-Likta.* New York: Harcourt, 1965.

Huber, Miriam B. *Story and Verse for Children.* New York: Macmillan, 1955.

Hull, Eleanor. *Cuchulain, the Hound of Ulster.* New York: Crowell, 1910.

Hutchinson, Veronica. *Candlelight Stories.* New York: Putnam, 1928.

———. *Chimney Corner Fairy Tales.* New York: Minton, Balch, 1925.

———. *Chimney Corner Stories.* New York: Minton, Balch, 1926.

———. *Fireside Stories.* New York: Putnam, 1927.

Hyde, Mark. *The Singing Sword*. Boston: Little, Brown, 1930.

Ireson, Barbara, comp. *Haunting Tales*. New York: Dutton, 1974.

Irving, Washington. *The Legend of Sleepy Hollow*. New York: Macmillan, 1963.

——. *Rip van Winkle*. Illustrated by Leonard E. Fisher. New York: Watts, 1966.

Ishii, Momoko. *Issun Boshi, the Inchling*. New York: Walker, 1967.

Ish-Kishor, Judith. *The Carpet of Solomon*. New York: Pantheon, 1966.

Jablow, Alta. *Gassire's Lute*. New York: Dutton, 1971.

Jacobs, Joseph. *A Book of Wonder Voyages*. New York: Putnam, n.d.

——. *Celtic Fairy Tales*. New York: Putnam, n.d.

——. *The Crock of Gold*. Illustrated by William Stobbs. Chicago: Follett, 1976.

——. *English Fairy Tales*. 3rd ed., rev. New York: Putnam, n.d.

——. *European Folk and Fairy Tales*. New York: Putnam, 1916.

——. *Indian Fairy Tales*. New York: Putnam, n.d.

——. *Master of All Masters*. Illustrated by Marcia Sewell. New York: Grosset, 1972.

——. *More Celtic Fairy Tales*. New York: Putnam, n.d.

——. *More English Fairy Tales*. New York: Putnam, n.d.

——. *Reynard the Fox*. New York: Schocken, 1967.

——. *The Three Wishes*. New York: McGraw, 1961.

Jacobson, Helen. *The First Book of Mythical Beasts*. New York: Watts, 1960.

Jagendorf, Moritz. *Ghostly Tales*. Morristown, N.J.: Silver Burdett, 1968.

——. *The King of the Mountain*. New York: Vanguard, 1960.

——. *Kwi-Na the Eagle*. Morristown, N.J.: Silver Burdett, 1967.

——. *The Marvelous Adventures of Johnny Darling*. New York: Vanguard, 1949.

——. *The New England Bean Pot*. New York: Vanguard, 1948.

——. *Noodlehead Stories*. New York: Vanguard, 1958.

——. *The Priceless Cats*. New York: Vanguard, 1956.

——. *Tyll Eulenspiegel's Merry Pranks*. New York: Vanguard, 1938.

——. *Up-state, Down-state*. New York: Vanguard, 1949.

——, and Clark, Barrett. *A World of Stories for Children*. Indianapolis: Bobbs-Merrill, 1940.

——, and Tillhagen, C. *The Gypsies' Fiddle*. New York: Vanguard, 1956.

Jewett, Eleanore. *Which Was Witch?* New York: Viking, 1953.

Johnson, Clifton. *The Oak Tree Fairy Book*. Boston: Little, Brown, 1905. Dover, 1968.

Johnson, Edna, et al. *An Anthology of Children's Literature*. 3rd ed. Boston: Houghton, 1959.

Johnson, Sally Patrick. *The Princesses*. New York: Harper, 1962.

Judd, Mary C. *Wigwam Tales*. Boston: Ginn, 1901.

Kalibala, Ernest Balintuma, and Davis, M. G. *Wakaima and Clay Man*. New York: Longmans, 1946.

Kästner, Erich, ret. *Baron Munchausen*. New York: Messner, 1957.

Kavcic, Vladimir. *The Golden Bird*. Cleveland: World, 1969.

Kay, Helen. *An Egg Is for Wishing*. New York: Abelard, 1966.

Keats, Ezra J. *John Henry*. New York: Pantheon, 1965.

Kelly, Eric. *In Clean Hay*. New York: Macmillan, 1953.

——. *The Christmas Nightingale*. New York: Macmillan, 1932.

Kelsey, Alice G. *Once the Hodja*. New York: Longmans, 1943.

——. *Once the Mullah*. New York: Longmans, 1954.

——. *Thirty Gilt Pennies*. Nashville, Tenn.: Abingdon, 1968.

Khatchatrianz, Iokov. *Armenian Folk Tales*. Philadelphia: Colonial House, 1946.

Kijima, Hajime. *The Little White Hen*. New York: Harcourt, 1969.

Kingsley, Charles. *The Heroes*. New York: Macmillan, 1954.

Kipling, Rudyard. *The Jungle Book*. Garden City, N.Y.: Doubleday, 1932.

——. *Just So Stories*. Garden City, N.Y.: Doubleday, 1941.

Kirn, Ann. *Nine in a Line*. New York: Norton, 1966.

Krylov, Ivan A. *Fifteen Fables of Krylov*. Translated by Guy Daniels. New York: Macmillan, 1965.

La Fontaine, Jean de. *Fables*. Edited by Richard Scarry. Garden City, N.Y.: Doubleday, 1963.

Lamorisse, Albert. *The Red Balloon*. Garden City, N.Y.: Doubleday, 1957. McGraw, 1967.

Lang, Andrew. *The Arabian Nights Entertainments*. New York: Longmans, 1946.

——. *The Blue Fairy Book*. 1894. Reprint. New York: Longmans, 1946.

——. *The Brown Fairy Book*. 1904. Reprint. New York: McGraw, 1966.

——. *The Crimson Fairy Book*. 1903. Reprint. New York: Longmans, 1947.

——. *The Green Fairy Book*. 1892. Reprint. New York: Longmans, 1948.

————. *The Grey Fairy Book.* New York: Longmans, 1900.

————. *The Lilac Fairy Book.* New York: Longmans, 1910.

————. *The Olive Fairy Book.* 1907. Reprint. New York: Longmans, 1949.

————. *The Orange Fairy Book.* 1906. Reprint. New York: Longmans, 1949.

————. *The Pink Fairy Book.* New York: Longmans, 1897.

————. *The Red Fairy Book.* 1890. Reprint. New York: Longmans, 1947.

————. *The Rose Fairy Book.* New York: McKay, 1948.

————. *Tales of Troy and Greece.* New York: Longmans, 1907.

————. *The Violet Fairy Book.* 1901. Reprint. New York: McGraw, 1967.

————. *The Yellow Fairy Book.* 1894. Reprint. New York: McGraw, 1967.

Leach, Maria. *How the People Sang the Mountain Up.* New York: Viking, 1967.

————. *The Rainbow Book of American Folk Tales and Legends.* Cleveland: World, 1958.

Leach, MacEdward. *The Ballad Book.* New York: Harper, 1955.

Leekley, Thomas. *The World of Manabozo.* New York: Vanguard, 1965.

Lent, Blair. *Baba Yaga.* Boston: Houghton, 1966.

Lester, Julius. *The Knee-hi Man.* New York: Dial, 1972.

Lewis, Naomi, ret. *The Story of Aladdin.* Illustrated by Barry Wilkinson. New York: Walck, 1971.

Lexau, Joan. *It All Began with a Drip.* New York: McCall, 1970.

Lim, Sian-Tek. *Folk Tales from China.* New York: John Day, 1948.

————. *More Folk Tales from China.* New York: John Day, 1948.

Lifton, Betty J. *The Cock and the Ghost Cat.* New York: Atheneum, 1965.

————. *Jo-Ji and the Dragon.* New York: Morrow, 1957.

Lillie, Amy. *The Book of Three Festivals.* New York: Dutton, 1948.

Lionni, Leo. *Tico and the Golden Wings.* New York: Pantheon, 1964.

Lipkind, William. *Professor Bull's Umbrella.* New York: Viking, 1954.

Lobel, Arnold. *The Great Blueness.* New York: Harper, 1968.

Lobagola, *Folk Tales of a Savage.* New York: Knopf, 1930.

Lord, Priscilla, and Foley, Daniel. *An Easter Garland.* New York: Chilton, 1963.

Lowe, Patricia. *The Little Horse of Seven Colors.* Cleveland: World, 1970.

Luckhardt, Mildred. *Christmas Comes Again.* Nashville, Tenn.: Abingdon, 1962.

Lynch, Patricia. *The Turfcutter's Donkey.* New York: Dutton, 1935.

McCormick, Dell. *Paul Bunyan Swings His Ax.* Caldwell, Idaho: Caxton, 1936.

MacDonell, Anne. *The Italian Fairy Book.* London: Fisher, 1925.

MacManus, Seumas. *The Bold Heroes of Hungry Hill.* New York: Farrar, 1951.

————. *Donegal Fairy Stories.* Garden City, N.Y.: Doubleday, 1900.

————. *Donegal Wonder Book.* New York: Stokes, 1926.

————. *Hibernian Nights.* New York: Macmillan, 1963.

————. *In Chimney Corners.* Garden City, N.Y.: Doubleday, 1899.

————. *The Well o' the World's End.* New York: Macmillan, 1939.

McNeil, Edwin. *The Sunken City.* New York: Walck, 1959.

Maher, Ramona. *The Blind Boy and the Loon.* New York: Day, 1969.

Malcolmson, Anne. *The Song of Robin Hood.* Boston: Houghton, 1947.

Malory, Sir Thomas. *The Boy's King Arthur.* Illustrated by N. C. Wyeth. New York: Scribners, 1924.

Manning-Sanders, Ruth. *A Book of Charms and Changelings.* New York: Dutton, 1971.

————. *A Book of Dragons.* New York: Dutton, 1965.

————. *A Book of Dwarfs.* New York: Dutton, 1964.

————. *A Book of Ghosts and Goblins.* New York: Dutton, 1969.

————. *A Book of Giants.* New York: Dutton, 1963.

————. *A Book of Magical Beasts.* New York: Nelson, 1970.

————. *A Book of Mermaids.* New York: Dutton, 1968.

————. *A Book of Monsters.* New York: Dutton, 1976.

————. *A Book of Princes and Princesses.* New York: Dutton, 1970.

————. *A Book of Witches.* New York: Dutton, 1966.

————. *A Book of Wizards.* New York: Dutton, 1967.

————. *A Choice of Magic.* New York: Dutton, 1971.

————. *Gianni and the Ogre.* New York: Dutton, 1970.

————. *Jonnikin and the Flying Basket.* New York: Dutton, 1969.

————. *Peter and the Piskies.* New York: Roy, 1958.

————. *Tales from the English and Scottish Ballads.* New York: Dutton, 1968.

Marchant, Ralph, and Marchant, Jill. *The Little Painter.* Minneapolis: Carol Rhoda, 1971.

Margolis, Ellen. *Idy, the Fox-chasing Cow*. Cleveland: World, 1962.

Marmur, Mildred. *Japanese Fairy Tales*. New York: Golden, 1960.

Marriott, Alice. *Winter Telling Stories*. New York: Sloane, 1947.

Martin, Frances. *Nine Tales of Coyote*. New York: Harper, 1950.

——. *Nine Tales of Raven*. New York: Harper, 1951.

Matsuno, Masako. *Oniroku and the Carpenter*. Englewood Cliffs, N.J.: Prentice-Hall, 1963.

Mehdevi, Ann S. *Persian Folk and Fairy Tales*. New York: Knopf, 1965.

Melzack, Ronald. *The Day Tuk Became a Hunter*. New York: Dodd, 1968.

Milhous, Katherine. *The Egg Tree*. New York: Scribners, 1950.

——. *Patrick and the Golden Slippers*. New York: Scribners, 1951.

Miller, Alice B. *Heroes, Outlaws, and Funny Fellows*. Garden City, N.Y.: Doubleday, 1934.

Milne, A. A. *Winnie the Pooh*. New York: Dutton, 1957.

Mosel, Arline. *Tikki-Tikki-Tembo*. New York: Holt, 1968.

Mother Goose. *The Old Woman and Her Pig*. Illustrated by Paul Galdone. New York: McGraw, 1960.

Mukerji, Dhan Gopal. *Rama, the Hero of India*. New York: Dutton, 1930.

Munchausen, Baron. *Baron Munchausen*. Retold by Doris Orgel. Reading, Mass.: Addison-Wesley, 1971.

Ness, Evaline, ret. *Mr. Miacca*. Illustrated by the author. New York: Holt, 1967.

Newell, Hope. *The Rescue of the Sun*. Chicago: Whitman, 1970.

Nic Leodhas, Sorche (Alger, Le Claire). *By Loch and Lin*. New York: Holt, 1969.

——. *Claymore and Kilt*. New York: Dutton, 1967.

——. *Gaelic Ghosts*. New York: Holt, 1964.

——. *Ghosts Go Haunting*. New York: Holt, 1965.

——. *Heather and Broom*. New York: Holt, 1960.

——. *Sea Spell and Moor Magic*. New York: Dutton, 1968.

——. *Thistle and Thyme*. New York: Holt, 1962.

——. *Twelve Great Black Cats*. New York: Dutton, 1971.

Norton, André. *Rogue Reynard*. Illustrated by L. Bannon. Boston: Houghton, 1947.

Olcott, Frances J. *Good Stories for Great Holidays*. Boston: Houghton, 1914.

——. *The Red Indian Fairy Book*. Boston: Houghton, 1917.

——. *Wonder Tales from Baltic Wizards*. New York: Longmans, 1930.

——. *Wonder Tales from China Seas*. New York: Longmans, 1925.

——. *Wonder Tales from Goblin Hills*. New York: Longmans, 1930.

——. *Wonder Tales from Persian Genii*. Boston: Houghton, 1917.

——. *Wonder Tales from Windmill Lands*. New York: Longmans, 1926.

Osma, Lupe de. *The Witches' Ride*. New York: Morrow, 1957.

Otsuka, Yuzo. *Suho and White Horse*. Indianapolis: Bobbs-Merrill, 1969.

Palmer, Robin. *Dragons, Unicorns and Mythical Beasts*. New York: Walck, 1966.

Panchatantra. *The Panchatantra*. Translated by Arthur Ryder. Chicago: Univ. of Chicago Pr., 1925.

Parker, Arthur C. *Skunny Wundy*. Chicago: Whitman, 1970.

Parkin, Rex. *The Red Carpet*. New York: Macmillan, 1948.

Peck, Leigh. *Don Coyote*. Boston: Houghton, 1942.

Perrault, Charles. *All the French Fairy Tales*. Retold by Louis Untermeyer. New York: Didier, 1946.

——. *Perrault's Complete Fairy Tales*. Translated by A. E. Johnson. New York: Dodd, 1961.

Picard, Barbara L. *Hero Tales from the British Isles*. New York: Criterion, 1963.

Potter, Miriam. *Mrs. Goose*. Philadelphia: Lippincott, 1947.

Power, Effie. *Bag o' Tales*. New York: Dutton, 1934.

——. *Blue Caravan Tales*. New York: Dutton, 1935.

——. *From Umar's Pack*. New York: Dutton, 1937.

——. *Stories to Shorten the Road*. New York: Dutton, 1936.

Price, Christine, ret. *The Valiant Chattee-maker*. New York: Frederick Warne, 1965.

Pridham, Radost. *A Gift from the Heart*. Cleveland: World, 1967.

Purnell, Idella. *The Talking Bird*. New York: Macmillan, 1930.

Pyle, Howard. *King Stork*. Illustrated by Trina S. Hymen. Boston: Little, Brown, 1973.

——. *The Merry Adventures of Robin Hood*. New York: Scribners, 1946.

——. *Pepper and Salt*. New York: Harper, 1923.

——. *The Story of King Arthur and His Knights*. New York: Scribners, 1933.

——. *The Wonder Clock*. New York: Harper, 1943.

Pyle, Katherine. *Charlemagne and His Knights*. Philadelphia: Lippincott, 1932.

Quiroga, Horacio. *South American Jungle Tales*. New York: Dodd-Mead, 1922.

Rackham, Arthur. *Arthur Rackham's Fairy Book*. Philadelphia: Lippincott, 1950.

Ralston, W. R. Sheddon. *Russian Fairy Tales*. London: Smith-Elder, 1873.

Ransome, Arthur. *The Fool of the World*. Illustrated by Uri Shulevitz. New York: Farrar, 1968.

———. *Old Peter's Russian Tales*. New York: Nelson, 1917.

Raspé, Rudolph Erich. *Baron Munchausen*. Retold by Stella Humphries. New York: Dutton, 1971.

Reeves, James. *A Golden Land*. New York: Hastings, 1958.

———. *Secret Shoemakers*. New York: Abelard-Schuman, 1966.

Renninger, Elizabeth. *Rustem*. New York: Scribners, 1928.

Ritchie, Alice. *The Treasure of Li-Po*. New York: Harcourt, 1949.

Robbins, Ruth. *Baboushka and the Three Kings*. Berkeley, Calif.: Parnassus, 1960.

Rockwell, Anne. *The Dancing Stars*. New York: Crowell, 1972.

———. *When the Drum Sang*. New York: Parents, 1970.

Roehrenbeck, William. *Christmastide*. New York: Day, 1948.

Ross, Eulalie S. *The Buried Treasure*. Philadelphia: Lippincott, 1958.

———. *The Lost Half Hour*. New York: Harcourt, 1963.

Rostron, Richard. *The Sorcerer's Apprentice*. New York: Morrow, 1941.

Rounds, Glen. *Ol' Paul*. New York: Holiday, 1949.

Rushmore, Helen. *The Dancing Horses of Acoma*. Cleveland: World, 1963.

Sandburg, Carl. *Rootabaga Stories*. New York: Harcourt, 1936.

———. *The Wedding Procession of the Rag Doll and the Broom Handle*. Illustrated by Harriet Pincus. New York: Harcourt, 1967.

Savory, Phyllis. *Congo Fireside Tales*. New York: Hastings, 1962.

Sawyer, Ruth. *Journey Cake, Ho!* New York: Viking, 1953.

———. *Joy to the World*. Boston: Little, Brown, 1966.

———. *The Long Christmas*. New York: Viking, 1967.

———. *My Spain*. New York: Viking, 1967.

———. *Picture Tales from Spain*. Philadelphia: Lippincott, 1936.

———. *This Is the Christmas*. Boston: Horn Book, 1945.

———. *This Way to Christmas*. New York: Harper, 1967.

———. *The Way of the Storyteller*. New York: Viking, 1962.

Schvarts, Evgeny. *A Tale of Stolen Time*. Englewood Cliffs, N.J.: Prentice-Hall, 1966.

Sechrist, Elizabeth. *Heigh-ho for Hallo'een*. Philadelphia: Macrae, 1948.

———. *It's Time for Christmas*. Philadelphia: Macrae, 1959.

———. *It's Time for Easter*. Philadelphia: Macrae, 1961.

———. *It's Time for Thanksgiving*. Philadelphia: Macrae, 1957.

———. *Once in the First Times*. Philadelphia: Macrae, 1969.

Seeger, Elizabeth. *The Five Sons of King Pandu (Mahabbarata)*. New York: Scott, 1967.

Sellew, Catherine. *Adventures with the Gods*. Boston: Little, Brown, 1945.

Sendak, Maurice. *Where the Wild Things Are*. New York: Harper, 1963.

Seredy, Kate. *The Good Master*. New York: Viking, 1935.

———. *The White Stag*. New York: Viking, 1937.

Seton, Ernest Thompson. *Ernest Thompson Seton's America*. New York: Devin-Adair, 1954.

———. *Wild Animals I have Known*. New York: Random House, n.d.

Seuss, Dr. (Geisel, Theodore). *The King's Stilts*. New York: Random House, 1939.

Shedlock, Marie. *The Art of the Storyteller*. New York: Dover, 1952.

Sherlock, Philip. *Anansi, the Spider Man*. New York: Crowell, 1954.

Sherwood, Miriam. *Cid Campeador: Tale of the Warrior Lord*. New York: McKay, 1930.

Simon, Solomon. *The Wise Men of Helm and Their Merry Pranks*. New York: Behrman, 1945.

Sleator, William. *The Angry Moon*. Boston: Little, Brown, 1970.

Sleigh, Barbara. *North of Nowhere*. New York: Colliers, 1966.

Slobodkin, Louis. *The Horse with the High-heeled Shoes*. New York: Vanguard, 1954.

Smith, Dorothy H. *The Tall Book of Christmas*. New York: Harper and Row, 1954.

Smith, Elva S. *Mystery Tales for Boys and Girls*. New York: Lothrop, 1946.

Smith, Nora, and Wiggin, Kate D. *The Story Hour*. Boston: Houghton, n.d.

Spellman, John. *The Beautiful Blue Jay*. Boston: Little, Brown, 1967.

Sperry, Margaret. *Scandinavian Stories*. New York: Watts, 1971.

Spicer, Dorothy. *13 Ghosts*. New York: Coward-McCann, 1965.

———. *13 Giants.* New York: Coward-McCann, 1966.

———. *13 Goblins.* New York: Coward-McCann, 1969.

———. *13 Jolly Saints.* New York: Coward-McCann, 1970.

———. *13 Rascals.* New York: Coward-McCann, 1971.

———. *13 Witches.* New York: Coward-McCann, 1963.

Stamm, Claus. *The Dumpling and the Demons.* New York: Viking, 1964.

Steel, Flora Annie. *English Fairy Tales.* New York: Macmillan, 1962.

Stockton, Frank. *Ting-a-ling Tales.* N.Y.: Scribners, 1955.

Stoutenberg, Adrien. *American Tall Tale Animals.* New York: Viking, 1968.

———. *Fee-Fi-Fo-Fum.* New York: Viking, 1969.

Sugimoto, Chiyono. *Japanese Holiday Picture Tales.* New York: Stokes, 1933.

———. *Picture Tales from Japan.* New York: Stokes, 1928.

Surany, Anico. *The Golden Frog.* New York: Putnam, 1963.

———. *Monsieur Jolicoeur's Umbrella.* New York: Putnam, 1967.

———. *Ride the Cold Wind.* New York: Putnam, 1964.

Sutcliff, Rosemary. *Beowulf.* New York: Dutton, 1964.

———. *The High Deeds of Finn McCool.* New York: Dutton, 1967.

Tashjian, Virginia. *Once There Was and Was Not.* Boston: Little, Brown, 1966.

Tazewell, Charles. *The Small One.* New York: Whitman, 1947.

Thayer, Jane. *Popcorn Dragon.* New York: Morrow, 1953.

Thomas, William J. *The Welsh Fairy Book.* New York: Stokes, 1908.

Thompson, Stith. *One Hundred Favorite Folktales.* Bloomington, Ind.: Indiana Univ. Pr., 1968.

Thompson, Vivian. *Hawaiian Myths of Earth and Sky.* New York: Holiday, 1966.

Thorne-Thomsen, Gudren. *East o' the Sun and West o' the Moon.* Evanston, Ill.: Row, Peterson, 1946.

Tolstoi, Alexei. *Russian Tales for Children.* New York: Dutton, 1947.

Tooze, Ruth. *The Wonderful Wooden Peacock Flying Machine.* New York: Day, 1969.

Topelius, Zacharius. *Canute Whistlewinks.* New York: Longmans, 1927.

Toye, William. *The Mountain Goats of Temlaham.* New York: Walck, 1969.

Tregarthen, Enys. *Piskey Folk.* New York: Day, 1940.

Tresselt, Alvin. *The Legend of the Willow Plate.* Garden City, N.Y.: Doubleday, 1965.

Tudor, Tasha. *Tasha Tudor's Book of Fairy Tales.* New York: Platt and Munk, 1961.

Uchida, Yoshiko. *The Dancing Kettle.* New York: Harcourt, 1949.

———. *The Magic Listening Cap.* New York: Harcourt, 1955.

———. *The Sea of Gold.* New York: Scribners, 1965.

Undset, Sigrid. *True and Untrue.* New York: Knopf, 1945.

Untermeyer, Louis. *Legendary Animals.* New York: Golden, 1963.

———. *The World's Great Stories.* Philadelphia; Lippincott, 1964.

Van Dyke, Henry. *The Other Wise Man.* New York: Harper, 1922.

Van Stockum, Hilda. *The Cottage at Bantry Bay.* New York: Viking, 1938.

Vance, Marguerite. *Jared's Gift.* New York: Dutton, 1965.

Walker, Barbara. *Just Say Hic!* New York: Follett, 1965.

Walters, Maude A. *A Book of Christmas Stories.* New York: Dodd, 1930.

———. *Clever and Foolish Tales for Children.* New York: Dodd, 1941.

Watts, Mabel. *The Patchwork Kilt.* New York: Dutton, 1954.

Weilerstein, Sadie. *The Adventures of K'tonton.* New York: Women's League Press, 1935.

Weisner, William. *Green Noses.* New York: Four Winds, 1969.

Weiss, Harvey. *The Sooner Hound.* New York: Putnam, 1959.

Werner, Jane. *The Giant Golden Book of Elves and Fairies.* New York: Golden, 1951.

Wernecke, H. H. *Christmas Stories from Many Lands.* Philadelphia: Westminster, 1961.

Werth, Kurt. *The Cobbler's Dilemma.* New York: McGraw, 1967.

———. *The Valiant Tailor.* New York: Viking, 1965.

Westwood, Jennifer. *Tales and Legends.* New York: Coward-McCann, 1971.

White, Anne T. *The Golden Treasury of Myth and Legend.* New York: Golden, 1959.

———. *Sinbad the Seaman—The Ebony Horse: Two Arabian Tales.* Champaign, Ill.: Garrard, 1969.

Whitney, Thomas. *In a Certain Kingdom.* New York: Macmillan, 1972.

———. *The Tale of Prince Ivan, the Firebird, and the Grey Wolf.* New York: Scribners, 1968.

Wibberley, Leonard. *The Ballad of the Pilgrim Cat.* New York: Curtis, 1962.

Wiese, Kurt. *Fish in the Air.* New York: Viking, 1948.

Wiggin, Kate D., and Smith, Nora. *The Fairy Ring.* Garden City, N.Y.: Doubleday, 1951.

———. *Magic Casements.* Garden City, N.Y.: Doubleday, 1942.

———. *Tales of Laughter.* Garden City, N.Y.: Doubleday, 1950.

———. *Tales of Wonder.* Garden City, N.Y.: Doubleday, 1942.

———, and Smith, Nora, reteller. *The Arabian Nights.* New York: Scribners, 1909.

Williston, Teresa. *Hindu Folk and Fairy Tales.* New York: Rand McNally, 1917.

Withers, Carl. *Painting the Moon.* New York: Dutton, 1970.

Yamaguchi, Tohr. *The Golden Crane.* New York: Holt, 1963.

Yaroslava. *Tusya and the Pot of Gold.* New York: Atheneum, 1971.

Yashima, Taro. *Seashore Story.* New York: Viking, 1967.

Yolen, Jane. *Greyling.* Cleveland: World, 1968.

Zemach, Harve. *Nail Soup.* New York: Follett, 1964.

Zemach, Margot. *The Fisherman and His Wife.* New York: Norton, 1966.

GENERAL ANTHOLOGIES AND STORY LISTS
(Some have exceptional background material.)

Arbuthnot, May Hill. *The Arbuthnot Anthology of Children's Literature.* Rev. ed. Chicago: Scott, Foresman, 1961. See also 3rd and 4th ed.

———. *Time for Fairy Tales.* Chicago: Scott, Foresman, 1961.

———, and Taylor, Mark. *Time for Old Magic.* Chicago: Scott, Foresman, 1970.

Baker, Augusta, comp. *Stories: A List of Stories to Tell and to Read Aloud.* 5th ed., rev. New York: New York Public Library, 1960. See all editions.

Cathon, Laura, and Hodges, Margaret. *Stories to Tell to Children.* 7th ed. Pittsburgh: Carnegie Library, 1960. See also 8th ed., 1974.

Hollowell, Lillian. *A Book of Children's Literature.* New York: Holt, Rinehart, 1966.

Huber, Miriam B. *Story and Verse for Children.* New York: Macmillan, 1955.

Jagendorf, Moritz, and Clark, Garrett. *A World of Stories for Children.* Indianapolis: Bobbs-Merrill, 1940.

Jinette, Isabella, et al. *Stories to Tell.* Rev. ed. Baltimore: Enoch Pratt Free Library, 1956. See all editions.

Johnson, Edna, et al. *An Anthology of Children's Literature.* 3rd ed. Boston: Houghton, 1959. Also 4th ed., 1970.

Rugoff, Milton. *A Harvest of Folk Tales.* New York: Viking, 1949.

Thompson, Stith. *One Hundred Favorite Folktales.* Bloomington, Ind.: Indiana Univ. Pr., 1968.

STORYTELLERS' GENERAL COLLECTIONS

Bailey, Carolyn S. *Favorite Stories for Children.* New York: Platt and Munk, 1965.

———. *The Storytelling Hour.* New York: Dodd, 1934.

Baker, Augusta. *The Golden Lynx.* Philadelphia: Lippincott, 1960.

———. *The Talking Tree.* Philadelphia: Lippincott, 1955.

Bryant, Sara Cone. *Best Stories to Tell to Children.* Boston: Houghton, 1912.

———. *How to Tell Stories to Children.* Boston: Houghton, 1905.

Chase, Richard. *Grandfather Tales.* Boston: Houghton, 1948.

———. *The Jack Tales.* Boston: Houghton, 1943.

Colwell, Eileen, comp. *A Second Storyteller's Choice.* New York: Walck, 1965.

———. *A Storyteller's Choice.* New York: Walck, 1964.

Cothran, Jean. *Magic Bells.* New York: Aladdin, 1955.

———. *The Magic Calabash.* New York: McKay, 1954.

———. *With a Wig, with a Wag.* New York: McKay, 1954.

Davis, Mary Gould. *A Baker's Dozen.* New York: Harcourt, 1930.

De la Mare, Walter. *Animal Stories.* New York: Scribners, 1940.

———. *Told Again: Old Tales Told Again.* New York: Knopf, 1927.

Hardendorff, Jeanne B. *The Frog's Saddle Horse.* Philadelphia: Lippincott, 1968.

———. *Tricky Peik.* Philadelphia: Lippincott, 1967.

Hutchinson, Veronica. *Candlelight Stories.* New York: Putnam, 1928.

———. *Chimney Corner Fairy Tales.* New York: Minton, Balch, 1925.

———. *Chimney Corner Stories.* New York: Minton, Balch, 1926.

———. *Fireside Stories.* New York: Putnam, 1927.

MacManus, Seumas. *Donegal Fairy Stories.* Garden City, N.Y.: Doubleday, 1900.

———. *In Chimney Corners.* Garden City, N.Y.: Doubleday, 1899.

———. *The Well o' the World's End.* New York: Macmillan, 1939.

Power, Effie. *Bag o' Tales.* New York: Dutton, 1934.

———. *Blue Caravan Tales.* New York: Dutton, 1935.

———. *From Umar's Pack.* New York: Dutton, 1937.

———. *Stories to Shorten the Road.* New York: Dutton, 1936.

Pyle, Howard. *Pepper and Salt*. New York: Harper, 1923.

——. *The Wonder Clock*. New York: Harper, 1943.

Ross, Eulalie S. *The Buried Treasure*. Philadelphia: Lippincott, 1958.

——. *The Lost Half Hour*. New York: Harcourt, 1963.

Sawyer, Ruth. *The Way of the Storyteller*. Rev. ed. New York: Viking, 1962.

Shedlock, Marie. *The Art of the Storyteller*. New York: Dover, 1952.

Thorne-Thomsen, Gudren. *East o' the Sun and West o' the Moon*. Evanston, Ill.: Row, Peterson, 1946.

SERIES FOLK AND FAIRY TALES

Carpenter, Frances. *Tales of a Basque Grandmother*. Garden City, N.Y.: Doubleday, 1930.

——. *Tales of a Chinese Grandmother*. Garden City, N.Y.: Doubleday, 1937.

——. *Tales of a Korean Grandmother*. Garden City, N.Y.: Doubleday, 1947.

——. *Tales of a Russian Grandmother*. Garden City, N.Y.: Doubleday, 1933.

——. *Tales of a Swiss Grandmother*. Garden City, N.Y.: Doubleday, 1940.

Haviland, Virginia. *Favorite Fairy Tales Told in Czechoslovakia*. Boston: Little, Brown, 1966.

——. *Favorite Fairy Tales Told in Denmark*. Boston: Little, Brown, 1971.

——. *Favorite Fairy Tales Told in England*. Boston: Little, Brown, 1959.

——. *Favorite Fairy Tales Told in France*. Boston: Little, Brown, 1959.

——. *Favorite Fairy Tales Told in Germany*. Boston: Little, Brown, 1959.

——. *Favorite Fairy Tales Told in Greece*. Boston: Little, Brown, 1970.

——. *Favorite Fairy Tales Told in India*. Boston: Little, Brown, 1973.

——. *Favorite Fairy Tales Told in Ireland*. Boston: Little, Brown, 1961.

——. *Favorite Fairy Tales Told in Italy*. Boston: Little, Brown, 1965.

——. *Favorite Fairy Tales Told in Japan*. Boston: Little, Brown, 1967.

——. *Favorite Fairy Tales Told in Norway*. Boston: Little, Brown, 1961.

——. *Favorite Fairy Tales Told in Poland*. Boston: Little, Brown, 1963.

——. *Favorite Fairy Tales Told in Russia*. Boston: Little, Brown, 1961.

——. *Favorite Fairy Tales Told in Scotland*. Boston: Little, Brown, 1963.

——. *Favorite Fairy Tales Told in Spain*. Boston: Little, Brown, 1962.

——. *Favorite Fairy Tales Told in Sweden*. Boston: Little, Brown, 1966.

Lang, Andrew. *The Blue Fairy Book*. 1894. Reprint. New York: Longmans, 1946.

——. *The Brown Fairy Book*. 1904. Reprint. New York: McGraw, 1966.

——. *The Crimson Fairy Book*. 1903. Reprint. New York: Longmans, 1947.

——. *The Green Fairy Book*. 1892. Reprint. New York: Longmans, 1948.

——. *The Grey Fairy Book*. New York: Longmans, 1900.

——. *The Lilac Fairy Book*. New York: Longmans, 1910.

——. *The Olive Fairy Book*. 1907. Reprint. New York: Longmans, 1949.

——. *The Orange Fairy Book*. 1906. Reprint. New York: Longmans, 1949.

——. *The Pink Fairy Book*. New York: Longmans, 1897.

——. *The Red Fairy Book*. 1890. Reprint. New York: Longmans, 1947.

——. *The Rose Fairy Book*. New York: McKay, 1948.

——. *The Violet Fairy Book*. 1901. Reprint. New York: McGraw, 1967.

——. *The Yellow Fairy Book*. 1894. Reprint. New York: McGraw, 1967.

(Also all are available unabridged and unaltered in Dover paperback, 1967.)

Manning-Sanders, Ruth. *A Book of Charms and Changelings*. New York: Dutton, 1971.

——. *A Book of Dragons*. New York: Dutton, 1965.

——. *A Book of Dwarfs*. New York: Dutton, 1964.

——. *A Book of Ghosts and Goblins*. New York: Dutton, 1969.

——. *A Book of Giants*. New York: Dutton, 1963.

——. *A Book of Magical Beasts*. New York: Nelson, 1970.

——. *A Book of Monsters*. New York: Dutton, 1976.

——. *A Book of Mermaids*. New York: Dutton, 1968.

——. *A Book of Princes and Princesses*. New York: Dutton, 1970.

——. *A Book of Witches*. New York: Dutton, 1966.

——. *A Book of Wizards*. New York: Dutton, 1967.

Olcott, Frances J. *Wonder Tales from Baltic Wizards*. New York: Longmans, 1930.

——. *Wonder Tales from China Seas*. New York: Longmans, 1925.

——. *Wonder Tales from Goblin Hills*. New York: Longmans, 1930.

——. *Wonder Tales from Persian Genii*. Boston: Houghton, 1917.

——. *Wonder Tales from Windmill Lands*. New York: Longmans, 1926.

Spicer, Dorothy. *13 Ghosts*. New York: Coward-McCann, 1965.

——. *13 Giants*. New York: Coward-McCann, 1966.

——. *13 Goblins*. New York: Coward-McCann, 1969.

——. *13 Jolly Saints*. New York: Coward-McCann, 1970.

——. *13 Rascals*. New York: Coward-McCann, 1971.

——. *13 Witches*. New York: Coward-McCann, 1963.

Wiggin, Kate D., and Smith, Nora. *The Fairy Ring*. Garden City, N.Y.: Doubleday, 1951. Rev. ver., Doubleday, 1967. These titles comprise *The Fairy Library*.

——. *Magic Casements*. Garden City, N.Y.: Doubleday, 1942.

——. *Tales of Laughter*. Garden City, N.Y.: Doubleday, 1950.

——. *Tales of Wonder*. Garden City, N.Y.: Doubleday, 1942.

Picture Tales Series

Carrick, Valery. *Picture Tales from the Russian*. Philadelphia: Lippincott, 1913.

Chamoud, Simone. *Pictures Tales from France*. New York: Stokes, 1933.

Hart, Johan. *Picture Tales from Holland*. Philadelphia: Lippincott, 1935.

Sawyer, Ruth. *Picture Tales from Spain*. Philadelphia: Lippincott, 1936.

Sugimoto, Chiyono. *Picture Tales from Japan*. New York: Stokes, 1928.

STOREHOUSE OF SAGAS, EPICS, AND HEROIC TALES

Almedigen, E. M. *Treasure of Siegfried*. Philadelphia: Lippincott, 1964.

Baldwin, James. *The Story of Roland*. New York: Scribners, 1930.

——. *The Story of Siegfried*. New York: Scribners, 1882.

Bryson, Bernarda. *Gilgamesh*. New York: Holt, 1966.

Bulfinch, Thomas. *Age of Fable*. Garden City, N.Y.: Doubleday, 1948.

——. *Legends of Charlemagne*. Illustrated by N. C. Wyeth. New York: Cosmopolitan Book Corp., 1924.

Church, Alfred J. *The Aeneid for Boys and Girls*. New York: Macmillan, 1942.

——. *The Iliad for Boys and Girls*. New York: Macmillan, 1964.

Collier, Virginia, and Eaton, Jeanette. *Roland, the Warrior*. New York: Harcourt, 1934.

Colum, Padraic. *Adventures of Odysseus*. New York: Macmillan, 1918.

Dalgleish, Alice. *St. George and the Dragon*. New York: Scribners, 1941.

De la Mare, Walter. *Stories from the Bible*. New York: Knopf, 1961.

Deutsch, Babette. *Heroes of the Kalevala*. New York: Messner, 1940.

French, Allen. *Story of Grettir the Strong*. New York: Dutton, 1936.

——. *Heroes of Iceland*. Boston: Little, Brown, 1905.

Gaer, Joseph. *Adventures of Rama*. Boston: Little, Brown, 1954.

Hazeltine, Alice, and Smith, E. S. *Hero Tales from Many Lands*. Nashville, Tenn.: Abingdon, 1961.

Henderson, Gertrude. *The Ring of the Nibelungen*. New York: Knopf, 1932.

Hosford, Dorothy. *Sons of the Volsungs*. New York: Holt, 1949.

Hull, Eleanor. *Cuchulain, the Hound of Ulster*. New York: Crowell, 1910.

Hyde, Mark. *The Singing Sword*. Boston: Little, Brown, 1930.

Kingsley, Charles. *The Heroes*. New York: Macmillan, 1954.

Lang, Andrew. *Tales of Troy and Greece*. New York: Longmans, 1907.

Macleod, Mary. *Book of Ballad Stories*. London: Wills Gardner, n.d.

Malory, Sir Thomas. *The Boy's King Arthur*. Illustrated by N. C. Wyeth. New York: Scribners, 1924.

Mukerji, Dhan Gopal. *Rama, the Hero of India*. New York: Dutton, 1930.

Norton, André. *Rogue Reynard*. Illustrated by L. Bannon. Boston: Houghton, 1947.

Picard, Barbara L. *Odyssey of Homer*. London: Oxford Univ. Pr.; New York: Walck, 1952.

——. *Hero Tales from the British Isles*. New York: Criterion, 1963.

Pyle, Howard. *The Merry Adventures of Robin Hood*. New York: Scribners, 1946.

——. *Story of King Arthur and His Knights*. New York: Scribners, 1905, 1933.

Pyle, Katherine. *Charlemagne and His Knights*. Philadelphia: Lippincott, 1932.

Renninger, Elizabeth. *Rustem*. New York: Scribners, 1928.

Seeger, Elizabeth. *Ramayana*. New York: Scott, 1969.

——. *The Five Sons of King Pandu (Mahabbarata)*. New York: Scott, 1967.

Sherwood, Miriam. *Cid Campeador: Tale of the Warrior Lord.* New York: McKay, 1930.

Sutcliffe, Rosemary. *Beowulf.* New York: Dutton, 1964.

———. *The High Deeds of Finn McCool.* New York: Dutton, 1967.

———. *Hound of Ulster.* New York: Dutton, 1962.

Tappan, E. M. *Old Ballads in Prose.* Boston: Houghton, 1901.

Weber, Henrietta. *Die Meistersinger: the Prize Song.* New York: Oxford Univ. Pr., 1935.

Wilson, Calvin D. *Story of the Cid for Young People.* Boston: Lothrop, 1901.

HOLIDAY ANTHOLOGIES

Association for Childhood Education. *Told Under the Christmas Tree.* New York: Macmillan, 1948.

Child Study Association. *The Holiday Story Book.* New York: Crowell, 1952.

Corrigan, Adeline. *Holiday Ring.* Chicago: Whitman, 1975.

Dalgleish, Alice. *Christmas.* New York: Scribners, 1950.

Eaton, Anne. *The Animals' Christmas.* New York: Viking, 1944.

Fenner, Phyllis. *Feasts and Frolics.* New York: Knopf, 1949.

Harper, Wilhelmina. *Easter Chimes.* New York: Dutton, 1942.

———. *Ghosts and Goblins.* New York: Dutton, 1965.

———. *The Harvest Feast.* New York: Dutton, 1938.

———, and Hazeltine, Alice. *Merry Christmas to You.* New York: Dutton, 1935.

Hazeltine, Alice, and Smith, E. S. *A Christmas Book of Legends and Stories.* New York: Lothrop-Lee, 1944.

Hoke, Helen. *Spooks, Spooks, Spooks.* New York: Watts, 1966.

———. *Witches, Witches, Witches.* New York: Watts, 1966.

Johnson, Lois. *Christmas Stories Around the World.* Chicago: Rand McNally, 1970.

Lillie, Amy. *The Book of Three Festivals.* New York: Dutton, 1948.

Lord, Priscilla, and Foley, Daniel. *An Easter Garland.* New York: Chilton, 1963.

Luckhardt, Mildred. *Christmas Comes Again.* Nashville, Tenn.: Abingdon, 1962.

Olcott, Frances J. *Good Stories for Great Holidays.* Boston: Houghton, 1914.

Roehrenbeck, William. *Christmastide.* New York: Day, 1948.

Sawyer, Ruth. *Joy to the World.* Boston: Little, Brown, 1966.

———. *The Long Christmas.* New York: Viking, 1941.

———. *This Is the Christmas.* Boston: Horn Book, 1945.

———. *This Way to Christmas.* New York: Harper, 1967.

Sechrist, Elizabeth. *Heigh-ho for Hallo'een.* Philadelphia: Macrae, 1948.

———. *It's Time for Christmas.* Philadelphia: Macrae, 1959.

———. *It's Time for Easter.* Philadelphia: Macrae, 1961.

———. *It's Time for Thanksgiving.* Philadelphia: Macrae, 1957.

Smith, Dorothy H. *Tall Book of Christmas.* New York: Harper, 1954.

Smith, Irene. *Santa Claus Book.* New York: Watts, 1948.

Walters, Maude A. *A Book of Christmas Stories.* New York: Dodd, 1930.

Wernecke, H. H. *Christmas Stories from Many Lands.* Philadelphia: Westminster, 1961.

Wyon, Olive. *The World's Christmas.* Philadelphia: Fortress, 1964.

BASIC SOURCES FOR STORYTELLERS

Aesop. *The Fables of Aesop.* Selected by Joseph Jacobs. New York: Macmillan, 1950.

Af'anasev, Aleksandr N. *Russian Fairy Tales.* Translated by N. Guterman. New York: Pantheon, 1945.

Andersen, Hans Christian. *Complete Andersen.* Edited and translated by Jean Hersholt. New York: Heritage, 1949.

Arabian Nights Entertainment. Edited by Andrew Lang. New York: Longmans, 1946.

Asbjörnsen, Peter, and Moe, Jorgen. *Popular Tales from the Norse.* Translated by Sir George Dasent. Edinburgh: D. Douglas, 1903.

Babbitt, Ellen C., ret. *Jataka Tales.* New York: Appleton, 1912.

———. *More Jataka Tales.* New York: Appleton, 1922.

Bay, Jens C. *Danish Fairy and Folk Tales.* New York: Harper, 1899.

Borski, Lucia. *The Jolly Tailor.* New York: Longmans, 1928.

Bowman, Cloyd, and Bianco, M. *Tales from a Finnish Tupa.* Chicago: Whitman, 1936.

Brooke, L. Leslie. *The Golden Goose.* London: Warne, 1906.

Chrisman, Arthur B. *Shen of the Sea.* New York: Dutton, 1925.

Colum, Padraic. *The Arabian Nights.* New York: Macmillan, 1923.

Field, Rachel. *American Folk and Fairy Tales*. New York: Scribners, 1929.

Fillmore, Parker. *The Laughing Prince*. New York: Harcourt, 1921.

———. *Mighty Mikko*. New York: Harcourt, 1922.

———. *The Shepherd's Nosegay*. New York: Harcourt, 1958.

———. *The Shoemaker's Apron*. New York: Harcourt, 1928.

Finger, Charles. *Tales from Silver Lands*. Garden City, N.Y.: Doubleday, 1924.

Grierson, Elizabeth. *The Scottish Fairy Book*. Philadelphia: Lippincott, 1910.

Grimm, Jakob L., and Grimm, Wilhelm. *Complete Grimm's Fairy Tales*. Translated by Margaret Hunt. New York: Pantheon, 1944.

———. *Household Stories*. Translated by Lucy Crane. New York: Macmillan, 1926.

Harris, Joel Chandler. *Brer Rabbit*. Retold by M. W. Brown. New York: Harper, 1941.

———. *Favorite Uncle Remus*. Boston: Houghton, 1948.

———. *Nights with Uncle Remus*. Boston: Houghton, 1883.

Hatch, Mary C. *More Danish Tales*. New York: Harcourt, 1949.

———. *13 Danish Tales*. New York: Harcourt, 1947.

Hearn, Lafcadio. *Japanese Fairy Tales*. New York: Boni and Liveright, 1924.

Hogner, Dorothy C. *Navajo Winter Nights*. New York: Oxford Univ. Pr., 1935.

Jacobs, Joseph. *A Book of Wonder Voyages*. New York: Putnam, n.d.

———. *Celtic Fairy Tales*. New York: Putnam, n.d.

———. *English Fairy Tales*. 3rd ed., rev. New York: Putnam, n.d.

———. *European Folk and Fairy Tales*. New York: Putnam, 1916.

———. *Indian Fairy Tales*. New York: Putnam, n.d.

———. *More Celtic Fairy Tales*. New York: Putnam, n.d.

———. *More English Fairy Tales*. New York: Putnam, n.d.

Kelsey, Alice S. *Once the Hodja*. New York: Longmans, 1943.

———. *Once the Mullah*. New York: Longmans, 1954.

Kipling, Rudyard. *The Jungle Book*. Garden City, N.Y.: Doubleday, 1932.

———. *Just So Stories*. Garden City, N.Y.: Doubeday, 1941.

MacDonell, Anne. *The Italian Fairy Book*. London: Fisher, 1925.

MacManus, Seumas. *The Bold Heroes of Hungry Hill*. New York: Farrar, 1951.

———. *Hibernian Nights*. New York: Macmillan, 1963.

Malcolmson, Anne. *Yankee Doodle's Cousins*. Boston: Houghton, 1941.

Marriott, Alice. *Winter-Telling Stories*. New York: Sloane, 1947.

Olcott, Frances J. *The Red Indian Fairy Book*. Boston: Houghton, 1917.

Panchatantra. *The Panchatantra*. Translated by Arthur Ryder. Chicago: Univ. of Chicago Pr., 1925.

Perrault, Charles. *All the French Fairy Tales*. Retold by Louis Untermeyer. New York: Didier, 1946.

———. *Perrault's Complete Fairy Tales*. Translated by A. E. Johnson. New York: Dodd, 1961.

Ransome, Arthur. *Old Peter's Russian Tales*. New York: Nelson, 1917.

Sandburg, Carl. *Rootabaga Stories*. New York: Harcourt, 1936.

Sellew, Catherine. *Adventures with the Gods*. Boston: Little, Brown, 1945.

Sewell, Helen, ret. *Book of Myths*. (Bulfinch Selections.) New York: Macmillan, 1942.

Shedlock, Marie. *Eastern Stories*. New York: Dutton, 1920.

Steel, Flora Annie. *Tales of the Punjab*. New York: Macmillan, 1894.

Sugimoto, Chiyono. *Japanese Holiday Picture Tales*. New York: Stokes, 1933.

Thomas, William J. *The Welsh Fairy Book*. New York: Stokes, 1908.

Uchida, Yoshiko. *The Dancing Kettle*. New York: Harcourt, 1949.

———. *The Magic Listening Cap*. New York: Harcourt, 1955.

Undset, Sigrid. *True and Untrue*. New York: Knopf, 1945.

Wheeler, Post. *Russian Wonder Tales*. New York: Beechhurst Pr., 1946.

PROFESSIONAL SOURCE BOOKS

Arbuthnot, May Hill. *Children and Books*. 3rd ed. Glenview, Ill.: Scott, Foresman, 1964. Also 4th ed. 1972, ed. Zena B. Sutherland; 5th ed. 1977, ed. Zena B. Sutherland.

American Library Association. *For Storytellers and Storytelling*. Chicago: A.L.A., 1968.

———. *Subject and Title Index to Short Stories for Children*. Edited by Julia Carter. Chicago: A.L.A., 1955.

Clarke, Kenneth. *Introduction to Folklore*. New York: Holt, 1963.

Colum, Padraic. "Storytelling Old and New" in his *The Fountain of Youth*. New York: Macmillan, 1927.

Cook, Elizabeth. *The Ordinary and the Fabulous.* Cambridge: University Pr., 1969.

Cooper, Frederick T. *An Argosy of Fables.* New York: Stokes, 1921.

Eastman, M. H. *Index to Fairy Tales, Myths, and Legends.* 2nd ed., rev. Boston: Faxon, 1926.

———. *Second Supplement.* Boston: Faxon, 1952.

———. *Supplement to Index.* Boston: Faxon, 1937.

Grinnell, George B. *Blackfoot Lodge Tales.* New York: Scribners, 1892. Reprint. Lincoln: Univ. of Nebraska Pr., 1962.

Hartland, Edwin S., ed. *English Fairy and Other Folktales.* London: W. Scott, 1890.

Haviland, Virginia. *Children's Literature: A Guide to Reference Sources.* Washington, D.C.: Library of Congress, 1966. Also supplements.

Ireland, N. O. *Index to Fairy Tales (1949–1972).* Westwood, Mass.: Faxon, 1973.

Meigs, C. L. *Critical History of Children's Literature.* Rev. ed. New York: Macmillan, 1953.

Opie, Iona, and Opie, Peter. *The Classic Fairy Tales.* London: Oxford Univ. Pr., 1974.

Ralston, W. R. Sheddon. *Russian Fairy Tales.* London: Smith-Elder, 1873.

Ramsey, Eloise. *Folklore for Children and Young People.* Biblio. series, vol. 3. Philadelphia: American Folklore Society, 1952.

Sawyer, Ruth. *My Spain.* New York: Viking, 1967.

Schoolcraft, Henry R. *Indian Legends from Algie Researches.* Edited by Mentor L. Williams. East Lansing: Michigan State Univ., 1956.

Thompson, Stith. *The Folktale.* New York: Dryden Pr., 1946.

Tolkien, J. R. R. *Tree and Leaf.* Boston: Houghton, 1964.

Ullom, J. C. *Folklore of the North American Indians.* Washington, D.C.: Library of Congress, 1969.

Ziegler, Elsie, ed. *Folklore Single Editions.* Westwood, Mass.: Faxon, 1973.

Index

The following index is to story titles and to authors. Anthologies are not listed, nor are editions or compilers.

Designed by John Grandits
Composed by Modern Typographers in Linotype Baskerville
Printed on 55# Hammermill Lock Haven
and bound in Joanna Devon, starch-filled cloth,
by The Book Press

Other important ALA publications keyed to young children's interests:

Handbook for Storytellers

Caroline Feller Bauer

A really different how-to-book. Shows parents, teachers, librarians and volunteers how to use effectively a variety of media—including films, music, crafts, puppetry and even magic—to bring stories alive. The storyteller is told how to create these media where possible and in all cases how to relate them to various stories.

400 pages   Cloth   ISBN 0-8389-0225-1 $15.00
400 pages   Paper   ISBN 0-8389-0293-6 $8.50

Storytelling

Readings, Bibliographies, Resources

Association for Library Service to Children, ALA

Emphasis is on the distinctive materials that will lend excitement to the craft and that will identify and locate good stories. Includes lists of books, articles and excerpts, recordings, films, and video-tapes to provide background information. Also contains lists of resources on the art of story-telling and sources of stories.

16 pages   Paper   ISBN 0-8389-3216-9 $1.00

More Films Kids Like

Maureen Gaffney, editor and compiler

The successor to *Films Kids Like* contains anno-tated lists of 200 short, recently produced 16mm films tested and proven effective for children from three to twelve years of age. Includes suggestions for classroom use and suggested follow-up activities.

168 pages   Paper   ISBN 0-8389-0250-2 $8.95

Start Early for an Early Start

You and the Young Child

Ferne Johnson, editor

Provides information on tested, effective methods and techniques and resources for developing pro-grams of library and library-related service to preschoolers and the adults responsible for their welfare. Contents range from the use of "scrounge" materials to such topics as Learning Experiences with Infants, Toys That Teach, and Dial-a-Story.

192 pages   Paper   ISBN 0-8389-3185-5 $7.50

A Multimedia Approach to Children's Literature

A Selective List of Films, Filmstrips, and Recordings Based on Children's Books, 2d edition

Ellin Greene and Madalynne Schoenfeld, editors

Contains annotated listings of more than 500 children's books, each followed by separately annotated listings of 16mm films, filmstrips, and recordings (disc and tape) based upon the books.

206 pages   Paper   ISBN 0-8389-0249-9 $6.00

British Children's Authors

Interviews at Home

Cornelia Jones and Olivia R. Way

Presents interviews with 20 British authors and illustrators in their homeland. Authors and illus-trators not only discuss their philosophies and methods of working, but also reveal something of their own culture and personalities.

192 pages   Cloth   ISBN 0-8389-0224-3 $10.00

American Library Association   50 East Huron Street, Chicago, Illinois 60611